CAREER AND COUNSELLING EDUCATION

CAREER AND COUNSELLING EDUCATION

Editor
SARLA GUPTA

KALPAZ PUBLICATIONS
DELHI-110052

Career and Counselling Education

ISBN: 81-7835-056-4

Reprinted in 2011 in India by
Kalpaz Publications,
C-30, Satyawati Nagar,
Delhi-110 052
E-mail: kalpaz@hotmail.com

Printed at: G. Print Process, Delhi

Preface

Career counselling and education are conducted with a wide variety of individuals in diverse settings. Career counselling is a hybrid discipline, often misunderstood and not always fully appreciated by many professionals or the public. Its present status is the result of a long and varied history and an ebb and flow of popularity. The process of career development begins in the preschool years and becomes more direct in elementary schools. It is a lifelong process that interacts dynamically with other life roles.

Career problems include career indecisions and undecidedness, work-performance, stress and adjustment, incongruence of the person and work-environment, and inadequate or unsatisfactory integration of life roles with other life roles. Career counselling has been known by a number of different names, including vocational guidance, occupational counselling, and vocational counselling.

Career counsellors must take many factors into consideration when helping an individual make a career decision. Career guidance and the dissemination of career information is traditionally pictured as a school activity. But this process is often conducted outside a classroom environment, for example, at governmental agencies, industries, libraries, and homes or with a private practitioner.

The ways of becoming informed about careers are extensive. Not all ways of learning are as effective as others, however, and those who fail to personalise career information to specific situations often have difficulty making vocational decisions. It is vital to provide qualitative and quantitative occupational information to individuals who are deciding about careers. Knowledge of career information does not guarantee self-exploration in career development, but good career decisions cannot be made without such data. A lack of enough information or up-to-date information is one reason that individuals fail to make decisions or make unwise choices.

The book provides an authoritative account of basic doctrines and theoretical principles of career counselling and education necessary to equip the reader with the requisite insight and understanding for effective functioning in the field. It also provides an extensive exploration of various guidance services, their appropriate methodologies and techniques to render them effectively.

Editor

Contents

1

Introduction

Introduction

Career counselling is a hybrid discipline, often misunderstood and not always fully appreciated by many professionals or the public Its present status is the result of a long and varied history and an ebb and flow of popularity. There is a national credentialing body for career counsellors: the National Council for Credentialing Career Counsellors (NCCCC). Potential candidates must first achieve the entry-level certification of National Certified Counsellors (NCC). Then they must pass the Career Counselling Speciality Exam and meet minimal educational course work and experience requirements to advance to the level of National Certified Career Counsellor (NCCC).

Career counselling is an interpersonal process designed to assist individuals with career development problems. Career development is that process of choosing, entering, adjusting to and advancing in an occupation. It is a lifelong process that interacts dynamically with other life roles.

Career problems include, but are not limited to, career indecisions and undecidedness, work performance, stress and adjustment, incongruence of the person and work environment, and inadequate or unsatisfactory integration of life roles with other life roles. Throughout its history, career counselling has been known by a number of different names, including vocational guidance, occupational counselling, and vocational counselling. Crites emphasizes that the word career is more modern and inclusive than the vocation.

Career is also broader than the occupation, which Herr and Cramer define as "a group of similar jobs found in different industries or organizations". Regardless of which term they use, career Counsellors dearly must take many factors into consideration when helping an individual make a career decision. To understand these factors, it is important first to define a career specifically. Super provides an excellent definition that incorporates a number of experiences.

The term *career information* has been defined by NCDA (then NVGA) as "information related to the world of work that can be useful in the process of career development, including educational, occupational, and psychosocial information related to working, e.g., availability of training, the nature of work, and status of workers in different occupations". The word *guidance is* usually reserved for activities that are primarily educational. Career guidance involves all activities that seek to disseminate information about present or future vocations in such a way that individuals become more knowledgeable and aware about who they are in relationship to the world of work.

Guidance activities can take the form of career fairs, library assignments, outside interviews, computer-assisted information experiences, and *career shadowing* as well as didactic lectures and experiential exercises such as role playing.

Career guidance and the dissemination of career information is traditionally pictured as a school activity. But this process is often conducted outside a classroom environment-for example, at governmental agencies, industries, libraries, and homes or with a private practitioner.

Career guidance is "for people who are pretty normal and have no emotional problems that would interfere with developing a rational approach to making a vocational or career choice". Many government and educational agencies (such as the National Career Information System computerise information about occupations and disseminate it through libraries.

Overall, the ways of becoming informed about careers are extensive. Not all ways of learning are as effective as others, however, and those who fail to personalize career information to specific situations often have difficulty making vocational decisions. The result may be unrealistic aspirations-goals beyond a person's capabilities. Therefore, it is vital to provide qualitative and quantitative occupational information to individuals who are deciding about careers. Knowledge of career information does not guarantee self-exploration in career development, but good career decisions cannot be made without such data. A lack of enough information or up-to-date information is one reason that individuals fail to make decisions or make unwise choices.

A number of computer-based programs offer career information and help individuals sort through their values and interests or just find job information. One of the beauties of computer-based career planning systems is their accessibility: There are available in many settings and with diverse people across cultures and the life span.

Career development theories try to explain why individuals choose careers. They also deal with the career adjustments people make over time. Modern theories, which are broad and comprehensive in regard to individual and occupational development, began appearing in the literature in the 1950s. The following four theories are among the most prominent:

The origin of trait-and-factor theory can be traced back to Frank Parsons. It stresses matching an individual with a job that fits that person's talents. Its most widespread influence occurred during the Great Depression when E. G. Williamson championed its use. It was out of favour during the 1950s and 60s but has resurfaced in a more modern form, as reflected in the work of researchers such as John Holland.

The trait-and-factor approach has always stressed the uniqueness of persons. Original advocates of the theory assumed that a person's abilities and traits could be measured objectively and quantified. Personal motivation was considered relatively stable. Thus, satisfaction in a particular occupation depended on a proper fit between one's abilities and the job requirements. In its modern form, trait-and-factor theory stresses the interpersonal nature of careers and associated life-styles as well as the performance requirements of a work position. Holland identifies six categories in which personality types and job environments can be classified: realistic, investigative, artistic, social, enterprising, and conventional.

Personal satisfaction in a work setting depends on the degree of congruence between the personality type and the work environment . For example, an artistic person will probably not fit well into a conventional job environment, such as that of office manager.

Psychodynamic theory

Roe theorized that vocational interests develop as a result of the interaction between parents and their children. Career choices reflect the desire to satisfy needs not met by parents in childhood.

From the psychodynamic point of view, the first few years, of childhood are primarily responsible for shaping the pattern of life. Roe believes there is an unconscious motivation from this period that influences people to choose a career in which these needs can be expressed and satisfied.

Three different parent-child relationship climates The first is characterised by an emotional concentration on the child. The pattern takes one of two forms. One is overprotection, in which the parents do too much for the child and encourage dependency. The other is overdemanding, in which the parents emphasize achievement. Children who grow up in these types of environments usually develop a need for constant feedback and rewards. They frequency choose careers that provide recognition from others, such as the performing arts. The second child-rearing pattern is avoidance of the child. There are two extremes within this pattern. One is neglectful parenting, in which there is little effort made to satisfy the needs of the child. The other is rejecting parenting, ill which no effort is made to satisfy the child's needs. The final pattern of child-parent relationships is acceptance of the child. Acceptance may be casual or more actively loving; in either case, independence is encouraged. Children from these families usually seek careers that balance the personal arid nonpersonal aspects of life, such as teaching or counselling.

The two most widely known career theories based on personal development are those associated with Donald Super and Eli Ginzberg. The original developmental theory proposed by Ginzberg and his associates has had great influence and has been revised. But Super's theory is examined in detail here because more extensive work has been done with it.

Developmental theory

Developmental theories are generally more inclusive, more concerned with longitudinal expression of career behaviour, and m inclined to highlight the importance of self-concept.

Super believes that career development is the process of implementing a self-concept. People's views of who they are reflected in what they do. He suggests vocational development unfolds in five stages, each of which contains a developmental task to be completed. The first stage is growth (from birth to 14).

During this stage, with its substages of fantasy (ages 4-10), interest (a 11-12), and capacity (ages 13-14), a child forms a mental picture of the self in relation to others. During the process of growth, the child becomes oriented to the world of work. The second stage is exploration (ages 15-24). It has three substages: tentative (ages 15-17), transition (ages 18-21), and trial (ages 22-24). The major task of this stage is a general exploration of the world of work and the specification of a career preference. The third stage is known as establishment (ages 25-44). Its two substages, trial (ages 25-30) and advancement (ages 31-44), constitute the major task of becoming established in a preferred and appropriate field of work. Once established, persons can concentrate on advancement until they tire or reach the top of the profession. The fourth stage, maintenance (ages 45-64), has the major task of preserving what one has already achieved.

The final stage, decline (age 65 to death), is a time for disengagement from work and alignment with other sources of satisfaction. It has two substages: deceleration (ages 65-70) and retirement (age 71 to death).

Cognitive and social-learning theories of career development were formulated in the 1960s. Two of the must prominent cognitive models have a developmental base. Tiedeman and O'Hara outline a seven-stage model of career decision: exploration (ages 14-18), crystallisation (ages 18-21), choice (ages 18-25), clarification (ages 18-25), induction (ages 21-30), reformation (ages 21-30), and integration (ages 30-40). There is some overlap among these stages, but each requires the individual to make a decision. This emphasis on the cognitive restructuring of the person from "within to without" is Tiedeman's unique contribution to career development theory. He and his associates view people as more active in the formation of careers than super does.

Knefelkamp and Slepitza also focus on a hierarchical structure of cognitive development 'in describing the development of career decision making in college students. Their model of career planning takes into account nine variables, such as locus of control, analysis, synthesis, and openness to alternative perspectives. A major weakness of the theory is its lack of measurement of the processes on which it focuses. Moreover, it has not been studied in a noncollege population. Krumboltz has formulated an equally comprehensive but less developmental social-learning approach. He takes the position that four factors influence a person's career choice: genetic endowment, conditions and events in the environment, learning experiences, and task-approach skills (such as values and work habits).

According to Krumboltz, career decisions are controlled by both internal and external processes: that is, one has some control over the events one finds reinforcing.

Career counselling has not enjoyed the same degree of prestige that other forms of counselling or psychotherapy have. This is unfortunate for both the counselling profession and the many people who need these services. Surveys of high school juniors and seniors and college undergraduates show that the counselling service they most prefer is career counselling. Brown also posits that career counselling may be a viable intervention for some clients who have emotional problems related to nonsupportive, stress-producing environments. The contribution of career counselling to personal growth and development is well documented.

Major aspects of career counselling

Crites lists important aspects of career counselling, which include the following:

1. *The need for career counselling is greater than the need for psychotherapy.* Career counselling deals with the inner and outer world of individuals, whereas other counselling approaches deal only with internal events.
2. *Career counselling can be therapeutic.* Super, Williams, Williams and Hills, Crites, and Krumboltz have all found a positive correlation between career and personal adjustment. Clients who successfully cope with career decisions may gain skill and confidence in the ability to tackle other problem areas. They may invest more energy into resolving noncareer problems because they have clarified career objectives. While Brown provides a set of assessment strategies that are

useful in determining whether a client needs personal or career counselling first, career and personal counselling are inextricably intertwined and often must be treated together. For example, people who lose jobs and fear they will never find other positions have both a career problem and a personal anxiety problem. It is imperative to treat such people in a holistic manner by offering information on the intellectual aspects of finding a career and working with them to face and overcome their emotional concerns about seeking a new job or direction in life.

3. *Career counselling is more difficult than psychotherapy* Crites states that to be an effective career counsellor a person must deal with both personal and work variables and must know how the two interact. "Being knowledgeable and proficient in career counselling requires that Counsellors draw from a variety of both personality and career development theories and techniques and that they continuously be able to gather and provide current information about the world of work.

The Association for Counsellor Education and Supervision (ACES) of ACA recognizes career counselling as a broad-based activity that is process-oriented. Herr and Cramer stress that a career-counselling viewpoint must be integrative.

— *Client-centered career counselling*: Client-centered career counselling was inspired by the writings of Carl Rogers and developed by C. H. Patterson. Client-centered career counselling deals in a complex but systematic fashion with both the emotional and cognitive aspects of making a career choice. Its major shortfalls are a failure to consider thoroughly the influence of outside phenomena on the career decisions of clients and an inconsistency in conveying career information to clients in a nondidactic Rogerian fashion.

— *Psychodynamic career counselling*: The model underlying psychodynamic career counselling was constructed primarily by Bordin. His view, which is based on psychodynamic theories such as Anne Roe's, holds that career choices involve a client's needs and are developmental in nature. A major limitation of the approach is its strong emphasis on internal factors, such as motivation, and its lack of attention to external variables. The process of career counselling from this perspective is considered overly complex.

One offshoot of psychodynamic career counselling, which is more concrete but still complex, is based on the work of Murray Bowen and has been amplified by McGoldrick and Gerson.

According to this approach, the uniqueness of people is interconnected with their family of origin. One way of mapping family-of-origin patterns is to draw a genogram.

— *Developmental career counselling*: The major contributions of developmental career counselling are its emphases on the importance of the life span in career decision making and on career decisions that are influenced by other processes and events in a person's life. This "life pattern paradigm for career counselling encourages Counsellors to consider a client's aptitudes and interests in a matrix of life experiences, not just in comparison to some normative group".

The developmental approach can be conceptualised as career-pattern counselling. While this method has been criticized for its historical and descriptive emphases, these features, along with the conceptual depth of the theory, have also been considered strengths. Overall, developmental career counselling is strong. With the further elaborations of Super and his associates, an even more comprehensive *rainbow theory* has emerged.

— *Comprehensive career counselling*: In contrast to these five theories, Crites developed his own model. It is based on the five major approaches just discussed; the more general systems of counselling and psychotherapy, such as those described by Corsini and Wedding; and his own wide experience as a career counsellor.

Counsellors make three diagnoses of a client's career problems: *differential* (what the problems are), dynamic (why problems have occurred), and *decisional* (how the problems are being dealt with). Such diagnoses result from a close working relationship between client and counsellor and are facilitated by open communication. Once made, diagnoses form the basis for problem-resolution strategies that can be expected to produce more further functioning individuals-intellectually, personally, socially, and vocationally. Crites employs eclectic methods in his career counselling. He uses client-centered and developmental counselling at the beginning to identify problems. The middle stage of his process is dominated by psychodynamic techniques, such as interpretation, to clarify how problems have occurred. The final stage of the process uses trait-and-factor and behavioural approaches to help the client resolve problem areas. Comprehensive career counselling also advocates the use of tests in working with clients.

The focus in test use, however, is on interpreting the tests without the tests: that is, letting the client and counsellor share responsibility for interpreting what the test results mean independently of standardized norms.

Finally, this model of career counselling stresses the use of career information and recommends that counsellors orient clients to such information and reinforce them when they make use of it.

Crites developed the Career Maturity Inventory to help Counsellors determine how knowledgeable clients are about career information and themselves. Overall, this model represents one of several eclectic approaches in career counselling.

Career counselling and education are conducted with a wide variety of individuals in diverse settings. Brown observes that career counselling typically is offered in college counselling centres, rehabilitation facilities, employment offices, and public schools. He thinks it could be applied with great advantage in many other places as well, including mental health centres and private-practice offices. Jesser agrees and asserts there is a need to provide career information and counselling to potential users, such as the unemployed, the learning disabled, prisoners, and those released from mental hospitals who seek to reenter the job market. The concept of careers encompasses the life span, Counsellors who specialize in this area find themselves working with a full age range of clients, from young children to octogenarians. Consequently, many different approaches and techniques have been developed for working effectively with select groups. The process of career development begins in the preschool years and becomes more direct in elementary schools. Herr and Cramer cite numerous studies to show that during the first six years of school, many children develop a relatively stable self perception and make a tentative commitment to a vocation. These processes are observed whether career counselling and guidance activities are offered or not.

Nevertheless, it is beneficial for children, especially those who live in areas with limited employment opportunities, to have a broad, systematic program of career counselling and guidance in the schools. Levels of career awareness in elementary school children may be raised through activities such as field trips to local industries, bakeries, manufacturing plants, or banks. When such trips are followed up with appropriate classroom learning exercises, children become aware of a wider spectrum of related occupations. There are three key career development areas at the elementary school level: self-awareness (that is, one's uniqueness), career awareness and exploration, and decision making. Well-designed career guidance and counselling programs that are implemented at an early age and coordinated with programs across all levels of the educational system can go a long way toward dispelling irrational and decision-hindering career development myths, such as "a career decision is an event that should occur at a specific point in time". To meet the career needs of adolescents, the American School Counsellor Association developed a role statement on the expectations and responsibilities of school Counsellors engaged in career guidance. The five-point statement emphasizes that school Counsellors should involve others, both inside and outside the school, in the delivery of career education to students. Cole stresses that in the middle and junior high school, career guidance activities should include the exploration of work opportunities and students' evaluation of their own strengths and weaknesses in regard to possible future careers. Assets that students should become aware of and begin, to evaluate include talents and—skills, general intelligence, motivation level, friends, family, life experience, appearance, and health.

The greatest challenge and need for career development programs occur on this level. Herr and Cramer state that, in general, there are three emphases of career counselling at the high school level: "stimulating career development, providing treatment, and aiding placement".

More specifically, Counsellors provide students with reassurance, information, emotional support, reality testing, planning strategies, attitude clarification, and work experiences, depending on a student's needs and level of functioning. Several techniques have proven quite effective in helping adolescents crystallise ideas about careers.

Some involve the use of fantasies, such as imagining a typical day in the future, an awards ceremony, a midcareer change, or retirement. More concrete exercises might include completing an occupational family tree to find out how present interests compare with the careers of family members. Another career focus within high schools is youth apprenticeships, a popular approach that provides work-based learning for adolescents. They help students who are not college-bound make a smooth transition from high school to the primary work environment. Educational programs, such as Mann's four Cs (cash, care, computers, and coalitions), can help students at risk become involved in career exploration and development. According to Bloch, successful educational counselling programs for students at risk of dropping out should follow six guidelines:

— They make a connection between a student's present and future status (that is, cash-students are paid for attending).

— They individualize programs and communicate caring.

— They form successful coalitions with community institutions and businesses.

— They integrate sequencing of career-development activities.

— They offer age- and stage-appropriate career-development activities.

— They use a wide variety of media and career-development resources, including computers.

Undergraduates are likely to visit college counselling centers for career counselling.

Career-counselling services are valued by college students at all levels of study For example, a study conducted at the University of Georgia revealed that career-development needs far outweighed students' purely personal and academic concerns. Even students who have already decided on their college majors and careers seek such services. Counselling centre activities range from creating alumni career consultation programs to writing weekly informational columns for student newspapers.

Herr and Cramer list a number of services that a comprehensive career guidance and counselling program in an institution of higher education attempts to provide.

Among them are help with the selection of a major field of study; offering self-assessment and self-analysis through psychological testing; helping students understand the world of work; facilitating access to employment opportunities through career fairs, internships, and campus interviews; teaching decision-making skills; and meeting the needs of special populations. Another important service is exploring with students the role of leisure in proposed career and life-style plans. Anticipating problems related to work and intimate relationships, such as preparing to live in a dual-career family, have also been proposed as career-counselling services for college students.

Career interest patterns tend to be more stable after college than during college. Nevertheless, many adults continue to need career counselling. Indeed, adults experience cyclical periods of stability and transition throughout their lives, and career change is a developmental as well as situational expectation at this stage of life.

Adults may have particularly difficult times with their careers and career decisions when they find "themselves unhappy in their work yet feel appropriately ambivalent about switching directions". In such situations they may create illogical or troublesome career beliefs that become self-fulfilling and self-defeating. There are two dominant ways of working with adults in career counselling: the differential approach and the developmental approach. The *differential approach* stresses that "the typology of persons and environments is more useful than any life stage strategies for coping with career problems". It avoids age-related stereotypes, gender and minority-group issues, and the scientific and practical difficulties of dealing with life-span problems.

At any age, the level and quality of a person's vocational coping is a function of the interaction of personality type and type of environment plus the consistency and differentiation of each.

A career counsellor who is aware of typological formulations such as Holland's can predict the characteristic ways a given personal-cope with career problems. For example, a person with a well-defined social/artistic personality (typical of many individuals employed as counsellors) would be expected to "have high educational and vocational aspirations, to have good decision-making ability, to have a strong and lifelong interest in learning, to have, moderate personal competency, and to have a marked interest in creative and high level performance rather than in leadership". A person with such a profile would also have a tendency to remold or leave an environment in the face of adversity.

A major advantage of working from this approach is the ease with which it explains career shifts at any age. People who shift careers, at any point in life, seek to find more consistency between personality and environment. The *developmental approach* examines a greater number of individual and environmental variables. "The experiences people have with events, situations and other people play a large part in determining their identities (i.e., what they believe and value, how they respond to others, and what their own self images are)".

Developmental life-span career theory proposes that adults are always in the process of evaluating themselves in regard to how they are affected hi outside influences (such as spouse, family, and friends) and how they impact these variables. The theories of Donald Super and John Crites are prime examples of Viewpoints that address developmental career concerns. Likewise, Okun and Gladstein and Apfel believe the interplay of other people and events strongly influences career decisions in adulthood.

Gladstein and Apfel's approach to adult Career counselling focuses on a combination of six elements: developmental, comprehensive self-in-group, longitudinal, mutual commitment, and multimethodological. These elements work together in the process of change at this stage of life. This model, which has been implemented on a practical level at the University of Rochester Adult Counselling Center since 1977, considers the total identity of the person over time. In a related model, Chusmir stresses the interaction of multiple factors in the process that men undergo when choosing nontraditional careers (careers in which people of one gender are not usually employed). Whether or not careers are nontraditional, the fact is that many forces enter into career decisions.

Gender-based career counselling

Women and cultural minorities have historically received less adequate career counselling than white males have. The reason has often involved stereotypical beliefs and practices connected with these two groups. Gender-based career patterns have changed for several reasons. In 1987 the Hudson Institute issued a report, *Workforce* 2000, which calculated that, from the late 1980s to the year 2000, nonwhites, women, and immigrants will make up more than five-sixths of net additions to the U.S. work force. These statistics, along with growing social activism among women and cultural minority groups, are helping to challenge constraining negative forces.

Since 1970, there has been a dramatic rise in research on and interest in the career development of women. The trend parallels the increase in women's participation in the work force, from roughly 50 percent of all women in the early 1970s to approximately 75 percent in the 1990s.

Unfortunately, most theories of career development cannot be appropriately applied to women because they were formulated for men or are incomplete. In working with women, counsellors need to watch out for occupational sex-role stereotyping, even at the elementary school level. Many people often assume that as a group females prefer social, artistic, and conventional occupations (as opposed to realistic, investigative, and enterprising occupations for men). Therefore, girls and women are sometimes not challenged to explore their abilities and possibilities. As a result, many women fail to develop their abilities to the fullest.

Consequently, they never work; develop a low or moderate commitment to work; or focus on "safe," traditional, female-dominated occupations such as teaching, nursing, or social work. Only a relatively small portion of women are pioneers who become highly committed to working in nontraditional occupations.

To understand why many women choose career paths as they do, Scott and Hatalla surveyed an extensive number of women from a large, urban, mid-Atlantic university 30 years after their graduations in 1959 and 1960. They found that three factors were common to the sample group, regardless of work history: "the contingency factors of Perception of Interests and Awareness of Skills, and the chance factor of Unexpected Personal Events".

Service jobs are those such as sales clerk and computer operator. If young women take these jobs rather than pursue higher-paying, nontraditional careers in skilled trades, they will be subjected to economic forces such as poverty, social welfare, and dependence on men that are not in their best interest or society's. Therefore, there is "an urgent need for career counselling interventions" offered through live or video modelling "that will persuade young women to consider the economic benefits of nontraditional career choices". In addition to girls and young women, two other groups of women workers displaced homemakers and late entrants-have received and should continue to receive considerable attention. Displaced homemakers, who enter the job market out of necessity, and late-entry or delayed-entry women, who decide to enter the job market after considerable time at home, pose considerable challenges for career counsellors. The displaced homemaker often finds herself in a financial strain, uninformed about current job market trends, without a support system, and with a shaky self-concept.

Career counsellors must first help women sort out or resolve some of these problems before dealing with major career decisions. In the process, they may assist the women in finding temporary employment, but long-term solutions to career satisfaction take time.

Late-entry women, because of their own motivation and status, do not face the same problems to the same degree. Nevertheless, they usually need more information on careers and, like displaced homemakers have to identify skills and deal with self-concept and family responsibilities.

Cultural minorities are so diverse that it is impossible to focus on all the factors that career counsellors must deal with in working with them individually or collectively. Many minorities (and women) have difficulty obtaining meaningful employment because of employers' discrimination practices, lack of marketable skills, and limited access to informal networks that lead to good jobs. The interest patterns of cultural minorities (as a group) tend to fall within Holland's social, conventional, and enterprising categories, which can limit their choices for meaningful work. While about 27 per cent of adults in the United States express a need for assistance in finding information about work, the rate is much higher among specific minority populations. Counsellors must remember that cultural minorities have special needs in regard to establishing themselves in careers.

Counsellors must be sensitive to such issues and at the same time help individuals overcome artificial and real barriers that prohibit them from maximizing their potential. For instance, some African-American youths who have lived in poverty all their lives are characterized as vocationally handicapped because "they have few positive work-related experiences, limited educational opportunities, and frequently lack positive work role models". Structured programs for these individuals use positive role models and experiences to affirm cultural or ethnic heritage and abilities, thus working to address and overcome traditional restrictions.

2

Educational Guidance

Guidance is the systematic professional process of helping the individual through education and interpretative procedures to gain a better understanding of his own characteristics and potentialities and to relate himself more satisfactorily to social requirements and opportunities in accord with social and moral values. Traxler considers guidance as a help which enables "each individual to understand his abilities and interests, to develop them as well as possible and to relate them to life-goals, and finally to reach a state of complete and mature self-guidance as a desirable member of the social order." According to Jones, "Guidance involves personal help given by someone; it is designed to assist a person to decide where he wants to go, what he wants to do or how he can best accomplish his purpose; it assists him to solve problems that arise in his life."

Guidance is a process

It helps every individual to help himself, to recognise and use his inner resources, to set goals, to make plans, to work out his own problems of development.

It is needed right from early childhood, adolescence, adult-hood and even in old age. Choice and problem points are the distinctive concerns of guidance as here the individual's unique world of perceptions interacts with the external order of events in his life context. It is assistance to the individual in the process of development rather than a direction of that development: The aim is to develop the capacity for self-direction, self-guidance and self-improvement through an increased understanding of his problems and his resources as well as limitations to solve the problem.

Guidance is a service meant for all

It is a regular service which is required at every stage for every student, not only for awkward situations and abnormal students. It is a positive programme geared to meet the needs of all students. It is both generalised and a specialised service. It is a generalised service because everyone-teachers, tutors, advisers, deans, parents-play a part in the programme. It is a specialised service because specially qualified personnel as counsellors, psychiartists, psychologists join hands to help the individual to get out of his problem. Very few terms have been more loosely or inter-changeably used than the terms 'guidance' and 'counselling'.

According to Tolbert, "Guidance is the total programme or all the activities and services engaged in by an educational institution that are primarily aimed at assisting and individual to make and carry out adequate plans and to achieve satisfactory adjustment in all aspects of his daily life.

Guidance is not teaching but it may be done by teachers. It is not separate from education but is an essential part of the total educational programme.

Guidance is a term which is broader than counselling and which includes counselling as one of its services." Bulter makes a logical separation of the counselling process discerned as having two phases called 'adjustive' and 'distributive'. In the adjustive phase, the emphasis is on the social personal and emotional problems of the individual; in the distributive phase the focus is upon his educational, vocational and occupational problems.

Teachers in technical institutions develops instructional plans, implement them and evaluate the effectiveness of their instruction for the main purpose of enabling their students to acquire the knowledge and skill prescribed in the courses of study.

Students often encounter difficulties in understanding what is taught in the classrooms, laboratories and workshops. They will be found wanting in achieving the explicitly spelt out instructional objectives a, failures in examinations and tests, poor standards or assignments, unsatisfactory involvement in the academic work by students are some of the often noticed problems. These result in improper utilisation of institutional facilities and resources, unsatisfactory benefits of the efforts of instruction and frustration to students. Efforts must be made to ensure that problems of the above types are solved to the maximum extent.

Objectives of Educational Guidance

— To monitor the academic progress of students studying in the institution

— To acquaint the students with the prescribed curriculum

— To identify the academically gifted, backward, creative and other category of special learners

— To cater to the educational needs of special learners

— To assist students in getting information about further education

— To diagnose the learning difficulties of students and help them overcome the same

— To assist the students to maximise their scholastic achievement

— To help students to review and reflect on their performance on the course, and where appropriate to identify ways of seeking changes in work habits or behaviour.

— To help students face the consequence of acceptance of their role and to respond to the demands legitimately made on them.

Principles

The following are some of the principles on which educational guidance must be based

— Must be objective oriented

— Every student is capable of achieving the best of his ability

— Individual differences in academic achievement of students must be recognised

— Strategy must be student oriented

— The strategies must take into consideration the resources and facilities available to the students

— It is not for a few students only; it needs to be provided for all.

A class in which all students have more or less the same abilities for coping with instruction is ideal for teaching-learning. Teachers may employ the same instructional strategy for an entire group of students whose entry behaviour characteristics, learning ability, interest motivation, attitude to learning are the same. In such situations they do not encounter much difficulty in guiding students for optimal learning.

In reality, classes are never homogeneous and teachers have the challenging task of coping with a variety of students' characteristics. Students in any class can be ordinarily classified into three categories viz., the average, below average and above average on the basis of their academic performance.

The below average students are those whose performance is below the average performance of the class. Those whose performance is above the average of the class are categorised as above average. In this category, we may notice creative and gifted students as well. There are other types of students called slow learners, who have the ability to perform satisfactorily but are only slow in doing so. Their slowness may be attributed to a combination of a variety of causes. There may be some students, whose performance in comparison to that of the class may be satisfactory. Yet, their own performance may not be commensurate with their ability.

Problems in learning are most common in all categories of students. An above average student is likely to have as much of learning difficulties as a below average one. By providing educational guidance, efforts must be made to ensure that students maintain their level of academic performance. In all other cases, the efforts should be towards enabling the students to overcome their educational difficulties. In doing so it is important to identify those students who have problems and find solutions to their actual problems.

Identification of students is possible by continuous and careful observation of the 'academic behaviour' by teachers. The aspects of behaviour that may be observed include the interaction of students with the teacher during instruction, the types of questions put by them, interest shown for involvement in the teaching-learning activity, keenness exhibited for learning, alertness in grasping whatever is taught in the class, performance in tests and assignments, perusal of assignments and other assigned work.

Teachers can easily observe their students in the classes. However, care, must be exercised in drawing conclusions based only on observation. For, a student who may be shy to answer questions or ask questions should not be identified as a weak student.

It is important to spot out those students who require educational guidance not only on the basis of observation, but also on the basis of discussion with other faculty.

Achievement tests are used to find out what has been learned i.e. what habit and skills have been developed in students as a result of instruction. They are valuable as a means of determining to what extent the student has attained a certain degree of progress towards a desirable goal, whether he is ready to undertake the next step and how his attainment compares with that of other members of his group. These tests, based on the prescribed syllabus enable the teacher to find out the strengths and weaknesses of the student.

It is possible to find out the improvement on achievement. Diagnosis which forms one of the basic steps in providing guidance is possible through achievement testing.

Achievement tests serve a variety of purposes for use in educational guidance programmes. These are useful to survey students in order to find out those with educational problems, diagnose the actual difficulties and for prognosis.

The survey type of achievement tests comprise items that include the content covered in a subject area in order to find to what extent students meet the accepted norms and standards of academic performance. Diagnostic tests serve the purpose of finding out the actual weaknesses of students. Prognostic tests are to determine a student's readiness for learning.

Aptitude of a person is latent trait accounting for the probability of his Success in a field related to the traits on giving necessary training. Aptitude is a combination, of inborn capacities and developed abilities, skills etc., that makes the person what he is at any give time and predicts what he may become. Aptitude tests are expected to measure the potential for specific abilities and skills such as music, graphic arts, medicine, law, engineering, teaching etc. They tell us how well the individual is equipped to excel in a specific skill.

Intelligence tests are used to determine an individuals' learning capacity. The results of intelligence tests may be used to arginase learners into relatively homogeneous teaching learning groups. It is important to note that a fairly high degree of mental alertness is required in pursuing various courses of study. Learners who have low intelligence level experience learning difficulties, if they choose certain types of courses. It has also been found that success in certain vocational areas is dependent upon a high degree of intellectual ability.

Interest inventories is well known that success in any course of study or vocation depends to a considerable extent upon the interest the individual takes in it. Interests are closely related to aptitude. In certain cases interests are intrinsic. In most cases, interests to be created externally. This provides a constant incentive to continue until the goal is reached. It must be noted that worthwhile activities are better supported by intrinsic interest, because the pleasure continues even if the goal is not reached. Finding out the interest (or appraisal) is difficult. However the methods used are to ask the individual about their interests, to analyse the various activities in which the individual is involved, and measuring interest using interest inventories.

The first two methods have obvious limitations. While in the first case, the individual's oral explanation cannot be relied upon very much in the latter case, individual may be involved in work because of necessity. It would be difficult to find out whether the activity involved is freely chosen or chosen out of compulsion.

Information or data about an individual's personality achievement, interest, aptitude etc., are very vital for any guidance aciivily. The data obtained must be valid and reliable which, therefore, implies that the tools used for collecting such data must have high validity and reliability. Certain points are to be kept in mind about the information collected. Whenever a test has to be administered to an individual it should be done in a relaxed and friendly atmosphere. The test should never be thrust upon him. He should never be allowed to take it when he is under stress or strain. Readiness to take the test' is an important aspect. Test scores should not be disclosed to any other person than the student himself without the explicit knowledge and permission of the client. Strict confidentiality has to be maintained whenever the data needs to be used for research purposes, special care is to be taken to see that the identity of the student is not at all revealed. Any information provided by him either as responses to test items or interviews should be treated confidentially.

Guidance is a time consuming process and several sessions will be required to provide adequate guidance. Each session may result in some new facts emerging which can provide some nearer insights into the problems of the individual concerned. The information so emerging should be very carefully recorded. Obtaining information alone is riot important but storing the same is equally important. The work involved in recording and filing is tedious and uninteresting yet, most important.

The record should be cumulative and, in addition to up-to-date identifying data, should include important items concerning a student from the time he enters the institution until he leaves it. Such information about a student car, be stored in a guidance folder. This is designed to cover a period of years. Suggested items for guidance folder are: Identifying data, home background, economic condition, health record, academic record, out-of-class activities, character and personality traits, special or peculiar incidents (details), special interests and achievement, educational plans, vocational plans, experiences, details or outcome of each guidance/ counselling session. Particular care must be taken in maintaining the folder. The entries must be made as accurately as possible. Where tests are administered, the date, time and conditions under which the tests were administered has to be correctly recorded. When interpretation of information is recorded, it has to be done under specific headings.

Guidance folders should be made available to the concerned teacher as well, since the learner's aims, interest, potentialities, degree of accomplishment, application to work represent valuable data to teachers in evaluating classroom work and in guiding learning. There is one exception to this general procedure, confidential information about an individual that is of value only to the counsellor should either be removed from the folder before the latter is made available for general use or be kept in a separate file. The information collected about students must be properly recorded. It is suggested that a master register may be developed for the purpose. The register may contain information about the different aspects of all students such as their place of education, medium of instruction at the school, study habits, level of motivation, performance in tests and assignments. Great care must be exercised in filling up the record sheet for each student. This sort of a register can be used for maintaining information about all students of a class.

Teachers must build educational guidance as an integral Part of their everyday instruction. Every teacher consciously or otherwise, deliberately or not deliberately attempts to provide, guidance to their students in learning. Sometimes it may be given in a formal way and at. Other times in an informal manner.

The guidance may range from suggesting/ advising students to be systematic in their studies, to planning and implementing individualised instructional strategies. Educational guidance strategies to be used by teachers depend upon the nature of the problems, and the extent of their effect and the purposes of providing for such guidance. These strategies should be situation oriented and student-oriented. The strategies employed must help in enabling students to achieve to the best of their abilities in scholastic areas. Guidance and counselling strategies can be classified into two categories viz., group approach and individual approach.

Every student must have the freedom (and be helped) to choose the courses of study considering his educational ability, interest, future needs etc. The purposes of this type of guidance are

— Encourage students to utilise their abilities in specific areas

— Assist students in understanding and appreciating the instructional obligations which they are required to complete. This may include information regarding the assignments, tests, project work they are required to complete as part of the course work

— Provide information to students regarding further education programmes

— Give general orientation to students regarding the facilities and resources available such as library, laboratories, workshops, scholarships etc.

— Provide opportunities for group thinking in regard to common problems and experience

Group guidance approach for educational purposes must be organised for disseminating educational information of a general nature to students. Care must be exercised in organising group guidance;

Group guidance may be in the form of group discussion and talks to enable students to plan their educational activities. This is possible by giving them information about the courses of study, curriculum requirements, scheme of evaluation etc., by teachers.

It is advisable to organise group guidance sessions for students who have common problems by identifying, students. Poor achievers, students whose level of motivation is low, those whose study skills are not satisfactory may be provided guidance, through a group approach. Besides the general group guidance programmes, teachers may have to design and implement group guidance in their own class for the purpose of general improvement in academic performance. Such guidance must form an integral part of instruction. In these programmes, teachers may have to often focus on the progress of the students, common problems faced by them and suggestions for overcoming them, common mistakes, committed in tests and assignments and suggestions for improving their performance. For effective organisation of group guidance it may be necessary to have a team of faculty for planning, implementing and evaluating these programmes. The team members have to be properly identified with one of them, preferably a Head of Department as the coordinator of the programme. The task of the team would be:

— to identify the areas and scope of guidance for students

— to plan a schedule of guidance programmes spread throughout the year

— to decide the strategy such as lecture, conference, seminar, etc. appropriate for the spelt out objectives

— to conduct the guidance programmes as per the schedule drawn

— to evaluate the effectiveness of the programmes organised to get feedback for purposes of improvement

— to plan and monitor the follow up.

Several problems of students in the area of learning may be attributed to a lack of knowledge of what the institution can offer and how it can do so. This calls for a knowledge of the facilities and resources available in the institution. These facilities may be laboratories, workshops, library, recreation, cocurricular, hostel etc. Each of these are meant for specific purposes, work under a set of rules and regulations, have certain expectations from students.

It is important to have an understanding of the rules and regulations of the academic administration of the institution. Certain areas under which such information is required are attendance requirements, scholarship and stipend awards (conditions for award, criteria and mode) academic and extra curricular activities, guidance services rendered by the institution. It is not that such information is not provided by institutions. Some institutions give these as part of their prospectus which is supplied with the application form for admission.

Most often students do not go through the rules. It is taken as a routine information. Even when the same is read, it is read rather casually. Thus, the purpose of giving the information in the prospectus gets defeated. The practice that should be followed in institutions is to hand over a copy of the rules and regulations and get the students committed to these. It is only then that they try to adhere to the same. Institutional induction is an activity which is in tended to 'introduce' the institution in its totality to the students.

It is during such an activity that students come to know of the objectives of the institution, its development, traditions, resources, faculty etc. This activity enables the students to know the environment in which they are required to work/study. It lays the foundation for their continuous interactions at the institution. It enables them to accept the institution as a place where their needs would be met, their aspirations and goals fulfilled. Students will be able to see themselves in the context of the institutional environment.

The objectives spelt in the above paragraph can be realised if induction programmes are efficiently organised. The main intention of such programmes should be a mutual understanding involving the students, staff and the administration of the institution.

The beginning of the academic programme would be the most ideal period for the organisation of induction programmes. In fact, all the academic activities planned by the institute should follow this programme. Care should be taken to cover all aspects of the life of students during their stay in the institution.

It is also advantageous to introduce all members of the faculty and office of the institution to the students during these programmes. A visit to the different departments and laboratories including the library will be very useful. A well drawn time table for the induction programme goes a long way in its effective implementation. It is useful to involve all members of the faculty in the organisation of such a programme.

Special learners

Special learners are those who stand out as a distinct set from other students in a class and therefore require special attention. Educationally they deviate from the average students in their academic achievement. These learners require special attention by teachers. They do not profit much from learning in average group situations. Special learners in institutions may be classified as

Gifted students

Gifted students are those who show consistently remarkable performance in educational endeavours. They possess a superior intellectual potential and functional ability to achieve academically in the top 15 to 20 per cent of the students in the institution, and/or talent of a high order. Creative students are those who exhibit creativity.

Creativity

Creativity is the process of sensing gaps missing elements; forming ideas or hypothesies and testing, the same. It is the ability to change one's approach to a problem, to cope with ideas that are both relevant and unusual; to go beyond the immediate situation to redefine the problem.

Slow learners

Slow learners are those students who require more time for learning than the normal/average students in a class. Hence, they show marked educational deficiency. They learn at a slower rate than others. In order to provide guidance to the above category of learners it is important to identify them. For these learners, individual guidance will have to be arranged. Identification of the special learners will have to be carried out systematically. It may be based on teachers' observation, academic records and performance in mental ability traits.

3

Guidance and Counselling

Guidance is an assistance made available by competent counsellors to an individual of any age to help him direct his own life, develop his own point of view, make his own decisions, carry his own burdens. Guidance as that aspect of educational programme, which is concerned especially with helping the pupil to become adjusted to his present situation and to plan his future in the line with his interests, abilities, and social needs.

According to Hollis and Hollis, there are eight principles on which any guidance programme should be based. They can be modified to fit locally accepted beliefs.

Functions

Adjustmental function

Guidance and counselling are adjustmental in the sense that they help the student in making the best possible adjustment to the current situations in the educational institution and occupational world, in the home and the community.

Professional and individualised aid is given in making immediate and suitable adjustment at problem points.

Orientational function

Guidance and counselling have orientational function also. They orientate the students in problems of career planning, educational programming and direction towards long-term personal aims and values. Awareness of the need to plan in the context of the complexity of the world of work is an essential prerequisite of going through education and preparation for after-education career.

Developmental function

They should try not only to cure when the problems have occurred and done their damage, rather they should begin before the problems arise and maladjustments occur. If unsolved problems re allowed to accumulate, their total effect may lead the student to the point where his capacity for growth is blocked. In such cases, guidance and counselling have a very important developmental function for helping the students achieve self-development and self-realisation. Guidance and counselling also have to discharge the important function of furthering the welfare of the society and be important instruments of national development.

Scope

As the life is getting complex day by day, the problems for which expert helps is required are increasing proportionately. The scope of guidance, per necessity, is extending horizontally to much of the social context, to matters of prestige in occupations, to the broad field of social trends, and economic development. Guidance is assuming more and more responsibility for the individual in every direction-it helps in the selection of educational courses, and profitable occupation, in job placement; placement in the next stage of education and training; occupational surveys; improvement of study skills, maintenance of mental health; counselling regarding personal adjustment problems; identifying the gifted, the backward and help them achieve the maximum.

In short, educational, vocational, avocational, social, personal, moral and even marital problems of individual are the concerns of guidance and counselling. Their scope is indeed very vast. A cursory glance at our seats of higher learning will show the imperative need of instituting in them a well-organized programme of guidance and counselling.

Education is expanding its frontiers making it well-nigh impossible for an individual students to make a choice of courses and careers without expert guidance. Occupational scene too is changing so rapidly that yesterday's rocket circuitry electronics specialist considered as highly prized as a marks-man on the old frontier is to-day's unemployment statistic. One of the great stories in out midst is the dramatic increase in jobs. Not only that quite a big number of students at the threshold of a college or university are in for compelling and difficult life situations-they are shy, fearful, gullible, not skilled in managing their own affairs. They lack self-acknowledge which may enable them to form realistic life-goals and plans. They lack both focus and meaningful direction.

Occasionally they lose their way in the dark labyrinths of adolescence and do not know how and when to act. They have a grapple with complex social problems-living with and sharing facilities with peers, such as living in hostels and sharing extra-curricular experiences, adjustment to heterosexual relationships etc. Surveys of Indian students and alumni document the widespread feeling of dissatisfaction with college and university life.

A survey was conducted by the All India Educational and Vocational Guidance Association for gauging college student's needs. Three thousand students from seventeen Indian universities responded.

It is true that provision of guidance and counselling services in the colleges and universities cannot be seen as a panacea for all our educational ills nor can a counselling officer hope to give students a trouble-free or problem-free life, but where possible, he can help them to resolve their difficulties, or if that is not possible, to live with them. To help them resolve the stresses and strains does not require a nosey-parker intrusion of privacy but the response of an understanding and empathic person and an atmosphere of understanding, faith and sincerity. And this is what is needed. Guidance and counselling programme needs to be introduced in our colleges and universities to meet the varied needs of the educational system, administration and students:

— *To help in the total development of the student*: The emphasis on intellectual development through the teaching of subjects alone cannot help in the total development of the students. We have to evolve some method of helping students understand themselves and helping teachers understand the students. There has to be a basic and fundamental change in our entire system of education, change which recognises that matter how well a human being is educated in chemistry, physics, economics, history or literature, he remains a barbarian unless he knows something about himself. Self-knowledge in depth which has been the forgotten factor in our educational system must become its primary focus-and this is what can be done through a programme of guidance and counselling. Total development of the students are expected, accepted, understood and planned for and all types of experiences in an institution are so organised as to contribute to the total development of the student. That, all that a student needs in an educational institution is good teaching, is an exploded myth. Something much more and beyond this is needed to produce competent, mature and well-rounded citizens.

— *To help in the proper choice of courses:* Everyone knows that so far our educational system has grown up in a higgledy piggledy fashion. The subjects which are the least wanted humanities and the liberal arts-have been those most frequently offered and taken, both in the colleges and the universities because they were the oldest and relatively inexpensive areas of knowledge, taken because they require to specified intellectual equipment.

— *To help in the proper choice of careers*: We are living in a highly complex and rapidly changing world of work. There are changing requirements in industrial jobs, altered market conditions for professional manpower, the development of para-professional occupational selection more difficult than eve. The young students in colleges and universities need to be informed about various jobs and openings available to them and the requirements, responsibilities and the nature of work involved in them so that they could measure themselves up to them and develop and crystallise their occupational goals. They need to be helped in making meaningful occupational selection and preparation for an entry into them to have a fulfilling and rewarding career.

— *To help the students in vocational development:* The process of vocational development covers almost the entire span of life on an individual. It begins quite early in one's life and continue till sometimes after retirement. In this process, the individual passes through various stages—growth, exploration, maintenance and decline. Guidance services need to be provided to the colleges and universities to help the students in the process of vocational development-particularly the stage of growth and exploration, by making it possible for them to gain knowledge about themselves-their abilities, interests and needs on, the one hand and knowledge about the world of work on the other. By providing them opportunities for self-exploration as well as exploration of the world of work while they are still in an educational institution, their transition from education to work can be facilitated.

— *To develop readiness for choices and changes to face new challenges*: In a paper entitled The Need for Counselling in Higher Education, presented at the Third International Round Table of Educational Counselling and Vocational Guidance, Miss New Some, Counselling Officer at the University of Keels, North Strafford Shire, England, writes, "For the students of higher education the demands of life are likely to be great, in a most different way from the exacting demands of education itself. On graduating he will be called upon to make use of the kind of person he has become as much if not more than what he has learnt in his course of study-not only to make an initial choice of what he is to do on graduating but will be called upon to change his occupation several times in a life time. Readiness for these choices and changes is essential, not only to the student himself but to the society as a whole. To the extent to which he is able to capitalise on his experience and face new challenges with a realistic expectation of success, to that extent he will benefit society. If he is unable to meet the changing demands, not only of the working world but also of his other roles of life, to that extent he will be a liability and will fail to fulfil the expectations which society has for its most able people." Guidance services are needed to develop in the students the ability to cope with their new problems and concerns in such a way that they become more competent to meet the demands which will continue to be made upon them in the future.

— *To minimise the mismatching between education and employment and help in the efficient use of manpower:* The latest analysis done by Planning Commission reveals that the educated youth between 15 and 29 years of age constituted 11.5 per cent of the corresponding labour force but they accounted for 33.2 per cent of the total unemployment in the country. According to the Planning Commission's labour force projections, the total number of educated unemployed at the beginning of 1980 was estimated at 3.47 million. If there is no further deterioration in the unemployment rate, this number is likely to go upto 4.66 million in 1985. And this is the challenging situation we have to face.

— *To motive the youth for self-employment:* Considering the magnitude of educated job-seekers flowing into the job market in India every year, it is essential that a sizable fraction of enterprising youth is initiated into careers of self-employment. Some arrangement needs to be instituted in the colleges and universities to identify the deserving cases fit to take up self-employment, educate them on how to proceed about the job of setting up a venture, help them through the cooperation of the concerned agencies in this sphere to prepare technically sound and economically viable projects; sponsor their cases to the banks for loan assistance and guide them to overcome the teething troubles effective follow-up after the commencement of the venture.

— *To help freshers establish proper identity:* In our country the youngmen entering colleges and even universities are comparatively young in years. Young adolescents they are, they are passing through a stage between childhood and adulthood, between the morality learned as a child and the ethics to be developed by the adult. They find it extremely difficult to establish a satisfactory identity. Such failure or delay leads to what can be called "role diffusion". This crisis in role identity is perhaps very acute today. The uncertainties of the future, the conflicts in languages, culture, regions, castes, etc., and the erosion of traditional values has rendered Indian youth rootless.

— *To identify and motivate the students from weaker sections of society:* Students from weaker sections have their own problems and needs. They experience difficulty in adjustment with the peers, teachers and the environment. To communicate, make friends, utilise the time profitably, make the best use of lectures, make an effective use of library and other facilities available all pose problems for them. Guidance facilities are urgently needed for such type of students to enable them to adjust and utilise the available facilities properly.

— *To help the students in their period of turmoil and confusion*: The students undergo a great deal of turmoil and searching to give meaning to their lives. They have their conflicts and anxieties. They feel disillusioned regarding higher education. They find that colleges and universities, instead of imparting them education, just enable them to pass examinations-they feel sunk and cheated. When this education does not enable them to get immediate employment, they feel lost and bewildered.

— *To help in checking wastage and stagnation:* The average pass percentage at the graduate and post-graduate level is about 50 to 60. Thousands of our students, unfortunately, drop out, get pushed out, and fall out of the system. This problem is becoming more serious day by day.

This poor achievement may be due to so many reasons lack of proper study skills and effective study habits, lack of the knowledge for making full use of the facilities provided and so on.

Need for counselling

There are no accurate figure of the number of counsellors in our educational institutions. Under the umbrella of the British Association for Counselling, the National Association of Counsellors in Education and the Association for Student Counselling are the two groups particularly appropriate for people who work in educational settings. Their membership consists perhaps at most, of a thousand people who are sufficiently interested in counselling in education to join an appropriate association.

Some members of the National Association of Careers and Guidance Teachers may consider counselling as part of their work. It seems unlikely that there are more counsellors throughout the country than the number of people in these groups, certainly not a number to be justifiably considered a multitude.

The advent of professional counselling as a supplement to pastoral care has had a very mixed reception. There has been hostility and resentment from those teachers, tutors and parents who see the counsellor as one who is making a take-over bid for the personal relationships with children and students which hitherto have bee their concern. Others feel antagonistic towards the counsellors' acceptance of children as they are and towards the counsellor's effort to help young people to make their own choices and decisions and, within limits, to take responsibility for their own lives.

We remember being sharply taken to task by a school governor because we said that children should not have freedom to choose anything. Perhaps a look at some of the objection to counselling which people raise may be appropriate as an introduction to the needs. Not a great deal is known about counselling in education in this country, and one of the aims of this book is to provide an introduction to the work which may help people to decide what counselling can and cannot do in diverse educational settings.

Among those people who know a little about counselling and among those who know nothing there are some who raise strong objections to the introduction of counselling as a specialist activity in schools and colleges, which is what we advocate. Some of these objections merit attention, because they arise from very real fears and firm beliefs about the meaning of education and of life, and they are helpful in the sense that they enable counsellors, indeed sometimes force them, to re-examine their own beliefs and acknowledge their defences.

Counselling is of no value. This view is representative of those who believe that any helping relationship is detrimental both to individuals and to society because to need help is a sign of weakness and to provide it fosters deficiencies in charter; adversity is the means to strength and people should counter it along and unaided. Leona Tyler argues that 'Counselling is still to a large extent an art, dependent more on shared experience than on reported experiments..' and counsellors need to 'distinguish between the things we do simply because they seem to work well and things we so because of some definite research evidence'. Nevertheless counsellors can and should assess the value of what they are doing.

Counselling fosters conformity. This objection to helping professions is being voiced increasingly by some students, who suggest that the counsellors manipulates people for example, into taking up safe, secure occupations instead of 'doing their own thing', which seems to ignore the fact that for some people 'doing their own thing' lies in a secure occupation and conformity. It is true that counsellors encourage people to take into account the cognitive and affective aspects of a decision or problems and the likely consequences, which does to some extent encourage caution. The alternative is action by impulse, which in certain circumstances, such as immediate danger, or in response to another person's distress, may be appropriate.

Counselling perpetuates the myth of freedom. Those who object to the self concept theories of counselling suggest that counsellors deceive themselves by talking about freedom of choice, for in reality life is deterministic and each step affects the direction of the next one. Someone described the importance of previous experience by saying that 'as we walk into the future we come face to face with the past'. In suggesting that we have a human capacity to choose between two or more genuine alternatives we should acknowledge that the choice is always limited and freedom have been compared to a game of cards, in which the limits are imposed by the cards which you are dealt and the freedom comes in the way you choose to play those cards.

At the present time in this country, counselling is not a discipline; it draws upon knowledge from many areas but its main subject is people, and to may knowledge there is no subject which attempts to concern itself with people in the way in which counselling does.

Psychology is concerned with behaviour, not so much with the people who do the behaving, and sociology seems concerned to a large extent with people in groups and the problems which society creates for them, but not with solutions. Between psychology and sociology there seems to be a gap in our knowledge and our concern which social psychology to some extent may close, but into which counselling is a study of interpersonal relationships, their effects, their development and practice in education may grow. Much depends upon the activity of counsellors and counsellors educators and the importance that they themselves attach to the study of their subject.

The objection that counsellors are inadequately prepared for their work must inevitable in these early years have some validity. It is of vital importance to assess the needs in a particular school or college which a counselling service may realistically be expected to meet and it is essential to appoint a counsellor who is trained and capable of running the type of service needed. Of course counsellors are inadequately prepared to perform as psychiatrists, as educational psychologists, as nurses, as mind readers or as magicians.

Trained counsellors should be adequately educated to counsel students who may wish to talk with them about personal, educational or vocational problems, but they are not trained to solve all these problems; they should be adequately educated in the administration and interpretation of certain tests, and in their liaison work with outside social services and with school staff. Counsellors are always learning and one of the things that a few years' experience as a counsellor reveals very painfully is that the counsellor who tries to be many things to many people sometimes ends up being nothing to anybody.

The objection that in theory counselling is available to all children or students but in practice is limited is a valid one. Counselling is often regarded as a source of help for those with problems or crises, but it can have a preventive as well as a remedial function, and it is only one source of help; students and children alike will turn for help to any one of a number of people within the institution, according to their temperament and inclination. The relationship and help provided by a counsellor are not for everyone and cannot compensate in the long term for other relationships which may be inadequate.

The charge that counsellors pamper students often arises from those who equate understanding with softness and over-indulgence, and acceptance with the sanctioning of any kind of behaviour. The understanding and acceptance offered by a counsellor are an attempt to encourage constructive ways of copying with problems rather than the negative or destructive ones which often seem to occur as a result of the blind application of moral judgements.

Since the end of World War II the majority of West European countries have revised their educational systems, attaching greater importance than ever before to the problems of guidance (of which counselling is a part) in schools. The introduction of comprehensive education is a development with which, in principle, we are in agreement, and we are aware that change is never made without inconvenience, even when it is a change is never made without inconvenience, even when it is a change for the better. Several years ago we worked in a school which was one of three to be reorganized and transferred to a new, purpose built, pleasant comprehensive school.

The reorganization of the three schools took place some eighteen months before the new building was completed and during this interim period the schools was housed in three separate buildings some distance apart, not an uncommon situation in reorganization schemes.

The transfer to the new building was organizationally fairly competent, considering the size of the enterprise and the inexperience and lack of training of teachers in such undertakings, and the school is now well established and bursting at the seams. Yet when we consider the cost of that experience in terms of human distress we have difficulty in justifying it. Everything seemed to be considered except the people; provision was made for the timetable, the furniture, the books, the equipment, but there was no one in a sufficiently detached position to consider the situation and say, 'Look at the way these children are behaving. What are we doing to them?' or 'This arrangement has placed these teachers under intolerable stress, what can we do to help them?' A counsellor is one of those who can be in a position to consider the 'people problems' of educational development. There is a significant association between the system of school authority as perceived by the class teachers, both as person and professionals. In other words, where teachers feel either that they have a hand in the internal running of the school, or that its outside directors are aware of their internal problems, they tend to be both liked by their pupils and to be seen as effective teachers. If the teachers see their superiors as remote or dictatorial, they, in their turn are seen by their pupils as unfriendly and in their turn are seen by their pupils as unfriendly and ineffective.

Awareness of the existence of this kind of situation could lead to an easing of the problem, and a counsellor is an appropriate person though not the only one to develop this awareness and to help people to cope with the resulting change in relationships.

The teacher/parent relationship is sometimes another difficult part of school life which could be made smoother with the help of a counsellor. In evidence given to the Plowden Committee on Primary Education, the Association of Educational Psychologists suggested that many teachers show defeatism in their attitudes towards parents, pleading that the parents who need to become involved in their children's education are the very ones who do not attend meetings, which of course is often the case. Schools must be encouraged, says the Association, 'to go out into their areas and ensure these contacts, without which much educational effort will be wasted'. Suitable teachers ought to be given the job of developing effective liaisons with parents and welfare, industrial and commercial interests in their areas, for 'with rare exceptions, there is a gross under-functioning of the school as a focal point for community interest and activity'.

Whilst we would not dispute this, we would like to suggest to the educational psychologists that to except a teacher to spend the day with some classes and then seek out parents in the evening is tantamount to inflicting the worst of tortures, and if they do not believe this, they are very welcome to test it empirically by doing it.

We are not saying that teachers should not visit the homes of children, but we do think it is an advantage for schools to have a counsellor or social worker to provide a regular means of communication. Joan Clerk, in describing her work as a Home School Liaison officer, gives her impression of the unwillingness of some parents to visit schools: 'Parents who had never visited the school at all, one found, were very often people who were genuinely scared of teachers. They felt that teachers "looked down" at them, and however wrong this may be, that is the way that they perceived the situation.

Daws suggests that the teachers' professional image is one of the most demanding of all the professions, requiring, as it does, that a teacher have a knowledge of his subject and a knowledge of his pupils and that he teach both it and them well. The increased pressure on teachers to be all things to all children, which is often self-inflicted and which, of course, is impossible, nevertheless indicates that it is becoming increasingly desirable for a teacher to have as great a knowledge of himself as he has of his subject and his pupils. This applies equally to the counsellor, but she is given the opportunity to gain self-knowledge during her training an opportunity not often presented in the course of teacher training.

This is not suggest that the socialisation of children is solely the job of the schools. It is initially the job of the parents, and most of them succeed, but where they fail or are inadequate then teachers and counsellors can be the safety net between the potential delinquent and his determined drive to self-destruction against the bulwark of society. Bryan Wilson suggests that the creation of large housing estates, large schools and the promotion of social mobility have all weakened community allegiances, and that the important aspect of this development has been the breakdown of the nexus between home and school.

Once the school ceases to belong to the community, parental moral training is much less reinforced by school training. As education is shorn of its moral concerns, and as teaching becomes subject to greater professional specialisations, so the personal knowledge of particular children by teachers becomes less intense.

As school size increases, so this context becomes increasingly impersonal. The individual child learns to look out for himself: if he acquires independence, he also learns the ropes according to the values of the peer groups and increasingly evident-of the entertainment dominated youth culture.

Many adults are well meaning considerate of and anxious for the welfare of children, particularly their own. However, parents are exhorted on all sides by child care experts, psychologists, women's magazines, newspapers, radio and television to treat their child in this way or that way, to feed him this food or that food in order that he may develop into a strong, healthy, stable-minded adult. So much so that the child is likely to need all these assets by the time he reaches maturity in order to cope with his neurotic parents.

Ambivalent feelings and attitudes are another difficult area of acceptance for all of us, but educators in particular seem to have a great dread of ambivalence and to deny its existence. It is much easier if things are either right or wrong, good or bad, yeas or no, do or don't, and people know their own minds. The failure to recognize and accept ambivalence as normal is perhaps one of the most prejudicial factors against making choices and decisions to which we can have some commitment.

The extent to which counselling is accepted and developed depends very largely on the work that counsellors themselves do to counteract the inertia of public opinion and/or the apathy of local and government authority.

Perhaps the most useful contribution to the growth of counselling will ultimately be found to be the publicity that counsellors themselves give to their own work and problems, and the energy with which they emphasize those important economic, social and above all human issues for which their work is vital. The quality of life in many of our school and colleges is sufficiently inadequate to arouse anger in the mildest of counsellors, and as people who are in everyday touch with the plan that this inadequacy creates for children, students, and staff, we could use some of that anger in a constructive enhancement of our own profession.

The provision of counselling services in education is not seen as a panancea for all or educational ills, nor does a counsellor hope to give children and students a trouble-or problem-free life, but where possible to help them to resolve their difficulties, or if that is not possible, to live with them.

We should help children and young people to cope with their everyday problems, for all lives bring crises which may be unexpected-illness, a death in a family, a missing parent- and most of us at some time suffer shattered dreams and frustrating or distressing experiences. Being aware of a child's stress situations and being sensitive to the individual thresholds of stress within human beings can be a complex and subtle process which requires not a 'nosey parker' instrusion of privacy but the response of an understanding and empathic person.

Teachers and tutors have an important task here in knowing when to try to decrease a child's internal burden by reducing his workload or when to recognize that disturbed behaviour may be his way of asking for help. Pain, hardship and failure can offer valuable learning experiences, but not in the negative way in which they are often used in education.

This does not imply that teachers or counsellors should attempt to be amateur psychiatrists or substitute parents, but that they should work together in an attempt to find educational answers to those psychological problems whicharise in the educational setting, for even when children are referred for psychiatric help they usually remain in attendance at school and have to cope with and be accommodated by the school community, except for the hour a week which they spend at the Child Guidance Clinic. The National Association for Mental Health in its proposal to involve schools in a positive mental health approach drew attention to the potential of the school as being of central importance in preventive measures because it is a community which caters for the total population of young people, it can compel their attendance over a long period of their childhood, and it more or less has a commitment to mental health goals.

Termination of counselling relationships

Historically, addressing the process of termination directly has been avoided for several reasons. Ward has suggested two of the most prominent. First, termination is associated with loss-a traditionally taboo subject in all parts of society.

Even though Hayes points out that loss may be associated with re-creation, transcendence, greater self-understanding, and new discoveries, counselling is generally viewed as emphasizing growth and development unrelated to endings. Second, termination is not directly related to the microskills that facilitate counselling relationships. Termination is not a process usually highlighted in counsellor education. Its significance has begun to emerge, however, because of societal trends, such as the aging of the American population, the wide acceptance of the concept of life stages, and an increased attention to death as a part of the life span. There are several important functions of termination. First, termination signals that something is finished. Life is a series of hellos and good-byes. Hellos begin at birth, and good-byes end at death. Between birth and death, individuals enter into and leave a succession of experiences, including jobs, relationships, and life stages. Growth and adjustment depend on an ability to make the most of these experiences and learn from them. To begin something new, a former experience must be completed and resolved. Termination is the opportunity to end a learning experience properly, whether on a personal or professional level. In counselling, termination "is more than. an act signifying the end of therapy"; it is also a motivator.

Both client and counsellor are motivated by the knowledge that the counselling experience is limited in time. This awareness is similar to that of a young person who realizes that he or she cannot remain a promising youth forever. Such realisations may spur one on to hard work while there is still time to do something significant. Some counsellors, such as those associated with strategic, systemic, and solution-focused family therapy, purposely limit the number of counselling sessions so that clients and counsellors are more aware of time constraints and make the most of sessions. Limiting the number of sessions in individual counselling is also effective. Second, termination is a means of maintaining changes already achieved and generalizing problem-solving skills acquired in counselling. Successful counselling results in significant changes in the way the client thinks, feels, or acts. These changes are rehearsed in counselling, but they must be practiced in the real world.

Termination provides an opportunity for such practice. The client can always go back to the counsellor for any needed follow-up, but termination is the natural point for the practice of independence to begin. It is a potentially empowering experience for the client and enables him or her to address the present in an entirely new or modified way. At termination, the opportunity to put "insights into actions" is created. In other words, what seems like an exit becomes an entrance. Third, termination serves as a reminder that the client has matured. Besides offering the client new skills or different ways of thinking about him or herself, effective counselling that ends with an appropriate termination marks a time in the client's life when he or she is less absorbed by and preoccupied with personal problems and more able to deal with outside people and events. This ability to handle external situations may result in more interdependent relationships that are mutually supportive and consequently lead toward a "more independent and satisfying life". Having achieved a successful resolution to a problem, a client now has new insights and abilities that are stored in memory and may be recalled on occasions.

When to terminate a relationship is a question that has no definite answer. If the relationship is ended too soon, clients may lose the ground they gained in counselling and regress to earlier behaviours. On the other hand, if termination is never addressed, clients can become dependent on the counsellor and fail to resolve difficulties and grow as persons. There are, however, several pragmatic considerations in the timing of termination. Have clients achieved behavioural, cognitive, or affective contract goals? When both clients and counsellors have a clear idea about whether or not particular goals have been reached, the timing of termination is easier to figure out. The key to this consideration is setting up a mutually agreed-upon contract before counselling begins.

Can clients concretely show where they have made progress in what the wanted to accomplish? In this situation, specific progress may be the basis for making a decision about termination. Is the counselling relationship helpful? If either the client or the counsellor senses that what is occurring in the counselling sessions is not helpful, termination is appropriate.

Has the context Of the initial counselling arrange-ment changed? In cases where there is a move or a prolonged illness, termination (as well as a referral) should be considered. Overall, there is no one right time to terminate a counselling relationship. The "when" of termination must be figured out in accordance with the uniqueness of the situation and overall ethical and professional guidelines.

Termination is an issue during individual counselling sessions. Initial sessions should have clearly defined time limits. A range of 45-50 minutes is generally considered adequate for an individual counselling session. It usually takes a counsellor 5-10 minutes to adjust to the client and the client's concerns.

Counselling sessions that terminate too quickly may be as unproductive is ones that last too long. Benjamin proposes two important factors in closing an interview. First, both client and counsellor should have be aware that the session is ending. Second, no new material should be introduced or discussed during this ending. If the client introduces new material, the counsellor needs to work to make it the anticipated focus of the next session. On rare occasions, the counsellor has to deal with new material on an emergency basis.

A counsellor can close an interview effectively in several ways. One is simply to make a brief statement indicating that time is up. For example, he or she might say, "It looks like our time is up for today." The simpler the statement, the better.

If a client is discussing a number of subjects in an open-ended manner near the end of a session, the counsellor should remind the client that there are only 5 or 10 minutes left. The client can then focus attention on important matters. As an alternative or in addition to the direct statement, the counsellor can use nonverbal gestures to indicate that the session is ending. These include looking at his or her watch or standing up. Nonverbal gestures are probably best used with verbal indicators. Each reinforces the other.

Toward the end of the interview it is usually helpful to summarize what has happened in the session. This summation may be initiated either by the counsellor or the client. A good summary ties together the main points of the session and "should be brief, to the point, and without interpretation". If done mutually, a summary allows counsellor and client to realize what each has gotten out of the session and provides a means of clearing up any misunderstandings. An important part of terminating any individual session is setting up the next appointment. Most problems are resolved over time, Clients and counsellors need to know when they will meet again to continue the work in progress. It is easier and more efficient to set up a next appointment at the end of a session than to do it later by phone.

Counselling relationships vary in length and purpose. It is vital to the health and well being of everyone that the subject of termination be brought up early so that counsellor and client can make the most of their time together.

Individuals need time to prepare for the end of a meaningful relationship. There may be some sadness, even if the relationship ends in a positive way. Thus, termination should not necessarily be presented as the zenith of the counselling experience. Hackney and Cormier stress that it is better to play down the importance of termination rather than play it up. The counsellor and client must agree on when termination of the relationship is appropriate and helpful. Generally, they give each other verbal messages about a readiness to terminate.

For example, a client may say, "I really think I've made a lot of progress over the past few months." Or a counsellor may state, "You appear to be well on your way to no longer needing my services." Such statements suggest the beginning of the end of the counselling relationship. They usually imply a recognition of growth or resolution. A number of other behaviours may also signal the end of counselling. These include a decrease in the intensity of work; more humour; and less denial, withdrawal, anger, mourning, or dependence. In a relationship that has lasted more than three months, the final three or four weeks should be spent discussing the impact of termination. For instance, counsellors may inquire how their clients will cope without the support of the relationship.

Counsellors may also ask clients to talk about the meaning of the counselling relationship and how they will use what they have learned in the future. Shulman suggests that, as a general rule of thumb, one-sixth of the time spent in a counselling relationship should be devoted to focusing on termination.

There are at least two ways to facilitate the ending of a counsellor-client relationship. One involves the use of fading. Dixon and Glover define fading as "a gradual decrease in the unnatural structures developed to create desired changes". In other words, clients gradually stop receiving reinforcement for behaving in certain ways. A desired goal of all counselling is to help clients become less dependent on the counsellor and the counselling sessions and more dependent on themselves and interdependent with others. From counselling, clients should also learn the positive reinforcement of natural contingencies. To promote fading, counselling sessions can be spaced further apart or simply shortened.

Another way to promote termination is to help clients develop successful problem-solving skills. Clients, like everyone else, are constantly faced with problems. If counsellors can help their clients learn more effective ways to cope with these difficulties, clients will no longer need the counselling relationship. This is a process of generalization from counselling experience to life. At its best, this process includes an emphasis on education and prevention as well as decision-making skills for everyday life and crisis situations.

Resistance to termination may come from either the counsellor or client. Patterson and Eisenberg note that resistance is especially likely when the counselling relationship has lasted for a long time or has involved a high level of intimacy. Other factors that may promote resistance include the pain of earlier losses, loneliness, unresolved grief, need gratification, fear of rejection, and fear of having to be self-reliant. Some of these factors are more prevalent with clients, while others are more likely to characterise counsellors.

Client resistance. Clients resist termination in many ways. Two easily recognized expressions of resistance are (1) asking for more time at the end of a session and (2) asking for more appointments once a goal has been reached. Another more troublesome form of client resistance is the development of new problems that were not part of his or her original concerns, such as depression or anxiety The manifestation of these symptoms makes termination more difficult; and in such situations, a client may convince the counsellor that only he or she can help. Thus, the counsellor may feel obligated to continue working with the person for either personal or ethical reasons. Regardless of the strategy employed, the termination process is best carried out gradually and slowly. Sessions can become less frequent over time; and client skills, abilities, and resources can be highlighted simulta-neously. Sometimes when clients are especially hesitant to terminate, the counsellor can "prescribe" a limited number of future sessions or concentrate with clients on how they will set themselves up for relapse. These procedures make the covert more overt and help counsellors and clients identify more clearly what issues are involved in leaving a helping relationship.

Counsellor resistance. Some counsellors are reluctant to say good-bye at the appropriate time. Clients who have special or unusual needs or those who are very productive may be especially attractive to counsellors. Goodyear lists eight conditions in which termination may be especially difficult for counsellors:

— When termination signals the end of a significant relationship

— When termination arouses the counsellor's anxieties about the client's ability to function independently

— When termination arouses guilt in the counsellor about not having been more effective with the client

— When the counsellor's professional self-concept is threatened by the client who leaves abruptly and angrily

— When termination signals the end of a learning experience for the counsellor (for example, the counsellor may have been relying on the client to learn more about the dynamics of a disorder or a particular subculture)

— When termination signals the end of a particularly exciting experience of living vicariously through the adventures of the client

— When termination becomes a symbolic recapitulation of other (especially unresolved) farewells in the counsellor's life

— When termination arouses in the counsellor conflicts about his or her own individuation

It is important that counsellors recognize any difficulties they have in letting go of certain clients. A counsellor may seek consultation with colleagues in dealing with this problem or undergo counselling to resolve the problem. The latter option is especially valuable if the counsellor has a personal history of detachment, isolation, and excessive fear of intimacy. Kovacs and Guy report that some persons who enter the helping professions possess just such characteristics.

The question of whether a client terminates counselling prematurely is not one that can be measured by the number of sessions the client has completed. Rather, premature termination has to do with how well the client has achieved the personal goals established in the beginning and how well he or she is functioning generally. Baruth and Huber note that there are some clients who show little, if any, commitment or motivation to change their present circumstances and request that counselling be terminated after the first session. Other clients express this desire after realizing the work necessary for change. Still others make this wish known more indirectly by missing or being late for appointments. Regardless of how clients express a wish for premature termination, it is likely to trigger thoughts and feelings within the counsellor that must be dealt with. Hansen, Warner, and Smith suggest that the topic of premature termination be discussed openly between a counsellor and client if the client expresses a desire to terminate before specified goals have been met or if the counsellor suspects that premature termination may occur. With discussion, thoughts and feelings of both the client and counsellor can be examined and a premature ending prevented.

Sometimes a client fails to keep an appointment and does not call to reschedule. In such cases, the counsellor should attempt to reach the client by phone or mail. If the counsellor finds that the client wishes to quit, an exit interview should be set up. Ward reports four possible benefits from such an interview:

— An exit interview may help the client resolve any negative feelings resulting from the counselling experience.

— It serves as a way to invite the client to continue in counselling if he or she so wishes.

— Another form of treatment or a different counsellor can be considered if the client so desires.

— An exit interview increases the chances that the next time the client needs help, he or she will seek counselling.

Cavanagh believes that, in premature termination, counsellors often make one of two mistakes. One is to blame either the counsellor or the client for what is happening'. A counsellor is more likely to blame the client; but in either case, someone is berated and the problem is compounded. It may be more productive for the counsellor to think of the situation as one in which no one is at fault. Such a strategy is premised on the idea that some matches between clients and counsellors work better than others.

A second mistake on the part of the counsellor is to act in a cavalier manner about the situation. An example is the counsellor who says, "It's too bad this client has chosen not to continue counselling, but I've got others." To avoid making either mistake, Cavanagh recommends that counsellors find out why a client terminated prematurely. Possible reasons include the following:

— To see if the counsellor really cares

— To try to elicit positive feelings from the counsellor

— To punish or try to hurt the counsellor

— To eliminate anxiety

— To show the counsellor that the client has found a cure elsewhere

— To express to the counsellor that the client does not feel understood

Cavanagh believes that counsellors need to understand that, regardless of what they do, some clients terminate counselling prematurely. Such a realization allows counsellors to feel that they do not have to be perfect and frees them to be more authentic in the therapeutic relationship.

It also enables them to acknowledge overtly that, no matter how talented and skillful they are, some clients find other counsellors more helpful. Ideally, counsellors are aware of the anatomy of termination. With such knowledge, they become empowered to deal realistically with situations concerning client termination. Not all people who seek counselling are equally ready to work in such a relationship, and the readiness level may vary as the relationship continues. Some clients need to terminate prematurely for good reasons, and their action does not necessarily reflect on the counsellor's competence. Counsellors can control only a limited number of variables in a counselling relationship. The following list includes several of the variables most likely to be effective in preventing premature termination:

Appointments. The less time between them and the more regular they are the better.

Orientation to counselling. The more clients know about the process of counselling, the more likely they are to stay with it.

Consistency of counsellor Clients do not like to be processed from counsellor to counsellor. Therefore, the counsellor who does the initial intake should continue counselling the client if at all possible.

Reminders to motivate client attendance. Postcards, telephone calls, or e-mail can be effective reminders. Because of the sensitivity of counselling, however, a counsellor should always have the client's permission to send an appointment reminder.

Counsellor-initiated termination is the opposite of premature termination. A counsellor sometimes needs to end relationships with some or all clients. Reasons include illness, working through countertransference, relocation to another area, an extended trip, or the realization that client needs could be better served by someone else. These are what Cavanagh classifies as "good reasons" for the counsellor to terminate. There are also poor reasons for counsellor-initiated termination. They include a counsellor's feelings of anger, boredom, or anxiety. If a counsellor ends a relationship because of such feelings, the client may feel rejected and even worse than he or she did in the beginning. It is one thing for a person to handle rejection from peers; it is another for that same person to handle rejection from a counsellor. Cavanagh notes that, although a counsellor may have some negative feelings about a client, it is possible to acknowledge and work through those feelings without behaving in an extreme or detrimental way.

Both London and Seligman present models for helping clients deal with the temporary absence of the counsellor. These researchers stress that clients and counsellors should prepare as far in advance as possible for temporary termination by openly discussing the impending event and working through any strong feelings about the issue of separation.

A client may actually experience benefits from counsellor-initiated termination by realizing that the counsellor is human and replaceable, understanding that a person has choices about how to deal with inter-personal relationships, exploring previous feelings and major life decisions, and learning more clearly that new behaviours carry over into other life experiences. There may also be a refocusing during the termination process that helps clients see issues on which to work more clearly

Seligman recommends a more structured way of preparing clients for counsellor-initiated termination than London does, but both models can be effective. It is important in any situation like this to make sure a client has the names and numbers of a few other counsellors to contact in case of an emergency.

The process of termination, like counselling itself, involves a series of check points that counsellors and clients can consult to evaluate the progress they are making and determine their readiness to move to another stage. It is important that termination be mutually agreed upon, if at all possible, so that all involved can move on in ways deemed most productive. Nevertheless, this is not always possible. Patterson and Eisenberg present eight guidelines a counsellor can use to end an intense counselling relationship in a positive way,

— Be clearly aware of the client's needs and wants. At the end of a counselling relationship, the client may need time to talk to the counsellor about the impending termination. This may require a few sessions to complete.

— Be clearly aware of your own needs and wants." Counselling is not a one way street, and counsellors who take care of others without taking care of themselves will most likely experience difficulty in terminating relationships. It is vital that a counsellor acknowledge personal feelings and needs about a counselling relationship before it ends.

— Be aware of your previous experiences with separation and your inner reaction to these experiences. The feelings generated from one intense relationship may be similar to those that occur in another. A counsellor should be emotionally self-aware to avoid counter-transference and be genuine in relationships.

— Invite the client to share how he or she feels about ending the experience. This guideline is similar to the first, but it focuses on the emotions, not the thoughts, of the client. Clients need to express themselves as completely as possible if closure is to be of maximum benefit.

— Share honestly with the client how you feel about the counselling experience. This is another aspect of the counsellor's being real in the relationship. Part of this sharing includes revealing to the client what you, as a counsellor, have learned from this particular experience.

Review the major events of the counselling experience and bring the review into the present." The focus of this process is to help a client see where he or she is now as compared to the beginning of counselling and realize more fully the growth that has been accomplished. The procedure includes a review of significant past moments and turning points in the relationship with a focus on personalizing the summary.

Supportively acknowledge the changes the client has made. At this point the counsellor lets the client know that he or she recognizes the progress that has been achieved and actively encourages the client to maintain it.

Invite the client to keep up to date on what is happening in his or her life, counselling relationships eventually end, but the caring and concern the counsellor has for the client are not automatically terminated at the final session. Clients need to know that the counsellor continues to be interested in what is happening in their lives. Updating can be accomplished in part through follow-up sessions.

Issues related to termination

"Follow-up entails checking to see how the helpee is doing, with respect to whatever the problem was, sometime after termination has occurred". In essence, it is a positive monitoring process that encourages client growth. Follow-up is a step that some counsellors neglect. It is important because it reinforces the gains clients have made in counselling and helps both counsellor and client reevaluate the experience. It also emphasizes the counsellor's genuine care and concern for the client. Follow-up can be conducted on either a short-or long-term basis. Short-term follow-up is usually conducted three to six months after a counselling relationship terminates. Long-term follow-up is conducted at least six months after termination. Follow-up may take many forms, but there are four main ways in which it is usually conducted. The first is to invite the client in for a session to discuss any progress he or she has continued to make in achieving desired goals. A second way is through a telephone call to the client. A call allows the client to report to the counsellor, although there is only verbal interaction. A third way is for the counsellor to send the client a letter asking about the client's current status. A fourth and more impersonal way is for the counsellor to mail the client a questionnaire dealing with current levels of functioning. Many public agencies use this type of follow-up as a way of showing accountability. Such procedures do not preclude the use of more personal follow-up procedures by individual counsellors. Although time consuming, a personal follow-up is probably the most effective way of evaluating past counselling experiences. It helps assure clients that they are cared about as individuals and more than just statistics. Sometimes, regardless of the type of follow-up used, it is helpful if the client monitors his or her own progress through the use of graphs or charts. Then, when relating information to the counsellor, the client can do so in a more concrete and objective way. If counsellor and client agree at the end of the last session on a follow-up time, this type of self-monitoring may be especially meaningful and give the client concrete proof of progress and clearer insight into current needs.

Counsellors are not able to help everyone who seeks assistance. When a counsellor realizes that a situation is unproductive, it is important to know whether to terminate the relationship or make a referral. A referral involves arranging other assistance for a client when the initial arrangement is not or cannot be helpful. There are many reasons for referring, including the following:

— The client has a problem the counsellor does not know how to handle.

— The counsellor is inexperienced in a particular area and does not have the necessary skill to help the client.

— The counsellor knows of a nearby expert who would be more helpful to the client.

— The counsellor and client have incompatible personalities.

— The relationship between counsellor and client is stuck in an initial phase of counselling.

Referrals involve a how and a when. The how involves knowing how to call on a helping resource and handle the client to maximize the chances that he or she will follow through with the referral process. A client may resist a referral if the client feels rejected by the counsellor. Patterson and Eisenberg suggest that a counsellor spend at least one session with the client in preparation for the referral. There are some clients for whom it will be necessary to spend several sessions. The when of making a referral involves timing. The longer a client works with a counsellor, the more reluctant the client may be to see someone else. Thus, timing is crucial. If a counsellor suspects an impasse with a certain client, he or she should refer that client as soon as possible. On the other hand, if the counsellor has worked with the client for a while, he or she should be sensitive about giving the client enough time to get used to the idea of working with someone else.

Recycling is an alternative when the counsellor thinks the counselling process has not yet worked but can be made to do so. It means reexamining all phases of the therapeutic process.

Perhaps the goals were not properly defined or an inappropriate strategy was chosen. Whatever the case, by reexamining the counselling process, counsellor and client can decide how or if to revise and reinvest in the counselling process. Counselling, like other experiences, is not always successful on the first attempt. Recycling gives both counsellor and client a second chance to achieve what each wants: positive change.

4

Group Counselling

Group counselling is not simply individual counselling applied to groups, nor is it merely an economical use of counsellor time. Many of the features of group counselling are quite unique and it would be wrong to think of it as 'individual' counselling in the mass. Because of the differences in the two processes, a counsellor trained in the skills of individual counselling might find herself in difficulty is she attempted group counselling without having some training in group interaction. It is essential that a counsellor wishing to work with individuals and groups should have a thorough theoretical and practical grounding in individual counselling theory and practice together with some experience of principles and practices of group dynamics.

The term multiple counselling is sometimes used to describe counselling carried out in groups. This seems a misleading term since it is not clear whether it is the counsellors or the students who are 'multiple'. It is used in this book to denote a situation in which there are two counsellors working either with one student, as in the chapter on training, or with a group. The term group counselling is used here to describe a situation in which there is one counsellor working with a group of students.

Group counselling is a relatively new way of working to help people ad although it has a unique contribution to make to our range of helping skills, it is not the complete answer for all psychological ills or needs.

Carkhuff has written quite strongly that Group processes are the preferred mode of working with difficulties in interpersonal functioning. We can do anything in group treatment that we can do in individual treatment-and more. Since groups are inherently interpersonal, they offer the helpee the means not only to relate to the helper and himself wit the helper's guidance but also to relate to other members of the group and to the group as a whole. Group processes offer the prospect for the greatest amount of learning for the greatest number of people at one time.

Carkhuff's unqualified approval as inappropriate and potentially damaging as attempting to gather peaches with a combine harvester. Certainly group counselling is sometimes successful with students who have not responded well to individual counselling, and there are several combinations of group and individual counselling in use. The two extremes are to use either group counselling or individual counselling only as a main technique. Some counsellors feel that it is unwise to make the two methods available to the same students at the same time because students may not bring out their deepest problems in the group, reserving them for the individual counselling sessions, which could inhibit the work of the group. Other counsellors feel that individual counselling offered concurrently with group counselling gives opportunity for a student to discuss more deeply and extensively personal problem areas which they have been unable to bring out in the group, either because of their own inability or because of a lack of opportunity and a need to share the time of the group with other members.

Group counselling overlaps with group guidance in its partial cognitive and factual content and with group therapy in its emphasis on feelings and emotion, and it has some similarities to the individual counselling situation, with the addition of the interaction of other members of the group and the sharing of counsellor. The effectiveness of group counselling may be partly attributable to the fact that, theoretically, it makes available the services of a number of potential helpers in the form of other group members, one or several of whom may be able to offer more help to a particular person at a particular point than is the counsellor herself.

Group counselling is a particularly useful, way of helping adolescents for whom peer group values are important. The interaction which takes place in a counselling group offers the students a means of gaining insight and understanding into his own problems through listening to other students discussing their difficulties. Ideas and values which a student has previously found unacceptable may become more understandable and sometimes more acceptable. The counselling group not only helps the individual student to change, but also often encourages both his desire an his ability to help social situation, for any group is more than the sum of its members: it is also the sum of its interactions.

The physical arrangements which are desirable for a counselling group are similar to those which pertain to the individual counselling situation namely, a warm, sound-proofed room with fairly comfortable chairs. It is difficult, though not impossible, to conduct a counselling group in the average classroom, and even more difficult to conduct it in a cupboard. It is helpful if the same room can be used each time the group meets, because of the effect of a changed environment on the functioning of the group if their meeting place is not a familiar setting.

The time factor in the group counselling situation is related to the purpose of the group. If it is intended that most of the 'work' of the individual members is to take place in the actual group counselling session, it is necessary for the group to meet more often than it would if the counsellor and the group members feel that the students need time between meetings to absorb and test some of the experiences learned. IT is usual for the counselling groups used in education to meet once, or perhaps twice a week. If the group meets too often, or example more than three times a week, there is the possibility that the frequency of sessions will restrict the group members' external social contacts and limit their opportunities for social reality testing outside the group. The length of each group meeting will be related to the age of the people involved, and the frequency with which the group meets, but sixty to ninety minutes is probably a reasonable time span for college students, thirty to sixty minutes for secondary school pupils and no more than thirty minutes for junior school children.

The composition of a counselling group is another practical consideration which is related to the purpose of the group. Sometimes it is felt that a homogeneous group consisting of students of the same age or sex, or students who seem to have similar problems is the most helpful, whilst other counsellors find that the wider talents of a heterogeneous group make for a better counselling situation. It is necessary to look carefully at the desired outcomes for the group, and to try to ensure that the purposes of the counsellor and those of the students are the same. It is important to recognize that groups can be homogeneous only in certain limited respects. A group chosen for homogeneity in sex or age is likely to be heterogeneous in other factors such as socio-economic background, maturity, motivation and, of course, temperament. It has been suggested that it is unwise to include in a counselling or therapy group people who are excessively aggressive or hostile because they are likely to destroy the atmosphere of a acceptance in the group; people who are psychologically sophisticated or those who are not sufficiently in contact with reality have also been seen as undesirable group members, but it is difficult for the school or college counsellor to exclude students on these grounds unless they know them personally. A preliminary interview can help, though this may be more appropriate as screening for therapy groups than as a means of choosing members for a counselling group in an educational setting.

The size of a counselling group, like that of any guidance group, is related to the methodology used. A directive counsellor or one who prefers task oriented discussion may choose to work with a larger action. A group of six to eight students is probably the best size for maximum group interaction.

The term group counselling has become very popular and practices under this name have been introduced in a variety of settings. There is still variation in what it means to different individuals.

Professionals working in counselling and related fields have been asked to reach a consensus as to what a group is beyond the definition that a group consists of three or more members who influence each other and are influenced by others. Such a group of individuals who meet and interact with one another in a face-to-face setting tend to believe that they belong to a particular group for the purpose of achieving some objective or goal.

Most professionals would agree that individuals meet to satisfy personal needs and to develop an interdependence upon one another. As will be shown in later chapters, these individuals establish roles and norms as a result of sharing common attitudes, feelings, and times. In addition, these groups go through stages that can be observed and described by those who study such group behaviour. Before looking at some specific definitions of group counselling, it may be valuable to look at distinctions between three major types of group activities. Gazda says that *group guidance is* "organized to prevent the development of problems".

Gazda suggests three major differences between group guidance and group counselling, while acknowledging that they share a great deal of similarity. First, he points out that group guidance is recommended for all individuals on a regular basis, while group counselling is generally recommended only for those who are experiencing some coping difficulties in their lives. Second, he points out that group guidance makes an indirect attempt to change attitudes and behaviours, while group counselling makes a direct attempt to modify attitudes and behaviours. Third, Gazda says that group guidance can be done with large, classroom-size groups; whereas group counselling is most effective in small, intimate groups.

A third type of group activity is that of group psychotherapy. Used primarily as part of in-patient treatment for individuals who are suffering from severe emotional distress, group psychotherapy is most often seen to be remediative-adjustive-therapeutic, while counselling is thought of as developmental-educative-preventive. While most professionals in the field believe that there is a difference between group counselling and group psychotherapy, most also agree that there is a great deal of overlap between them. The distinctions between group counselling and group therapy are difficult to define, although it is generally accepted that such differences exist. George and Cristiani suggest that a clear distinction between the two can best be made by giving counselling and psychotherapy as points on a continuum in regard to various elements: goals, clients, settings, practitioners, and methods.

Overall, differences may be best understood in terms of the kind of goals that are seen for each. Whereas counselling is most often described as being educational, supportive, vocational, problem- solving, conscious awareness, and short-term in nature; psychotherapy is most often perceived as being reconstructive, analytical, and long term, with an emphasis on severe emotional problems. The confusion resulting from a lack of agreement concerning a definition of group counselling can be seen by looking at various definitions that have already been offered.

Most individuals work as a part of a group, most individuals interact with social acquaintances as part of a group, and most individuals spend much of their leisure time as part of a group. Since the realities of community existence require community interaction, people are highly concerned with the nature of their relationships with family, friends, and colleagues. These relationships produce and/or reduce stress, feelings of loneliness, low self-esteem, a sense of failure, or a desire to improve their lives. In a sense, the counselling group provides an opportunity for the individual to participate in a small microcosm of society the individual experiences daily. As such, the group process reflects the world beyond and adds an ingredient of realism to a setting and interaction which can often be seen as artificial.

Group counselling can make factors such as peer group pressure, social influence, and conformity come into play as part of the therapeutic process, just as they influence and affect the individual's attitude and behaviour change outside the group.

Corey points out that "the group process provides a sample of reality. The struggles and conflicts that people experience in the group situation are no different from those they experience outside of it". In such a setting, participants have the opportunity to explore their styles of relating with others and to learn more effective behaviours in those relationships.

The group setting becomes an opportunity to receive feedback and support from others concerning their perceptions of one another of how each is experienced in the group. As such, the individuals often learn to take risks regarding new attitudes such as trusting, caring, and helping, as well as new behaviours. Group members have the opportunity to get to know others at a relatively intimate level, if they wish, as a result of experiencing one another in a highly safe environment. Thus, a group setting provides a good setting for the individual to learn and practice new skills. In a group setting the peer pressure that is involved often brings about a greater push to action both within the group and outside the group. Thus, members of the group are urged toward activity involved in facing and acting on the real issues and concerns in their lives. Likewise, the possibility of learning new behaviours is increased by the opportunity to observe other members of the group who may be seen as role models in terms of the specific behaviours which the individual wishes to change. Group discussion can strengthen discrimination learning as members come to compare effective behaviour with behaviour that does not achieve desired goals. Most important in this process, group members develop a sense of belonging, and the kind of closeness that develops provides a caring, but challenging environment for personal growth and development. Part of this results from individuals becoming aware of similarities between their problems and the problems of other group members, which leads to decreased feelings of isolation and peculiarity and a sense of commonality with others. The economic advantages to a group format may be overstated.

Many professionals agree that it is generally less expensive when the counsellor/leader is able to meet with a number of individuals simultaneously. This is particularly true when the purpose of the group is such that there is material to be learned and common skills to be developed. It is important to point out that group approaches are not the answer to limited members of professional personnel or to the limited financial resources of individuals seeking help. Although group settings enable counsellors to see more individuals in the same amount of time than would be possible in individual therapy, group experiences are generally less efficient than individual approaches because they cannot be tailored to meet the individual needs of the patient.

The goals of a particular counselling group should be established by the members and leaders of those groups themselves. There is some agreement in terms of general goals to be accomplished via group settings.

Frank suggested general treatment goals as being

(a) to facilitate the constructive release of feelings,

(b) to strengthen patients' self-esteem,

(c) to encourage patients to face and resolve their problems,

(d) to improve their skills in recognizing and resolving both interpersonal and intrapersonal conflicts, and

(e) to fortify them to consolidate and to maintain their therapeutic gains.

Kelman continued the focus on clients' means for improving interpersonal skills by establishing the following goals: (a) to overcome feelings of isolation, (b) to enhance self-esteem and increase acceptance of self, (c) to develop hope for improved adjustment, (d) to help each client learn to be himself and to express his feelings, (e) to accept responsibility for himself and for solving his problems, (f) to develop, practice, and maintain new relationship skills, and (g) to enhance his commitment to change his attitudes and behaviours, and to generalize his insight and skills by implementing them in daily life.

General goals have to do with establishing a psychological environment within which individuals can work toward achieving their personal goals. Process goals have to do with clients learning appropriate self-disclosures, being willing to share feelings with other members of the group, being willing to talk about themselves in a personal way, being willing to talk about current feelings, providing feedback to others within the group, learning how to confront with care and respect, and expressing reactions to what is going on in the group. Perhaps the best list of general goals shared by most counselling groups is one proposed by Corey.

The term *therapeutic group is* used as a general term for any of a wide variety of groups. By *therapeutic*, it is not meant that the group is used for the treatment of severe emotional and psychological disorders, but rather that the group's overall purpose is to have a positive, healing effect on whatever issues the members of the group may bring to it. These issues may have to do with individuals' wanting to learn more about themselves by increasing their awareness of their feelings, values, and beliefs. Other therapeutic experiences might also include providing information to individuals that will enable them to make more appropriate decisions about the course of their lives, as well as giving them tools necessary to make the kind of changes they would like.

As a result, the term therapeutic group may be utilized for such diverse counselling groups as growth and development groups, T-groups, encounter groups, awareness groups, sensitivity training groups, consciousness- raising groups, therapy groups, and task-oriented groups, as well as groups where the focus is on specific behaviour change and/or the learning of specific new skills. Before looking at some of the various types of groups that exist, it is important to note that one major difference among the various kinds of groups has to do with the degree of structure of the various group activities. Most growth and development groups utilize minimal structuring in which the direction and progress of the group is generally left to the input and expressed needs of the group members.

Only general goals related to the growth and development of those group members are verbalized. Behaviour-change groups often provide greater structuring to the group process. Leaders of these groups often convey precisely what they expect of group members, what group members can expect of the leader, how previous group members have been helped through these experiences, and a relatively formalized outline of planned activities.

Perhaps the greatest emphasis in counselling groups during the past few decades has been in group experiences that focus on the personal growth of the individual. Such groups are not specifically designed for the rehabilitation of individuals suffering from specific psychological or emotional difficulties, but are intended for relatively normal people who are hoping to enhance their personal living skills particularly as these skills involve relating to others. Such growth-centered groups tend to focus on helping individuals gain specific skills; develop insights into their own sets of values, beliefs, and attitudes; enhance their socialisation abilities; and learn how to become more aware of the feelings that they are experiencing. Groups for such growth purposes have been identified by several names depending on the areas of growth which are emphasized.

T-groups, or laboratory training groups, tend to emphasize the development of human relations skills which enable the individual to be more effective in a business organization. Focusing more on group process than on personal growth per se, T-groups emphasize education through experience in an environment in which experimentation can occur while receiving support and feedback from the other members of the group. Individuals are encouraged to try out new behaviours, and those behaviours are analysed so that the individual learns how his or her behaviour is seen by others in the group. T-group members usually increase their sensitivity to the feelings and behaviours of other group members, as well as increase their understanding of group behaviour dynamics. Thus, in a sense the T-group provides an opportunity for group members to learn how to learn by discovering that the only real answers in terms of becoming more effective as a leader are answers that are provided by their own experiences and not answers that come from some authority figure. Likewise, T-group members are encouraged to focus on the "here and now" as a means of becoming more aware of what is happening to them at the moment and how they feel about it. Encounter groups, which are the type of groups most often known as personal growth groups, generally offer an intense group experience in which the emphasis upon personal growth through expanding awareness and the release of dysfunctional inhibitions is utilized as a means of helping relatively healthy individuals gain more effective, valid contact with themselves and others. While such groups are diverse in their methods, in the experiences of their members, and in the styles of leadership involved, their common goal is to teach individuals how to deal with themselves and others in a more open, honest manner.

The emphasis is on eliciting emotions and on expressing these emotions fully. Frequent confrontations within the group are often encouraged so that the members of the group learn that such confrontation is not only acceptable but also effective in improving relationships with other people.

Thus, encounter groups usually encourage intimacy and sharing, openness, honesty, and intense interpersonal relating, with an emphasis on the spontaneous expression of one's feelings, especially risk-taking expressions and living in the present.

In addition to the verbal interaction that occurs in an encounter group, nonverbal techniques are often utilized to foster interaction. These may include touching, the use of fantasy, massage, dance, art, meditation, centering, and various encounter games.

Various types of interpersonal communication exercises are frequently used to hasten members' awareness of themselves, to promote contact with the feelings of those members, and to promote increased group participation.

In particular, marathon groups focus on individuals' learning more about the mask they wear in daily life, the social facades they present to others, the genuine aspects of themselves that are often hidden by those masks and facades, and how to give up some of these pretenses as they reenter their normal living activities. Other types of growth and development groups have included sensitivity training, awareness groups, Gestalt groups, and transactional analysis groups. Sensitivity groups generally refer to the kind of experiences provided by both T-groups and encounter groups, but with a particular focus on individuals' becoming more sensitive to their own emotional experiencing as well as to the impact of their behaviour on other individuals. Awareness groups, on the other hand, tend to emphasize awareness and expression of one's physical body through movement, spontaneous dance, and other physical activities. Gestalt groups focus on a concept of awareness, in which an expert therapist focuses on one individual at a time, while utilizing other members of the group to provide additional input that will enable the individual on the "hot seat" to become more aware of the total experiencing that he or she is going through. Likewise, transactional analysis (TA) groups provide a framework based on a TA therapeutic model in which members of the group become more aware of their behaviour in terms of the ego state they utilize in various interactions with others as well as the kind of interactional patterns they prefer. This is done in such a way that group members examine their pasts, their current ego states, scripts, games, and so forth.

Systematic human relations training is closely related to T-groups, but differs in placing much greater emphasis on specific skill development. It is largely based on the work of Carkhuff, who, expanding on Rogers's work regarding the conditions for therapeutic success, developed a systematic model for training people in various interpersonal skills.

Gazda and Egan have translated the Carkhuff model to the group experience in such a way that group members are able through experiential learning to develop these skills. Some of the same psychological conditions that exist in the T-group—a small group, feedback, the encouragement of experimentation, psychological safety, and here-and-now focus—are provided so that individuals develop the kind of skills which will enable them to be more effective in their interaction with other persons and thus develop a more satisfying life experience for themselves.

Task-centered groups are those which focus on the successful development of a performance or product through collaborative efforts of the group members, while little effort is used in changing the various group members as individuals. Examples of such task groups would include committees, industrial work groups, conflict resolution groups, community interest groups, and various task forces. These groups are important, not because of the counselling experiences that are provided, but because the successful working of these groups depends on the kind of group dynamics that occur.

Behaviour-change groups are distinguished from other group approaches in that they specify desirable changes in the behaviour of each group member that are to occur as a result of the group experience. Generally, individuals who become part of such a group know in advance what the focus of the group will be and therefore why they are there.

While the focus is on the successful change in behaviour of the various members of the group, a major aspect or dynamic is support from other group members. Alcoholics Anonymous, Overeaters Anonymous, and Smoke Enders are examples of support groups which exist. Other groups may focus on the development of such specific behaviours as study habits, social interaction skills, and parenting skills.

Learning groups are those in which the focus is on the acquisition of specific information and knowledge, especially in terms of vocational and academic information. Such groups are typically more structured, with carefully defined goals and more explicit, generally accepted expectations of the group members. Although the focus is on learning specific information, the process involves a great deal of group interaction, with members of the group sharing feelings, attitudes, and values.

A group that is focused on developing job-seeking skills, in which participants learn how to find job leads, prepare a resume, prepare for an interview, and present themselves to the employer, will also focus on individuals discussing the kind of fears they have about the total experience. In addition, the members will be continually discussing the kind of internal forces that affect the type of jobs in which they are interested as well as the kind of jobs they will actually seek.

Other learning groups might include mid-life career change groups, career exploration groups, work adjustment groups, and various kinds of child-raising groups. One structured group that has received a great deal of attention is parent - effectiveness training, in which parents meet to learn better ways of relating to and managing their children. Group members learn definable skills, while participating in a process that includes group interaction and support.

Psychotherapy groups are usually made up of psychiatric patients who are hospitalized as a result of their difficulties and outpatients who have more severe emotional or psychological problems. Generally, therapy groups are aimed at reconstructing the personality, although many people who participate in group therapy do so in an attempt to alleviate specific symptoms or problems, such as depression, anxiety, psychosomatic disorders, eating disorders, chemical dependency, and sexual problems. In such groups, the focus is on identifying and correcting the emotional or psychological difficulties that impede the individual's functioning. Thus the goal may be a minor or a major change in the personality structure both depending on the nature of the difficulty of the individual and the specific theoretical orientation of the therapist. Psychotherapy groups tend to be of longer duration than the other kinds of groups that have been discussed.

By re-experiencing these situations and the accompanying feelings, the individuals are given the opportunity to resolve "unfinished business" and to express the kinds of intense feelings that have stayed below the surface for a long period of time.

As members become aware of and gain insight into their past, they are able to reconstruct a more healthy emotional attitude about themselves and those experiences and to eliminate the emotional blocking that has interfered with the group members' current functioning.

Many psychotherapy groups utilize psychoanalytic concepts and procedures, such as working with dreams, focusing on the earliest memories of the individual, trying to uncover the unconscious, and symbolically reliving, thus reconstructing, unhappy significant relationships. Other groups may utilize cognitive techniques, behavioural techniques, and other psychotherapeutic modalities to bring about therapeutic change. Many psychotherapy groups are made up of individuals who are relatively healthy and are not experiencing severe emotional or psychological problems.

These individuals participate in group therapy for many of the same reasons that others participate in growth and development groups; that is, to be part of an experience in which a safe climate is provided so that they can become healthier, more effective individuals who live more satisfying lives.

Guidance is concerned with presenting information in a way which will enable each individual student to find some personal meaning in what he has read, seen or heard.

It is not sufficient to present information to students, and to assume that they have all heard and understood the same thing, for each one reads personal meanings in the what may be considered 'objective' facts. If we exclude group counselling, then group guidance becomes a set of activities used with a group of students to help each in his individual learning.

It is mainly a cognitive process with little attention given to feelings or emotions and is concerned with helping people to discuss the meaning of various kinds of information. The focus is on ideas, explanations, and verbal expression as an aid to a personal understanding of information or to the completion of a set task.

There are certain problems which are common to adolescents as part of the developmental processes of the developmental process of this age group, there are also certain kinds of educational, vocational and social information which can be of help to young people as they grow up. These may be presented in a group situation and discussed with the realization that their difficulties are not peculiar to them as individuals, as they often think, but are shared by fellow students.

There are essentially two types of information needed for intelligent decision-making: information regarding oneself as a person with assets and liabilities, talents and limitations; and information regarding the particular situation about which a decision is to be made, or to which the self is related. When a person has this information he needs some way of dealing with it. There are various models of choice or decision-making used by people in making vocational or other choices, which vary according to the individual concerned and his circumstances.

The trait and factor model is based on the idea that any individual possesses a variety of traits and any occupation demands certain requirements of those who enter it.

The individual can match his traits with the occupational or educational requirements and determine which job or course he is best fitted for. This model is often used in vocational guidance in our schools and its main disadvantage is that it is too static and does not take into account the changing and developing nature of neither the student or the environment to which he must relate.

An individual using the economic model chooses an occupation or a college which will maximize his gain minimize his loss; for example, going to college might be a means of achieving greater status and mobility. The gains achieved are not necessarily economic or financial but may consist of anything which is of value to the person concerned.

The individual using a social structure model of choice is restricted in the decisions he can make because his knowledge of the various opportunities available is limited by family, social and economic circumstances.

This is particularly so as disadvantaged students for whom narrowness of cultural or social class horizons places restrictions on their educational or vocational selection had often leads to the equally narrow perspective of immediate gratification as the basis for choice.

A person may be forced into using the information processing model of choice when the facts necessary for him to make a decision are so overwhelming that he is pressured into a premature decision. Some students chose a particular college or job because their friends have done so, or because they are vaguely aware that a college has a particular college or job because their friends have done so, or because they are vaguely aware that a college has a particular reputation. This type of choice supports the individual's rationalization and reduces his anxiety.

The need reduction model is a comprehensive one which subsumes certain elements of the other models. It assumes that an individual has a self-concept and that he implements this picture of himself in his choice of course or occupation, by gravitating towards a career, or a course of study which he sees as compatible with his needs and interests. This may be a result of unconscious motivation, or a relatively rational conscious choice. This provides for change in the person's behaviour, environment and expectations between the individual and his environment. It suggests that making decisions about important areas of one's life is a complex and on-going process forming part of a developmental sequence extending from childhood through adulthood and not an isolated event at a particular point in time.

It is no good giving information to students who see no need for it, so motivation should precede instruction in group guidance. The presentation of information is only part of the process and must be followed by some feedback to ensure that it reached each student accurately.

Whilst large groups offer an economical way of disseminating information, large group audiences tend to be passive listeners, or merely passive. We need to supplement this type of presentation by work in smaller groups and with individuals in which there is more opportunity for interaction and feedback.

Unless tutors in school have one period each day with their students the tutorial group is not an effective way of providing information on which to base choices, or of providing help in other areas. Tutors also need training in group work, and the support of a carefully planned, effectively led guidance programme.

Orientation usually takes the form of large group information giving, plus smaller orientation groups which continue throughout the year and are aimed at helping the students to develop independence. This applied at all levels of education, not just at the school level. American studies indicated that three out of the four college students had difficulties with the transition from the orderly, fairly directive secondary school to the non-directive environment of college. Some of the reasons given for these difficulties were unrealistic expectations of college social and education life; an inability to organize their time; going to college without a strong desire to attend; and financial difficulties. Closed circuit television can be a useful medium for orientation purposes.

Guidance groups are concerned with effective discussion about the impact of information and also about problems arising from some personal adjustment and difficulties. Affective discussion groups can be useful in this area, as they form a bridge between the purely intellectual discussion group and the counselling group with its emphasis on empathy. They need planning ad structuring, and some of the techniques for initiating affective discussion are role-playing, case-studies, role-models, literature and audio-visual media. Although the two concepts of group guidance and group counselling overlap to some extent in the area of affective discussion, group guidance tends to be more cognitively oriented and is usually used in an attempt to personalise information, whereas group counselling is used in an attempt to meet emotional needs and is often closer to group therapy it is to group guidance.

There are two basic assumptions upon which a counsellor may choose to build her role. One is that it is the task of the counsellor to work with the group to encourage the students to be more self-sufficient and self-directed, so that the counsellor herself may then become another group member and the interaction of the group itself will provide any help which members need. An alternative assumption is that the counsellor works towards the development of the students' self-sufficiency, but because she considered that the group members are not always able to help each other she does not abdicate her special helping role.

There are six phases which are involved in group counselling:

1. rapport.
2. acceptance.
3. listening and observing.
4. promoting group and individual understanding.
5. problem solving skill development.
6. closing evaluation and procedures.

Whilst the counsellor's acceptance of all the group members and their problems is assumed in the nature of the role of the counsellor, as is the acceptance of the student in individual counselling, the creation of rapport and acceptance within and amongst the group members themselves, and between them and the counsellor, is a unique experience which differs from the one-to-one counselling relationship in its patterns of development.

Rapport involves the gradual building of an association of mutual respects and trust and it can be introduced by initial discussion of the group, whether the group should be 'open', so that members may leave when they wish or new members may be brought into the group as it proceeds, or whether it could be 'closed', retaining its initial membership for a specified period of time.

Questions directed at the counsellor can be referred to the group for discussion and decision by means of a counsellor response such as 'What does the group feel about this?' If multiple counselling is being done, the role and function of the co-counsellor may be discussed. The structuring of the group by the counsellor in the early stages may also help in the growth of rapport. Structuring should be brief and should focus attention on the particular goals of the group, which may be self appraisal, to encourage the free expression of feelings by group members to each other and to the counsellor, and the avoidance of purely intellectual discussion. The limits of the group may be expressed, for example, in terms of the permitting of verbal but not physical expression of hostile feelings. The emphasis of the observance by all group members and the counsellor of confidentiality about the proceedings of the group is also a part of structuring which can help to bring about trust.

Initial resistance is a natural phenomenon of groups and the creation of an accepting climate is a gradual process which the counsellor tries to encourage by her own acceptance of each student's feelings an his expression of them. From the counsellor the students learn to accept and help one another.

Listening and observing actively and intensely are two of the essential skills of the counsellor, and a group situation gives an added complexity to the use of these in order to promote both group and individual understanding. 'The counsellor's task is more complicated in group counselling. He not only has to understand the speaker's feelings and help him become aware of them, but he must also observe how the speaker's comments influence the group members.

The counsellor must not only be aware of the discussion, he must be perceptive of the interplay of relationships among the members.' The counselling group can make little significant progress in developing the skills for solving problems until the initial stages of rapport, acceptance, understanding and insight have been established. It may be that the process of group counselling itself will uncover more problems that it actually solves, but if it is effective it also helps to bring about the attitudes and draws out the resources which will enable students to work at these problems themselves once they have been brought to conscious awareness. Alternatively it may lead them to seek individual counselling help for these.

Types of groups

There are a number of group models appropriate for a wide variety of situations.

Guidance/psycho-educational groups

These groups are preventive and educational. Their purpose is to teach group participants how to deal with a potential threat (such as AIDS), a developmental life event (such as growing older), or an immediate life crisis (such as the death of a loved one). These types of groups are often found in educational settings. One of the most important parts of the process in such groups revolves around group discussions of how members will personalize the information presented in the group context. In school settings, instructional materials such as unfinished stories, puppet plays, films, audio interviews, and guest speakers are employed in guidance/psycho-educational groups. In adult settings, other age-appropriate means are used.

Counselling/interpersonal problem-solving groups

These groups "seek to help group participants to resolve the usual, yet often difficult, problems of living through interpersonal support and problem solving. An additional goal is to help participants to develop their existing interpersonal problem-solving competencies so they may be better able to handle future problems. Non-severe career, educational, personal, social, and developmental concerns are frequently addressed".

Gazda distinguishes group counselling from group guidance in the following ways:

- Group counselling is recommended for individuals who are having temporary or continuing problems, whereas group guidance is recommended on a regular basis as a personal educational measure.
- Group counselling is more direct than group guidance in attempting to modify attitudes and

behaviours. For instance, group counselling stresses the affective involvement of participants, whereas group guidance concentrates more on the cognitive understanding of its members.

— Group counselling is conducted in a small, intimate setting, whereas group guidance is more applicable to classroom-size environments.

Psychotherapy/personality reconstruction groups

These groups are set up to help individual group members remediate in-depth psychological problems. "Because the depth and extent of the psychological disturbance is significant, the goal is to aid each individual to reconstruct major personality dimensions". Group psychotherapy often takes place in inpatient facilities, such as hospitals or mental health facilities, because greater control may be necessary for the people involved. Certain types of individuals are poor candidates for outpatient, intensive group psychotherapy. Among them are depressives, incessant talkers, paranoids, schizoid and sociopathic personalities, suicidals, and extreme narcissists.

It may be easier to identify group psychotherapy candidates who should be excluded than choose those who should be included. Regardless, group psychotherapy is an American form of treatment and has provided much of the rationale for group counselling. The relationships among group guidance, group counselling, and group psychotherapy.

Task/work groups

Task/work groups help members apply the principles and processes of group dynamics to improve practices and accomplish identified work goals.

The task/work group specialist is able to assist groups such as task forces, committees, planning groups, community organizations, discussion groups, study circles, learning groups, and other similar groups to correct or develop their functions.

Several traditional and historical groups belong in one of the four categories of speciality groups just described. Some of these groups, however, do not fit into any category well. Furthermore, all these types of groups developed before groups were classified as they are today. T-groups and encounter groups are seldom conducted in their original forms any more but are important because of their contributions to the field of group work. Psychodrama, group marathons, and support/self-help groups continue to be used in their traditional ways and are important therapeutically

T-groups. The first T-group (the T stands for training) was conducted at the National Training Laboratories (NTL) in Bethel, Maine, in 1947. These groups appeared at a time when neither group counselling nor group psychotherapy was popular. Kurt Lewin's ideas about group dynamics formed the basis for the original groups. Since that time, T-groups have evolved from a focus on task accomplishment to a primary emphasis on interpersonal relationships.

It is difficult to classify T-groups in just one way, members of such groups are likely to learn from the experience how one's behaviour in a group influences others' behaviour and vice versa. In this respect, T-groups are similar to forms of family counselling in which the emphasis is on both how the system operates and how an individual within the system functions.

Encounter groups. According to Lynn and Frauman, encounter groups emerged from T-groups in an attempt to focus on the growth of individual group members rather than the group itself Encounter groups are intended for "normally functioning" people who want to "grow, change, and develop". These groups took many forms in their heyday, from the minimally structured groups of Carl Rogers to the highly structured, open-ended groups of William Schutz.

Group marathon. A group marathon is an extended, one-session group experience that breaks down defensive barriers that individuals may otherwise use. The concept was pioneered by Frederick Stoller and George Bach in the 1960s. Group marathons have been used successfully in working with substance abusers in rehabilitation programs and normally functioning individuals in group counselling settings.

Self-help/support groups. Since the 1970s, self-help and support groups has counsellors grown in prominence. A self-help group usually develops spontaneously, centers on a single topic, and is led by a layperson with little formal group training but with experience in the stressful event that brought the group together. For example, residents in a neighbourhood may meet to help each other make repairs and clean up after a natural disaster, or they may assemble to focus government attention on an issue, such as toxic waste, that directly affects the quality of their lives.

Self-help groups can be either short or long term, but they basically work to help their members gain greater control of their lives. Yalom reports that over 10 million people were involved in approximately 500,000 such groups in 1980 and the number continues to increase. A support group is similar to a self-help group in its focus on a particular concern or problem, but it is organized by an established professional helping organisation or individual. Some support groups charge fees; others do not. The involvement of lay people as group leaders varies. Like self-help groups, support groups center around topics that are physical, emotional, or social.

Self-help and support groups partly fill the needs of populations that can best be served in group formats and that might otherwise not receive services. They meet in churches, recreation centers, schools, and other community buildings as well as in mental health facilities.

Theoretical approaches to counselling in groups vary as much as individual counselling approaches. In many cases, the theories are the same. For instance, within group work there are approaches based on psycho-analytic, Gestalt, person-centered, rational-emotive, transactional analysis, and behavioural theories. Because the basic positions of these theories are examined elsewhere in this text, they will not be reviewed here. In an evaluation of seven major theoretical approaches to groups, Ward analyses the degree to which each approach pays attention to the individual, interpersonal, and group levels of the process. For instance, the psychoanalytic, Gestalt, and behavioural approaches are strong in focusing on the individual but weak on the other two components of the group process. On the other hand, the Rogerian approach is strong on the individual level and medium on the interpersonal and group level. Ward points out the limiting aspects of each approach and the importance of considering other factors, such as the group task and membership maturity, in conducting comprehensive group assignments.

Group leaders and potential group members must know how theories differ in order to make wise choices. Overall, multiple theoretical models provide richness and diversity for conducting groups. Three factors, in addition to the ones already mentioned, are useful for group leaders to consider when deciding on what approach to take:

1. Do need a theoretical base for conducting the group?
2. What uses will the theory best serve?
3. What criteria will be employed in the selection process?

A theory is a lot like a map. In A group, it provides direction and guidance in examining basic assumptions about human beings. It is also useful in determining goals for the group, clarifying one's role and functions as a leader, and explaining the group interactions.

Finally, a theory can help in evaluating the outcomes of the group. Trying to lead a group without an explicit theoretical rationale is similar to attempting to fly an airplane without a map and knowledge of instruments. Either procedure is foolish, dangerous, and likely to lead to injury. A good theory also serves practical functions. For example, it gives meaning to and a framework for experiences and facts that occur within a setting. Good theory helps make logical sense out of what is happening and leads to productive research. With so many theories from which to choose, the potential group leader is wise to be careful in selecting an approach.

Groups, like other living systems, go through stages. If an individual or group leader is not aware of these stages, the changes that occur within the group may appear confusing rather than meaningful and the benefits may be few. Leaders can maximize learning by either setting up conditions that facilitate the development of the group or "using developmentally based interventions, at both individual and group levels". In either case, group members and leaders benefit.

There is debate in the professional literature about what and when groups go through stages. Developmental stages have been identified in various types of groups, such as learning groups and training groups, yet much of the debate about stages centers around group counselling. Group counselling is most often broken into four or five stages, but there are models for as few as three stages and as many as six. Tuckman's stage model is considered mainstream. Tuckman was one of the first theorists to design a stage process for group counselling. He believed there were four stages of group development: forming storming, norming, and performing. This concept was later expanded to include a fifth stage: adjourning mourning/morning.

In each stage certain tasks are performed. For example, in the forming stage, the foundation is usually laid down for what is to come and who will be considered in or out of group deliberations. In this stage, members express anxiety and dependency and talk about nonproblematic issues. One way to ease the transition into the group at this stage is to structure it so that members arc relaxed and sure of what is expected of them. For example, before the first meeting members may be told they will be expected to spend three minutes telling others who they are. In the second stage, stoming, there is usually considerable turmoil and conflict, as in adolescence. Group members seek to establish themselves in the hierarchy of the group and deal successfully with issues concerning anxiety, power, and future expectations. Sometimes the group leader is attacked at this stage.

The third stage, norming, is similar to young adulthood, where "having survived the storm the group often generates enthusiasm and cohesion. Goals and ways of working together are decided on".

This stage is sometimes combined with the storming stage and leads to performing, which parallels adulthood in a developmental sense.

At this stage, the group members become involved with each other and with their individual and collective goals. This is the time when the group, if it works well, is productive. Finally, in the adjourning or mourning/morning stage, the group comes to an end, and members say good-bye to one another and the group experience. In this death stage, members feel either fulfilled or bitter. There is often a celebration experience at this point of the group or at least a closure ceremony. One of the easiest ways to conceptualise groups, regardless of the type being led, is through the four-stage group model: forming, norming, working, and terminating.

Overall, the developmental stages of a group are not readily differentiated, group does not necessarily move step by step through life stages, but may move backward and forward as a part of its general development". It is necessary that a group have at least a beginning, a middle, and a closing. After that, the question of what stage a group and where it is heading can best be answered through retrospection or insightful perception.

There are a number of issues involved in conducting successful groups. Some deal with producers for running groups; others deal with training and ethics.

Screening and preparation are essential for conducting a successful group. Some individuals who wish to be members of groups are not appropriates for them. If such persons are allowed to join a group, they may end up being difficult group members and cause the group leader considerable trouble. Or they may join with others who are at an equally low level of functioning and contribute to the regression of the group. When this happens, members become psychologically damaged, and the group is unable to accomplish its goals.

There are distinguishing qualities of effective and ineffective group leaders, instance, group leaders who are authoritarian, aggressive, confrontational, or emotionally removed from the group are ineffective and produce group casualties. On the other hand, four leadership qualities have a positive effect on the outcome of groups, if they are not used excessively:

— Caring: the more, the better

— Meaning attribution: Includes clarifying, explaining, and providing a cognitive framework for change

— Emotional stimulation: Includes activity, challenging, risk taking, self-disclosure

— Executive function: Includes developing norms, structuring, and suggesting procedures

It is vital that group leaders find a position between the two extremes of emotional stimulation and executive function for the well-being of the group. Leaders should not allow members to experience so much emotion that they are unable to process the material being discovered in the group nor structure the situation so rigidly that no emotion is expressed.

Effective leaders understand the forces operating within a group, recognize whether these forces are therapeutic, and, if they are not, take steps to better manage the group with the assistance of its members. His assessment of leadership complements that of Yalom's and Osborne's, who believe that good group leaders behave with intentionality because they are able to anticipate where the group process is moving and recognize group needs. An example of this phenomenon is the ability of group leaders to treat the group homogeneously when there is a need to manage group tensions and protect members and to emphasize heterogeneous qualities when the group has become too comfortable and is not working.

Effective group leaders are committed "to the never-ending struggle" to become effective as human beings. He lists a number of personal qualities that are "vitally related to effective group leadership". Among them are presence, personal power, courage, willingness to confront oneself, sincerity, authenticity, enthusiasm, sense of identity, and inventiveness/ creativity.

Therapeautic elements

A group approach to counselling individuals is a well-established mode of treatment. At the same time, the question of what it is about the group approach that makes group counselling effective is poorly understood. One part of the difficulty in answering the question results from the fact that any kind of therapeutic change is an enormously complex process and occurs through a multiple interplay of various experiences. Since this process is as complex as it is, efforts have been made to identify the crucial aspects of the group experience which are most important in promoting therapeutic change. One of the difficulties, however, in studying the literature related to group counselling results from a wide assortment of theories seeking to explain the therapeutic process. Likewise, empirical research sometimes tends to complicate the picture even further, since the research findings are often inconsistent and the quality of the research varies considerably.

One approach to the problem involves the overall concept of therapeutic elements. Researchers such as

Frank, Truax and Carkhuff, and Carkhuff, and Berenson have sought to identify and validate that certain elements are consistently related to effective individual counselling. However, there have been only limited efforts made to discover those same kinds of consistent, basic elements in group counselling that constitute the therapeutic process, no matter what theoretical model is being applied. Such research would not only provide a more solid scientific footing for group counselling, but would also enable the group leader to integrate into his or her counselling process those factors that have been shown to be most important in therapeutic change.

It is reasonable to believe that the more skillful the group leader is in utilizing therapeutic elements, the more effective the therapy process will be. The focus in this chapter is on those therapeutic elements which have been tentatively identified. These elements were originally proposed as the result of the group experiences that various individuals encountered. In some cases such elements are included because the observations made were done in a systematic, although not empirical, manner. Where empirical research is available to demonstrate the relationship of a particular therapeutic element to outcome, such research will be briefly summarized. Part of the difficulty in identifying those therapeutic elements results from a tendency among group theorists to use different language and different ideologies to describe the same phenomenon. Successful group leaders frequently attribute their success to the use of certain techniques or strategies. While these techniques and strategies may be extremely important in facilitating the group movement, an analysis of therapeutic elements must go beyond these specific strategies and look at the broader concept of what is happening within the group when such strategies are utilized. The concept of a therapeutic element is based on the assumption that the group process involves a specific set of elements that can be differentiated from one another as to their exerting specific effects on members of the group, thus facilitating change. These elements, while inherently therapeutic, may be misused by the group leader either because the leader lacks appropriate skill or because a group member is unable to accept that kind of therapeutic factor.

With this in mind, a definition of therapeutic element can be proposed. The definition that we are using is that proposed by Bloch. Bloch defines a therapeutic factor as "an element occurring in group therapy that contributes to improvement in a patient's condition and is a function of the actions of the group therapist, the patient, or fellow group members". This definition takes into account the fact that the means by which therapeutic elements arc important varies considerably. The definition also helps to distinguish between therapeutic elements and two other aspects of the group process which are closely related: conditions for change, and techniques. Conditions for change are important in the operation of therapeutic elements, but do not in themselves have therapeutic force. For instance, self-disclosure requires listeners, and the actual presence of several individuals to hear that self-disclosure increases its therapeutic effect. Similarly, a technique does not have direct therapeutic effect but is simply a strategy available to the group leader to increase the effectiveness of a therapeutic element. While therapeutic elements, conditions for change, and techniques can be isolated, they often overlap and are interdependent with one another.

Corsini and Rosenberg published the first major effort to produce a unifying classification of those therapeutic elements shared by group counsellors of various theoretical persuasions. Basically, Corsini and

Rosenberg conducted a "factor analysis" by abstracting the therapeutic factors identified in 300 pre-1955 group counselling articles from which they identified 220 statements reflecting therapeutic factors. They then reduced those to 166 by combining identical statements and then, through a set of hypotheses suggested by a study of those statements, clustered them into nine major categories. Those nine categories formed a classification system for identifying therapeutic factors in group counselling. These categories are:

1. Acceptance: A sense of belonging
2. Altruism: A sense of being helpful to others
3. Universalization: The realization that one is not unique in one's problems
4. Intellectualization: The process of acquiring knowledge about oneself
5. Reality Testing: The recognition of the reality of such issues as defenses and family conflicts
6. Transference: A strong attachment either to therapist or to co-members
7. Interaction: Relating within the group that brings benefit
8. Spectator Therapy: Gaining from the observation and imitation of fellow patients
9. Ventilation: The release of feelings and expression of previously repressed ideas

Hill attempted to take the classification further; he interviewed nineteen group therapists and proposed six therapeutic factors: catharsis, feelings of belongingness, spectator therapy, insight, peer agency (universality), and socialization. The next classification, produced by Berzon, Piovs, and Farson used group members rather than leaders as the source of information for determining the essential therapeutic elements. Berzon studied eighteen members of two outpatient, time-limited therapy groups which met for fifteen sessions. After each meeting the patients filled out a questionnaire in which they described that incident which was most important to them. As a result, 279 incidents were obtained. Judges then sorted those incidents into nine categories in order of frequency. The resulting nine categories closely resembled those of Corsini and Rosenberg and included:

1. Increased awareness of emotional dynamics
2. Recognizing similarity to others
3. Feeling positive regard, acceptance, sympathy for others
4. Seeing self as seen by others
5. Expressing self congruently, articulately, or assertively in the group
6. Witnessing honesty, courage, openness, or expressions of emotionality in others
7. Feeling responded to by others
8. Feeling warmth and closeness generally in the group
9. Ventilating emotions

The main therapeutic mechanisms were reported to result from the interaction among group members with few of the reports involving the group leader. To a large extent, the major focus was on the interpersonal feedback which group members received, enabling them to modify their self-image and to validate the universality of problems. Ohlsen proposed a somewhat different set of therapeutic forces which were based on a series of research conclusions that he summarized.

Yalom proposed his landmark classification of curative factors. Based primarily on a series of research studies which Yalom and his colleagues performed, Yalom emphasized an interactional dimension to the group process and, in particular, highlighted the interaction taking place among the group members themselves. He proposed the term "interpersonal learning" as a major curative factor which had two components: input, chiefly through feedback; and output, an actual process whereby the group member attempts to develop more effective modes of relating to others.

Yalom also included three new therapeutic factors that had not been earlier proposed: the installation of hope (the member feels optimistic about change as a result of observing progress in others); guidance (the member receives advice from the group leader or from fellow group members); and an existential factor (the member becomes aware that one alone is responsible for the way one lives one's life). Yalom's list of curative factors then included:

1. Installation of hope
2. Universality
3. Imparting of information altruism
5. The corrective recapitualization of the primary family group
6. Development of socializing techniques
7. Imitative behaviour
8. Interpersonal learning
9. Group cohesiveness
10. Catharsis
11. Existential factors

Bloch, Reibstein, and Crouch have sought to exploit the assets of the aforementioned classifications while avoiding the limitations they believed to exist. Their ten-factor classification resembled Yalom's classification but with certain modifications. For instance, they omitted Yalom's existential factor because they believed it did not correspond to their definition of a therapeutic factor; that is, it was not an element of the group process that exerts a beneficial effect. They suggested that the existential factor instead calls for the group member to think about life in a specific way along lines laid down by a particular theory and is therefore better conceptualized as a therapeutic goal. They also omitted family reenactment, since they felt this assumes that the group member should identify a specific cause of his or her difficulties- unresolved family conflict.

At the same time, they proposed a new factor of self-understanding which was all-embracing in quality in the sense that it was based on the members learning about some important aspect of the self. They also made a distinction between two forms of expression: *self-disclosure*, the members revelation of highly personal information reflecting honesty and openness; and *catharsis*, the members release of intense feelings, bringing about a sense of relief. Their final difference from Yalom's was one of emphasis and concerned interaction. Bloch and his colleagues saw interaction as an *attempt* by the member "to relate constructively and adaptively within the group either by initiating a pattern of behaviour or by responding to other group members".

In an attempt to build on the work of those individuals whose work we have just summarized, as well as others who have made significant contributions to our understanding of group counselling, we propose a somewhat simpler model for identifying those therapeutic elements which are necessary and sufficient for effective group counselling. Like some of the others who have preceded us, we are basing our ideas concerning therapeutic effectiveness elements on the research that we have reviewed, the conceptual ideas that others have presented, and our own experience in leading various kinds of groups. From our viewpoint, then, the essential elements that contribute to therapeutic effectiveness in group counselling include the following:

1. Installation of hope
2. Sense of safety and support
3. Cohesiveness
4. Universality
5. Vicarious learning
6. Interpersonal learning

Installation of hope is a therapeutic element through which the group member gains a sense of optimism about his or her progress or potential for progress through actual counselling experience. Although the concept has been emphasized by a number of theoreticians over the years, it has been virtually neglected by those individuals doing empirical research in group counselling. As Frank, Hoehn-Saric, and Imber have suggested—that hope may act as a placebo factor in psychotherapy generally—it is possible that the installation of hope in a group setting is even more of a placebo effect than in individual therapy since the potential sources of a group member's hope includes all of his or her peers.

If future research can somehow prove this placebo effect to be true, the installation of hope will still be an important element since, whether placebo or not, group leaders are only concerned about what it is that helps to bring about therapeutic change among the group members. Certainly the installation and maintenance of hope is crucial, since hope is required to keep the member in the group so that other therapeutic factors can take effect. When the individual remains within the group, other "hope-installing" factors can take place. For instance, other members of the group will have often suffered from some of the same concerns as the individual group member.

Such individuals who have had similar problems and have coped with those problems effectively provide hope for others that their own concerns and problems can be resolved. Effective group leaders frequently exploit this factor by calling attention to the improvement that group members have made. Likewise, if the group members are to possess a sense of hope about the group counselling experience, it is important that the group leader believe in himself and in the efficacy of the group. The belief that the group leader is able to help every member who commits himself to counselling and remains with the group for an appropriate period of time is important for the group leader; sharing this belief with each group member can be an important part of increasing that member's optimism about his group experience.

One of the great strengths of such support groups as Alcoholics Anonymous, Overeaters Anonymous, and Synanon is the fact that the leaders are almost always individuals who have suffered from the same disorders as the current members. These leaders then become living inspirations to the new members, who are able to believe that because the leader was able to overcome his or her problems they will be able to do so also.

A major part of the meetings of these groups is dedicated to testimonials from not only the group leader but from the various members of the group. These testimonials are of major importance in the effectiveness of these groups. Corey and Corey point out that hope is a belief that change is possible, that "one is not a victim of the past and that new decisions can be made". Such hope comes not only from a sense of identification with other individuals who have solved similar problems, but also emerges from the recognition that one has untapped reserves of spontaneity, creativity, courage, and strength. As individuals recognize and accept that they have the internal resources necessary to direct the course of their lives, their sense of hope greatly increases.

Because individuals enter group counselling with the hope that it will be helpful to them, it is important that the group leader build on that hope so it will block or destroy concurrent feelings of these group members that "maybe nothing can help. " One way of maintaining this hope is to develop clear-cut expectations of what will be expected from each member. The more members understand and adopt those expectations—to discuss their problems openly, to work toward specific behaviour change, and, when necessary, to confront other group members toward implementing new behaviours—the more those group members will increase their feelings of power and optimism about changing their own lives.

The need to feel reasonably secure within the counselling group—where individuals can be themselves, give up their facades, discuss their problems openly, accept other persons' frank reactions to them, and express considerately their own genuine feelings toward others—is a need that is clearly essential to a therapeutic experience within group counselling. Part of this sense of safety and security results from a feeling of genuine acceptance by other group members. This group acceptance not only enhances self-esteem, but provides quality support for various changes in behaviour which the individual wishes to attempt. Such acceptance ordinarily involves the affirmation of the individual's right to have his or her own feelings and values and to express them. It also comes from demonstrated caring. This caring is sensed when individuals believe that others are listening to them and have an involvement with their concerns. When group members are able to sense that their concerns are important to others and that they are valued as persons, they are more likely to risk the kinds of changes in their lives that will be therapeutic in the long run. Risking involves opening oneself to others and actively doing those things in the group experience that are necessary for change. As such, this kind of riskiness results in the person's feeling vulnerable to rejection. Perhaps the key word is trust. A sense of safety and support within the group can come only after the individual feels a large level of trust in the group. As Johnson and Johnson have pointed out, trust is a necessary condition for effective communication. They go on to add, "the higher the trust the more stable the cooperation and the more effective the communication. A group member will more openly express his thoughts, feelings, reactions, opinions, information, and ideas when the trust level is high".

When group members trust the group and feel this sense of safety and support, two particularly important behaviours or effects are likely to occur: self-disclosure and catharsis.

A number of studies indicate that successful group members self-disclose. Self-disclosure has two major effects: (a) a member is able to receive understanding and acceptance from the other group members that will let that member know that he is okay as a person and (b) group members discover that their fellow members whom they may admire have problems as difficult as their own and that they are not giving up. The effect of universality, which will be discussed later, can begin to take effect.

Catharsis—the release of strong feelings, bringing relief—can be therapeutic in that energy is released that has been tied up in withholding certain threatening feelings. Catharsis often permits an individual to realize that negative and positive feelings toward another person or situation may coexist. The relief that results from the individual's knowledge that other people now know about these intense feelings and the situations that brought them about is a major step in that individual's feeling understood and accepted. Although catharsis has been emphasized by a number of individuals, it has received little attention by those who do empirical research on group counselling variables. One reason for this may be the intrinsic nature of catharsis and the difficulty of measuring its impact. Another reason may be a feeling that catharsis by itself has little value; only when catharsis is complemented by subsequent cognitive reflection does it result in individual growth.

The Lieberman, Yalom, and Miles study is the major study which has attempted to clarify the value of catharsis *per se.* These researchers asked 210 Members of a thirty-hour encounter group to describe the most significant incident that occurred during the course of the group.

While experiencing and expressing feelings was frequently selected, this critical incident was not related to positive outcome. Incidents of catharsis were as likely to be selected by group members who showed little change as by those who showed good change. They point out that "catharsis was not unrelated to income; it was necessary but, in itself, not sufficient". They believed that their study showed that individuals who had profited most from their group experience showed a profile of catharsis plus some form of cognitive learning. Thus the open expression of feelings is without question vital to the group therapeutic process. In its absence, the group would flounder in a sterile nonmeaningful exercise. Rather, catharsis is intricately related to cohesiveness and provides the kind of bonding that enables the group to work honestly in the therapeutic change of its members.

Cohesiveness

Although Corsini and Rosenberg, as well as each of the other theorists summarized in this chapter, included the concept of cohesiveness in their classification of therapeutic elements, its precise definition remains elusive. Although acceptance is an element of the sense of safety and support, described earlier, we are including it in this section as part of an individual's feeling that he or she belongs and is part of a particular therapeutic group. This sense of togetherness, which we have labelled group cohesiveness, involves many aspects, including allegiance, agreement with the group's objectives, and attraction to the group leader as well as to peers.

Corey and Corey point out that a group is characterized by a high degree of togetherness at times, providing an environment in which "participants feel free to share problems, try new behaviours, and in other ways reveal the many dimensions of themselves". From a practical standpoint, cohesiveness is important because it has an impact on the attendance of individuals at group sessions as well as their involvement. Thus when a group feels a sense of cohesiveness, they are more likely to take those actions which result in therapeutic change. A number of research studies have been performed which support the idea that cohesiveness is an important element within group counselling. Dickoff and Lakin, for instance, in a study of former group psychotherapy patients, found that the patients believed that group cohesiveness was of major therapeutic value. They found that over half of those former patients indicated that the primary help they had received in group therapy was the result of mutual support.

Also, those patients who perceived their group as cohesive attended more sessions, experienced more social contact with other members, and judged their group as having been therapeutic. Likewise, a positive association was found by Kapp, Glaser, and Brissenden in their study of long-term members of discussion and therapy groups. In this study, members rated their own level of change as well as the degree of cohesiveness they perceived in the group. Kapp and his colleagues concluded that cohesiveness may be important in bringing about change.

However, a study by Yalom, Houts, and Zimerberg indicating that patients perceived cohesiveness as positively relating to self-ratings of change, also showed that there was no relationship between the degree of cohesiveness perceived by patients and independent judgments of therapeutic outcome. In 1977 Jones studied 130 patients who responded to questionnaires at a student mental health service. These patients had attended one of thirty therapy groups offered at the service, consisting of twenty two-hour sessions over a five-month period. The respondents stated that the most positive aspect of their group experience was the feeling of security and acceptance they had experienced in the group.

Jones concluded that the amount of cohesiveness was positively related to the degree of self-reported improvement; that is, that those groups that received high cohesion scores from its members were more likely to have a higher number of patients who improved during the course of therapy.

Yalom summarized a large segment of the research that has been done in laboratory groups and dyads related to group cohesiveness. He concluded that the overall evidence from this research demonstrates that the members of a cohesive group, in contrast to the members of a noncohesive group, will:

1. Try harder to influence other group members;
2. Be more open to influence by the other members;
3. Be more willing to listen to others and more accepting of others;
4. Experience greater security and relief from tension in the group;
5. Participate more readily in meetings;
6. Self-disclose more;
7. Protect the group norms and, for example, exert more pressure on individuals deviating from the norms;
8. Be less susceptible to disruption as a group when a member terminates membership.

Two factors that may contribute to the importance of cohesiveness as part of the therapeutic process arc intimacy and empathy. As people experience closeness in a group, an intimacy develops creating a stronger sense of trust in others. Individuals may become aware, as a result of this new sense of closeness to others, of the barriers in their outside lives that have prevented intimacy. Empathy may also be a part of cohesiveness, since a true sense of empathy Involves a deep understanding of the struggles of another individual. In the group setting, commonalities among the individuals emerge that unite them, forming a cohesive bond. The feeling that one is alone lessens with the realization that certain problems—such as fear of rejection, fear of intimacy, loneliness, or hurt resulting from previous experiences—are universal. We have also chosen to include, under the umbrella of cohesiveness, the concept of altruism, which various theorists have proposed as a separate therapeutic factor. In a cohesive group, the individual is more likely to become part of the therapeutic process of offering help to other group members.

As a result, the individual is more likely to engage in those activities that will enable him or her to benefit from the realization that he or she can be of value to his or her peers. This results in the realization that, in counselling groups, members receive through giving, not only as part of the reciprocal giving-receiving sequence, but also from the very intrinsic act of giving. Such giving undermines the sense of being demoralized and of having nothing of value to offer others. Thus for the group member, it is a refreshing, self-esteem-boosting experience to find that they can be of importance to others. Even more important, group members are enormously helpful to one another in the group process itself. By offering support, reassurance, suggestions, insight, and understanding, they provide spontaneous, truthful reactions and feedback, permitting other members to gain insight into how they relate to others.

Carkhuff pointed out this importance of altruism in the therapeutic process in his comments regarding training as a preferred mode of treatment. His basic concept was that by training individuals to help others, those individuals would receive the greatest degree of help themselves. Perhaps the major reason this occurs was pointed out by Frankl when he suggested that it is only when we as individuals have transcended ourselves, when we have forgotten ourselves in an absorption in someone or something outside of ourselves, that we obtain self-actualization and meaning in life.

Another key element in the therapeutic process of group counselling is that of universality, the sense that one is not unique in one's problems-that others share these problems. Since many clients enter a group setting with some reluctance because they believe that their problems are unique to themselves and have little relationship to the kinds of problems that other people experience the positive impact that occurs whenever those individuals learn that others do have concerns similar to their own is enormous.

A sense of relief often results as these clients hear the self-disclosure of other group members, and a growing insight into the nature of their own problems results. Yalom reports that clients often indicate that they feel more in touch with the world and see this process of commonality with other group members as one of a "welcome to the human race" experience. As trainers of counsellors, we have often had our counsellors- in training practice an empathy exercise in which each member of the training group would write a secret that he or she would be highly unlikely to share with the rest of the group.

After the secrets have been written, they are collected and redistributed, with each member receiving a secret other than his or her own to share with the group. The individual then reads someone else's secret and tries to describe the way he or she believes the other person feels with a secret such as that. Over the years, we have learned that one of the more positive outcomes has been that those who had shared the secrets in the first place discover that their secrets were not devastating to the other group members, but were accepted. In addition, the pattern over the years of those secrets seems to indicate that the kinds of issues which create the major problems for most of us have a great deal in common. Yalom reports having utilized a similar technique and finding that the most common secret revealed was that of basic inadequacy, followed by a sense of interpersonal alienation. Thus, as members of the group learn the kinds of feelings, thoughts, and concerns which have disturbed them and made them feel as if they were somehow less than other individuals, they begin to feel a sense of commonality with other people and to lose the sense that something is wrong with them.

Like several other of the therapeutic elements, universality has had little research that demonstrated its importance to group counselling. There has been a growing theoretical interest in it as a concept, especially in the study of self-help groups. Lieberman suggests that universality is a major feature of the self-help group in providing a supportive effect on the group's members. At about the same time, Robinson highlighted another dimension: The value of universality as a means of reducing a sense of stigma, so commonly associated with emotional, mental problems.

Vicarious learning has been called different things by different theorists. From the very beginning it has been recognized as an important element of group counselling. Corsini and Rosenberg spoke of " spectator therapy, " which they described as gaining from the observation and imitation of fellow patients.

George and Cristiani point out that while clients in groups are focusing on resolving their own interpersonal or intrapersonal difficulties, they are also exposed to interpersonal relationship skills being modelled by both the group leader and the other group members. In a previous work, we reviewed some of the research that had been done on the effects of imitative learning as part of the group process. Modelling can be deliberately used in group counselling sessions as a means of demonstrating desirable behaviour before group members try out the new behaviour with the group providing feedback. Bandura, Ross, and Ross have been leaders in the emphasis on social learning as a major therapeutic technique. They demonstrated the power of imitation by successfully treating a large number of individuals with snake phobias by asking them to observe their therapist handle a snake. The effective group leader, then, is able to utilize this therapeutic element of vicarious learning by bringing into the group process other group members who may be experiencing similar concerns. In doing so, those clients not only gain additional insight into what is occurring with them, but may also learn what does not fit.

Jeske has conducted one of the most important studies of vicarious learning in group counselling. Jeske had each group member who was participating in short-term counselling press a button whenever that individual found himself or herself identifying with another group member. Those patients who showed the greatest improvement recorded twice the number of such identifications as did those who did not improve at all. Jeske concluded that the group leader should promote such intermember identification as a means of facilitating the therapeutic progress.

Although listed last in this set of therapeutic elements in group counselling, there is little doubt that interpersonal learning plays a major role in the course of group counselling. Several research projects have asked group members to evaluate those factors that have been most helpful to them during the group process. In eight major studies, six of them ranked interpersonal learning among the top three. Interpersonal learning was ranked among the top five in the other two studies. In personal growth groups, interpersonal learning is even more highly valued, ordinarily being ranked first by the members of the group.

Bloch points out that interpersonal learning has two components: input, chiefly through feedback; and output, an actual process whereby the group member attempts to develop more effective modes of relating to others. Certainly the attempt to relate constructively and adaptively within the group becomes an important aspect to many group counselling members as they attempt to develop new ways of interacting in a more satisfying manner with those around them. As gregarious persons who live our lives in a social setting, we are only able to develop self-esteem, a sense of satisfaction, and security from those social contacts that we make. Thus, as a group develops, individuals within the group begin to interact with one another in the same way they interact with others in their lives. Thus, the group becomes a laboratory in which is revealed maladaptive interpersonal behaviour and attitudes—arrogance, grandiosity, nonassertiveness, sexualization, overcompliance.

As individual group members receive feedback from the other members of the group, the individual learns the effects of his or her behaviour on others. When feedback is given honestly and with care, group members are able to understand more clearly the impact they have on others and to learn how often they create the kinds of reactions that they receive from other individuals. As a result, each group member can then decide what to do with this feedback. As group members become fully aware of the impact of their behaviour upon (a) the feelings of others, (b) the opinions that others have of them, and (c) the opinion they have of themselves, they become more aware of their own responsibility for what happens in their interpersonal worlds. Likewise, as each individual fully accepts personal responsibility for that interpersonal world, he or she can begin to struggle with the resulting implication that he or she is the only one thus able to alter that world.

In facilitating the interpersonal learning element of group counselling, the group leader must focus on the present the here-and-now-of the group interaction. If each group member is to learn as much as possible about the effects of his or her interactions with the group leader and with the other members, the group focus must be upon the immediacy of the interactions occurring in the group.

In doing so, the group de-emphasizes the past as well as de-emphasizes the current outside life of each of the members. This does not mean that group counselling undermines the importance either of the past or of the current life situation. Rather, it places a focus on the power and efficiency of the interpersonal interactions that are occurring right now. Such an immediate experience involves both an affective and a cognitive component. That is, group members not only share important emotional experiences, but they also step outside of that emotional experience and examine, understand, and integrate the meaning of that experience they have just undergone. Thus, the most effective here-and-now focus consists of a rotating sequence of affect followed by cognition. To facilitate both components of the here-and-now requires that the group leader have two different sets of techniques. For the first stage-the stage of emotional experiencing-the leader needs a set of techniques that will plunge the individual, and the group, into an intense awareness of what each experiencing. This involves the use of the same kinds of techniques that counsellors use in individual therapy for helping clients get in touch with their current experiencing.

The group leader must be active and continually work toward the shifting of material from the outside to the inside, from the abstract to the specific, from the generic to the personal. In addition, the therapist is often able to encourage a focus on the here-and-now by genuine self-disclosure of his own experiencing. The second component of the here-and-now—the understanding and clarification of the emotional experience—requires a set of techniques that enables the group to transcend itself in order to examine, explain, and interpret its own experience.

This demands reflection, explanation, and interpretation. This phase of group work is called "group process." It refers to what the content of a group discussion or of an individual's comments reveals about the nature of the relationship of the individuals involved in the discussion. In facilitating this cognitive stage of the here-and-now, the group leader must focus on process, listening to the group discussion with an ear toward examining how the words exchanged shed light on the relationships among the participating individuals.

To understand this process, the group leader needs to register all of the available data, both verbal and nonverbal. This includes such simple issues as choice of seats, attendance patterns, being on time, eye contact when talking, and socializing patterns after the group session. However, the most likely productive source of information concerning the group process comes from the group leader's own feelings. If, for example, the group leader feels impatient or discouraged or bored or frustrated, he or she must recognize this as important data about the working of the group and utilize this information to the group's advantage.

Catharsis, which involves the group member's release of intense feelings bringing about a sense of relief, can be an important process factor within several of the therapeutic elements. Even Yalom, who earlier had defined catharsis as a curative factor in group therapy, points out that catharsis is "intricately interwoven with other therapeutic factors". Certainly, strong expression of emotion is an important aspect of group counselling. It enhances the development of cohesiveness, by binding together members who express strong feelings toward one another. It often results in a sense of relief when the individual learns that his or her expression of intense feelings does not result in rejection by the other group members.

Likewise, we have not included as a therapeutic element what Yalom called 'imparting of information. " Again we believe that while imparting of information is important as part of the group experience, its function is to be part of various of the therapeutic elements. This aspect of group counselling can include information that is rather specific in its nature, for instance, information about various career issues that might be important to a career counselling group.

One other therapeutic element that occurs across the others and is therefore identified individually involves the use of humour in the group counselling process. Although humour can be a negative factor in group situations, especially when it consists of a pseudo-humour which is exercised at the expense of some person or subgroup, humour can become an important healing aspect of the group. There are some truly humorous dimensions of the human condition. When group leaders possess the ability to laugh at themselves and to see the humour in their own human frailties, the group becomes more likely to do so also. This humour is certainly not sarcasm, ridicule, or cynicism. Rather, spontaneous and natural laughter with one or more of the group members can help establish an additional bond of genuine caring for each other and confidence in the helping nature of human rapport.

The use of humour may allow the group leader to deal with the group member's irrational ideas by taking those ideas to ridiculous extremes or reducing them to absurdity. When this is done, the members are able to see the ridicule of their own ideas, not a ridicule of themselves. Such humour, as long as it is not used to derail an important immediate dynamic to express anger or to conceal an individual's deep feelings, has curative value all by itself.

Theoretical expectations

As a means of understanding the results of counselling, we can examine what outcomes of successful group counselling have been hypothesised by proponents of selected theories. The selected theories are Gestalt, Adlerian, Personal Growth, and Cognitive-Behavioural. Each section is divided into goals of the individual member, interactional goals between members of the group, and overall group goals or group process goals.

Gestalt groups

Although Frederick Perls was not himself a group therapist, many students may have the impression that Perls was conducting group counselling sessions. Instead, Perl's workshops had only one purpose: to demonstrate his Gestalt techniques. Nevertheless, by examining the writings of other Gestalt writers, it is possible to piece together an approximation of what a Gestalt group counsellor might include as a list of expectations for a successful group.

Individual goals

The major goal for a Gestalt group leader is to increase the self-awareness of each individual. This increased self-awareness is itself curative according to Gestalt concepts. For the most part, all the goals which follow are either process goals to help increase the self-awareness or they are specific examples of increased awareness.

Additional transparency for each individual is a major goal. Melnick has described how individuals come to recognize and accept more and more aspects of themselves and how these individuals also become more willing to communicate formerly hidden or self-disguised aspects of themselves. An increase in responsibility for one's self is another goal. This frequently comes about through interactions with the group leader and with other group members and can be seen through an increase in "I" statements. An increased integration of individual conflicts and greater self-reliance are additional goals for the Gestalt approach. Within each individual, inherent conflicts become split into polarities. These polarities are extreme tendencies that individuals hold simultaneously. For example, as one wishes to be loved by a person, there is a tendency to wish to dominate the same person. The top dog-underdog polarity is a commonly used example of such conflict. Increased integration has been called "the overriding objective of Gestalt counselling". The split in self-image concepts is gradually reduced as individuals come to accept the divergent, often contradictory, aspects of these images of self.

Gradually roles are reduced or eliminated as the person incorporates the other goals listed above. This results in increased integration of the self.

Interpersonal goals

Members will perform more and more self-disclosure in a Gestalt group as it develops. Increased communication which is focused on the immediate is a goal of a Gestalt group. As individuals become more aware about self, they will increasingly give here-and-now reactions to the group leader and to other group members as well as communicate about themselves in a here-and-now fashion.

As individuals interact within a Gestalt group they will invariably act out sibling rivalries and familial patterns. The interactions and the communications of conflict between group members will increase the self-understanding of each group member. Another goal of Gestalt counselling is to stimulate the investigation and exploration of polarities for each individual, mentioned earlier. Much of this exploration occurs as individuals compare and contrast themselves with other group members.

Group Process

Group process goals are centered on the climate which is most conducive to individual exploration and growth. A Gestalt group counsellor would be likely to stimulate group exploration of the group's structure and the group's process. As the group facilitator stimulates each member's self-exploration, the counselling group will also be involved in exploration and examination of the group itself. Just as the growth for individual members occurs through discovery, a group Process goal is for the group to make discoveries about its own functioning.

Adlerian groups

Much of the writing in Adlerian group counselling currently specializes in groups for elementary-aged children as well as groups for parents. Nevertheless, there are certain general goals which would be hypothesized for any Adlerian group, including groups for younger children.

Individual goals

An Adlerian group counsellor helps the client see the beliefs and feelings as well as the motives and goals that determine the individual's life-style. Clients develop insights into their mistaken goals and self-defeating behaviours. They are then helped to develop appropriate life goals. Group counsellors also try to maximize the responsible freedom and personal effectiveness of each individual group member. develop feelings of personal worth in each individual group member, and help each individual consider alternative life-styles and make a commitment towards change.

Interpersonal goals

As each group member is encouraged to explore his or her feelings and reactions to other group members, self-understanding is furthered. This goal could be described as providing opportunities for group members to learn about their own style of coping through exploring their interactions with other group members. In addition, self-understanding is increased by helping each individual member learn how he/she decided to belong to the group. To develop and to further social interest in group members through their encouraging others and becoming involved with other members' specific life changes is another Adlerian goal.

Group process

Although not emphasized as much as in Gestalt groups, process goals for Adlerian group counselling would include developing an empathic relationship between the group leader and each individual member, encouraging empathy and acceptance by the entire group for each individual member, developing the social interest of individuals through the group climate and the development of an encouraging group, providing a climate of encouragement for individual group members so that they will risk making a commitment to change their behaviours and their life-style, and developing a cooperative climate and norms within the group.

Personal growth groups

Several types of groups-including human potential, T-groups, and some types of encounter groups-are considered under the general heading of personal growth. Diversity of goals among groups of this type may very well be as large as the diversity of goals for the entire range of counselling theories. Nevertheless, a collection of selected goals representative of personal growth groups follows.

Individual goals

As members are given time in the group to relate personal information, self-understanding is an important goal, much as it is for individual client-centered counselling. Furthermore, as individual members are encouraged to explore the meaning of their interactions with other members, self-understanding is said to be increased. Several specific goals are usually included in personal growth groups. One of these is to increase self-awareness and the awareness of the individual's potential. A second is to increase individual self-exploration and there by heighten the ability of the individual to achieve greater self-awareness and communicate this awareness. A third goal is to increase individual acceptance of self. As the individual member experiences acceptance from other members of the group and from the leader, self-acceptance then leads to increased self- understanding.

Interpersonal goals

Interactions between group members are a means to increasing individual self-understanding. Interactions are explored and examined so that all group members are able to consider their own reactions and to incorporate individual learning. The goal of self-acceptance is furthered as the leader models an accepting individual, even within conflict situations. Individual members are encouraged to be less judgmental and more accepting of each group member. Encouraging the individual's reliance on self as a source of evaluation rather than the reliance on others' appraisal is a major goal as is increasing the frequency of spontaneous reactions and expressions of feelings to other group members.

Group process

For some proponents of personal growth groups, the totality of the group's interactions, including changes in group interactions over time, are an important focus. The mutuality of goals for individual members, namely, to foster and to spur individual growth and change, provides an emphasis on certain climate or group process goals. Another important group goal is to develop a climate of intermember support. The feeling of support from other members encourages individuals to explore and to communicate about themselves. To explore, examine, and increase individual awareness of the interdependence of members is still another goal. As individuals are encouraged to learn about themselves, many will offer help to other members and also learn to receive help. An important group process goal is to create an accepting atmosphere.

The reduced fear and self-consciousness in individual members that results is believed to increase self-disclosure and thereby to further individual self-understanding. Another goal mentioned frequently with growth groups is to increase the group leadership. Increasing self-direction by the group rather than relying heavily on group leaders for direction is seen as a process goal.

Although there has been some confusion as to the distinction between groups where interaction among members is encouraged and those where the only interaction is from leader to individuals, this focus on cognitive-behavioural groups is limited to groups in which members have clearly identified changes which they would like to make in their lives outside the group.

Individual goals

The central goal of a cognitive-behavioral group is to help individual members make changes in their lives in ways of their choosing. The emphasis is on change outside the group. Such changes would include the decrease of behaviours regarded by the individual as maladaptive and an increase in adaptive behaviours. To help an individual practice and receive reinforcement and encouragement would be a major goal so that the individual will succeed with the new behaviour outside the group. Another goal is to help the individual learn techniques to influence his or her own environment. Such techniques might help the individual to set up certain stimuli or change certain stimuli preceding crucial behaviours; to perform designated behaviours; to alter his or her own thinking, and to seek out or otherwise to provide reenforcement for targeted behaviours. To help individuals examine and carry out changes by interacting with other group members having similar problems is another goal

Interpersonal goals

To provide appropriate models for other group members is a behavioral goal. Use of multiple models could be encouraged so that an individual member could benefit from seeing more than one group member perform designated behaviours. Increasing the support for individual members through encouragement and social reenforcement is a goal. Interpersonal goals might also include members agreeing to check up with a member, to prompt another member, or to reinforce a member. The opportunity for rehearsal and practice is an important goal of behavioral groups. Members can be especially helpful by being willing to participate in role plays. An advantage of group counselling lies in the potential for feedback from other individuals. At times this goal will be directly influenced by the group leader's providing training for members in the skill of behavioral feedback.

Group process

Although it is often difficult to determine whether group behavioral counselling actually includes group interaction variables such as discussion, sharing feelings, and providing feedback, behavioral group counselling as defined in this section would focus on the group climate. Especially important would be a group climate which would encourage individual exploration and risk-taking which would further the specific goals of the particular group. At times group members would be trained in certain techniques such as, providing feedback, providing social reinforcement, or providing encouragement. It is desirable that the group provide a climate which seems safe enough for members to share personal concerns and to take risks as they attempt to practice new, and sometimes difficult, behaviours. The group process should be work-oriented. This requires commitment from individual members to stay on a task as well as to offer support and social reinforcement to other members of the group.

Reviewers of research in group counselling have puzzled over the poorly defined terms and concepts. They have lamented the lack of effective research methodology. Yet, the professional literature reflects a high interest in this area with long lists of studies and many reviews in many settings. What follows is a brief look at recent studies in the effectiveness of group counselling and psycho-therapy. Because of the infrequent use of comparative studies, the theoretical sections used earlier in this chapter are not used to organize the selected studies here. Instead the categories of goals used for each of the theories provide the organizing headings found later in the review: individual change, interpersonal change, and group process. Although a rich and extensive literature exists in the group counselling area, reviewers have consistently complained about the quality of this research. What makes research in group counselling so difficult? A few of the factors are the inability of writers in group counselling to agree upon definitions of terms; the difficulty in comparing theory to theory; complaints that group studies performed in a laboratory with six college sophomores, for example, or for one 20-minute session are not transferable to real groups; and finally, the extreme amount of effort and persistence needed to compare comparable counselling groups in a counselling setting.

When one writer uses a term such as *insight* in a specific way, other writers may very well invent or use their own special meaning for the term insight. When writers from varying theories of group counselling use similar terms, all too often the definitions do not agree. It has been pointed out that many widely used terms in the group area such as self-disclosure and cohesiveness have never had operational definitions which were agreed upon. This lack of operational, agreed-upon definitions, of course, makes comparing results from one study to another virtually impossible. In addition, there has been a tendency in the literature for writers to use group in the title or in their introductory paragraph but to never specify exactly what the group consisted of, or what the experience and style of the leader was, what specific interventions were used in the sessions, and whether the same members existed at the end of the group as in the beginning. In many areas of counselling great strides in research have been gained by looking in the laboratory at very narrow, specific aspects of complicated processes. For example, a study which looked at role taking or, even better, at varying aspects of role taking, might very well result in a hypothesis that could be tested by group leaders in the field or by researchers with the capability to conduct group counselling research in a help-giving setting. However, a lot of the practitioners, and several of the writers in the area of group counselling, have complained violently about the lack of practicality of laboratory studies for the group counselling practitioner.

The significant outcome studies of counselling and psychotherapy have compared counselling of three to five different theoretical backgrounds with one another at the end of counselling. To find on-going, comparable groups at the same time and then to compare results, has been an exceedingly difficult task for group studies. This task has been made even more complicated by the finding that theoretical labels have not differentiated between interventions and techniques used by group leaders. In his thorough review of therapeutic factors in group psychotherapy over a 25-year period, Bloch et al. confirmed how little definitive research has been done which indicates the effectiveness of various therapeutic factors within groups.

The studies which were included here, selected because they seemed like clear examples of the three headings, namely, individual change, interpersonal change, and group process; or because they were especially effective studies taken from agency or educational settings. Studies were not included which focused on family counselling and psychotherapy, on in-patient groups, or which featured special populations. Studies were included which had been published since 1977. In the event that a study does feature an in-patient client group or does focus upon a special population, the text will make note of this.

One recent study has been selected as an example which indicates the difficulties of conducting research in group counselling while at the same time providing an effective, exemplary sample. Shadish conducted an experiment using 49 undergraduates who had volunteered for the study. These subjects were randomly assigned to six groups. One research difficulty in counselling which is especially troublesome when conducting research in groups is that of design. Shadish assigned his six groups as follows: 10 subjects to a pretested control group, *8* subjects to an unpretested control group, eight subjects to a pretested verbal group (his treatment), eight subjects to an unpretested verbal group, seven subjects to a pretested nonverbal group, and eight subjects to an unpretested nonverbal group.

One of the troubling questions in successful research is that of a control group. This study met this by providing three controls-a pretested control group, an unpretested control group plus the two groups, one in each treatment, which had been pretested along with the other two groups which had not been pretested. This type of design allows the researcher to determine what effect the pretest may have had on the subsequent results of the findings. However in Shadish's study groups of unequal size were used. All too often, studies do not indicate the experience level of the group leaders. In this study, four pairs of group leaders were made up of clinical psychology graduate students. These pairs were counterbalanced by sex and experience. In addition, all eight group leaders went through an 18-hour educational experience which consisted of didactic and experiential training. In addition, this experiment used a follow-up. The follow-up in this study was of 3 weeks, not very long, but in our opinion better than no follow-up at all.

One difficulty in conducting research in counselling and psychotherapy is the ability to determine whether the treatment groups, as well as the control groups, actually did contain a treatment or, in the case of the control group, no treatment at all. In this study, Shadish had two senior psychology students observe meetings of the six groups. The two senior students were able to identify correctly whether they were viewing a control group, a nonverbal group, or a verbal group. The treatment consisted of three

3-hour sessions plus a marathon weekend session. Although no description was given of the control groups or the treatment groups, a sample nonverbal and verbal exercise is described.

Several measures were used in this study. A difficulty of comparing group outcomes is the tendency for researchers to use their own, home made measures of change. Shadish used standardized instruments. For example, the Personal Orientation Inventory (POI) resulted in no differences before the treatment, after the treatment or after the follow-up.

Individual changes

Sulzbacher, Wong, McKeen, Glock, and MacDonald used the POI as an outcome-measure as well as a self-concept instrument. The treatment was a 3-month intensive resident human growth program with 33 participants. Thirteen members of the participants' families served as the control group. The instruments were administered before the group program, at its conclusion, and at a 1 -year follow-up. Highly significant increases were found in self-actualization and self-concept for the participants. These increases were maintained at the end of 1 year. No changes were found at the time of the three testings in members of the control group.

Shapiro, Sank, Shaffer, and Donovan studied changes in group member depression, state anxiety, trait anxiety and assertiveness. Forty-four enrollees in a health maintenance organization were used as subjects. Of these, 35 completed all assessment inventories. The subjects were described as mildly depressed. Participants were randomly assigned to one of three treatment groups: cognitive behaviour therapy, traditional inter-personal process group, and individual cognitive behaviour therapy. The cognitive behaviour group was given relaxation training and cognitive restructuring practice. The traditional interpersonal group used an unstructured treatment which included elements of insight development, interpersonal feedback, and focus on group process. All three treatments, including the individual treatment, met for 10 weekly sessions (1½ hours for group treatment and 1 hour for individual treatment).

All three treatments resulted in reduced depression, less state anxiety, less trait anxiety, and a significant increase in assertiveness. In a 6-month follow-up, the experimenters found maintenance of several changes in the individual participants. Follow-up data was completed on 29 of the original 35 participants. The changes in anxiety and assertiveness were maintained. However, depression had returned towards but did not reach pretreatment levels.

Barrera also studied the effects of group therapy on depression. This study used a subscale of the same measure as Shapiro et al. The Minnesota Multiphasic Personality Inventory (MMPI) and a personal screening interview were used to diagnose participants as depressed. Twenty subjects were assigned to an immediate treatment group and 20 others to a delayed treatment group. Leaders for both groups were a male and female coleader.

At the end of four weeks, when the immediate treatment group was completed, and at the end of 8 weeks, when both groups had received treatment, there were no differences between the two groups. At the end of one month, the delayed-treatment group was described as much improved on the depression scale. The authors were unable to explain the lack of treatment effect in the immediate treatment group.

In a one year follow-up to a study comparing individual and group cognitive behavioral counselling, Kendall reported significant changes in a study conducted in a school. Teacher ratings of group participants indicated significant behavioral change at the end of the group and at a one year follow-up from pretreatment ratings. In addition, group and individual participants in the study were no longer viewed as different from other students by the teachers. However, teacher ratings indicated that the control subjects in the study continued to be rated as different from the majority of the students. The individual treatment and the group treatment were viewed as equally successful in this study.

Olson, Ganley, Devine, and Dorsey described a 4-year follow-up with 137 participants in a study which compared behavioral versus insight therapy. One hundred thirteen subjects were available from the original 137. The control group received the standard milieu treatment for 1 month. Treatment group 1 received two or three lectures a day plus "traditional group therapy" that focused on feelings. Treatment group 2 received transactional analysis (TA) sessions 3 times a week. Treatment group three received behavioral treatment conducted by two therapists. This treatment included covert desensitization—aversiveness, drinking-avoidant behaviour and social reinforcement. Treatment group three received transactional analysis combined with behavioral treatment under the same leaders. In addition, all treatment groups received bibliotherapy and attended daily Alcoholics Anonymous meetings, individual psychiatric consultations each week, recreational activities, and a weekly family group counselling session. The follow-ups were conducted on the telephone, with a second interviewer listening on an extension telephone. The reliability of the two interviewers was described as 0.86 and 0.94. No group differences were found 4 years after the treatment, although there was a nonsignificant trend for the TA group to do poorly.

Although interaction and interpersonal communication among group members is commonly described as a reason for group counselling, relatively few research studies in group counselling have focused on interpersonal change. Morran, Robison, and Stockton described a study which focused on feedback among counselling group members. "Interpersonal feedback occurs when one group member shares his or her perceptions of and reactions to another's behaviour with that other person". Earlier studies indicated that effective definitions of feedback must include informational aspects as well as motivational aspects. In addition, group members have been found to accept positive feedback more readily than negative; to respond to positive and negative feedback differently at different stages of group development; and to value behavioral rather than emotional feedback.

This study interrupted the group process in order to devote one session to gathering feedback at either the second, fourth, or sixth group session. Three groups participated in feedback at each of the three sessions (nine treatment groups). Sixty-three subjects participated in 6-week "personal growth groups," meeting 2 hours each week. The nine groups were co-led by male-female or female-female advanced doctoral students who were interns in a counselling agency. The study was interested in who provided feedback-the members or the leaders; the timing of the feedback-which session it was given in; and positive versus negative feedback.

During the special session, group members and the leader completed a form to give feedback to each member. After writing the feedback, each person in the group read his or her feedback to each member. Positive and negative feedback were separated with the order being randomly assigned. Recipients immediately rated the feedback. Results showed that the sex of feedback givers and receivers was not a factor. Recipients rated positive feedback as more accurate than negative.

In addition, feedback in Session four was rated as more helpful than feedback in Session two. Member and leader feedback was rated equally. Feedback from members was more specific when positive, while leader feedback specificity was the same for positive and negative. Negative feedback was less directive the later the session in which it was gathered.

A second example of studies regarding interpersonal change can be found in member attractiveness for the group (cohesion). Falloon used behavioral group therapy with 76 out-patients described as neurotically depressed or with inadequate personalities who reported having difficulties with their social skills. These results, rather than shedding light on differential group treatments causing different outcomes, can better be seen as an example of an outcome study for a treatment setting. Six role rehearsal groups (n = 6—10) and three discussion (control) groups were formed. Each group met for 10 weekly 75-minute sessions. The control groups used the same topics, handouts, and homework as the treatment groups. Leaders prompted and praised "constructive discussion and mutual help." The treatment groups were also structured around weekly topics. Patients exchanged information about homework but also participated in deep muscle relaxation, listening to MUSIC and other tension relieving activities. Leaders modelled effective behaviour each week followed by member rehearsal. Group attractiveness was greater for the behavioral groups than for control groups ($p < .05$). The authors suggest that cohesiveness can be improved by role rehearsal activities. No differences were found among the behavioral groups.

The final area of organization for expected goals of theories is group process. Only a few theories focused their expectations on specific group process goals. Likewise the research on group counselling has tended to slight this aspect of groups, an aspect that is unique to group counselling. Once again, definitions pose a problem in this area. Topics such as member interaction and cohesiveness, treated under interpersonal change above, could be viewed as elements of group process. While some authors focused on "group dynamic processes" or "group climate" little research exists on group process changes in the literature. Interpersonal learning is viewed as an important therapeutic factor by many group writers. However this concept is usually measured in any research by obtaining individual group members' self-estimates. In some studies, these measures may be averaged, with the resulting mean seen as an indication of group process change. Such a procedure is not really a group process measure, however. As summarized by Bloch et al. "... there is no evidence of how interpersonal learning occurs or its effect on outcome.... ". Coche and Dies point out the overemphasis on group research on the individual. Research in group counselling has exhibited several difficulties including a lack of studies which compare outcomes of groups using different theories, lack of studies which focus on expected outcomes for any theory, lack of agreed-upon definitions or measures, and difficulty in establishing comparable control groups. Nevertheless, a sample study was shown which illustrated the type of research which is lacking. In addition, research was described according to the categories used earlier for expected group theory outcomes; namely, individual change, interpersonal changes, and group process.

5

Counselling Profession

Counselling programs were set up to help employees adversely affected by personal problems, such as alcoholism, drug abuse, divorce, and financial pressures. Counsellors have the potential to play an important role and are doing so already. In a recent national survey, more than 60 per cent of the externally administered programmes reported hiring counselling graduates with master's and doctoral degrees.

Courses in multicultural counselling are frequently added to counsellor education programs nationwide. This increase stems from the realization that in a therapeutic relationship ethnicity can be part of the solution or the problem for the client and the counsellor.

Some counsellor training programs and the professionals associated with them are exemplary in providing multicultural education for their students. One of the most exciting developments in multicultural counselling is the renewed emphasis on theories specifically designed for different cultures. For example, traditional Asian psychotherapies, which have existed for more than 3,000 years, have recently become more popular in the West Newer Asian theories, such as the Japanese-originated Morita therapy, have also begun to be applied in the United States, especially for the treatment of eating disorders such as bulimia.

Marriage and family counselling is a popular trend as evidenced by the rapid membership growth of the International Association of Marriage and Family Counsellors, which reached about 8,000 in 1995. Hollis and Wantz cite marriage and family counselling as the area in which the greatest number of courses have been added in counselling programs since 1984. They note that by 1996 there will probably be at least one marriage and family counselling course in most counsellor education programs.

A high divorce rate, an increase in out-of-wedlock births, substantial cohabitation, and an increase in selecting a single life-style further attest to changes in the American family. Marriage and family life require commitment and hard work in the best of times and can be extremely difficult when unsettling changes are sanctioned by society at large. Another major reason for the popularity of marriage and family counsel h realization that persons become healthier when their families function better. Family counselling is economical, and its encompassing nature makes it intrinsically appealing. Computer use has grown rapidly since the late 1970s. What once was considered a promising technology has now became reality. User-friendly computers have made an impact on all facets of society.

In the 1980s, several special issues of Counsellor Education and Supervision, Journal of Counselling and Development, and The School Counsellor were devoted to the use of computers in counselling. Much of the material in these issues focused on record keeping, the manipulation of data, and word processing, although a few articles centered on client simulation and training counsellors with computers. In the 1990s more attention is being focused on factors affecting computer and client interaction. For instance, clients who are high in maturity and low in direction may especially benefit from computer programs such as SIGI-PLUS in career counselling.

Rehabilitation counselling

The Americans with Disabilities Act of 1990 is a major piece of federal legislation that protects people from job discrimination on the basis of their disabilities. In addition, it specifies that all people with disabilities have full and equal access to goods, services, facilities, privileges, advantages, and accommodations available to all Americans. This law will have a major impact on rehabilitation counselling both now and in the future, as disabled Americans and those who work directly with them encounter employment and testing situations that do not meet the guidelines of the act. Furthermore, this legislation and challenges to it may call into question the concept of what is and is not a disability. Another trend in rehabilitation, private practice, may also alter the focus of the profession, bringing with it the opportunity for more freedom and greater financial benefits.

In the 1980s, the federal government declared a war on drugs. In doing so, it admitted that its citizens widely use illegal substances that are harmful or dangerous. Therefore, academic programs that educate counsellors will continue to emphasize substance abuse counselling. There is some dispute about whether this speciality should be a major within a degree program or an emphasis under community/agency, mental health, or rehabilitation counselling. Realistically, it will probably occupy all these positions in the future, depending on the personnel who operate such programs.

In 1994 NBCC set up a certification process for becoming a substance abuse counsellor. On the surface, substance abuse appears to be an individual problem; in reality, however, it is a way of protecting and stabilizing dysfunctional families by keeping their attention off overall dynamics and on predictable problematic behaviours. In addition, substance abuse may serve as a substitute for sex and promote pseudo-individuation. Thus, it is difficult to help people caught up in substance abuse patterns to change behaviours without an intensive systems approach. Comprehensive ways of conceptualizing and treating chemical dependency will most likely become more prevalent in the future.

A feminist view of counselling sprang from the eruption of the women's movement in the 1960s. Initially, this movement was a challenge to patriarchal power; but as it grew, its focus centered on the development of females as persons with common and unique qualities. Beginning with the publication of Carol Gilligan's In a Different Voice there has been an increased integration of feminist theory into counselling.

One branch of this approach, liberal feminist counselling, encourages individuals to become more aware of socialisation patterns and personal options in altering traditional gender roles as they make changes. The other branch, radical feminist counselling, concentrates more on encouraging clients to become involved in social-change activities that stress equality as a way of bringing about change. Feminist theory is more an approach to counselling rather than a well-formulated set of constructs. It is assertive in challenging and questioning attitudes of traditional counselling theories because these models often advocate the maintenance of the status quo of a male-dominated, hierarchical society. Two main emphases in the feminist position distinguish it from other forms of helping: Its emphasis on equality in the helping relationship, which stems from a belief that women's problems are inseparable from society's oppression of women. Its emphasis on valuing social political and economic action as a major part of the process of treatment. Androgyny, the importance of relationships, the acceptance of one's body as is, and nonsexist career development are also stressed in feminist thought. Overall, feminist theory starts with the experience of women and uses women's values and beliefs as the assumptive framework. Although these emphases are covered by the umbrella of feminist theory, their underlying principles have universal appeal. Beneath the exterior and mystique of women and men is a commonality of emotion and experience that the feminist perspective and its counterparts seek to highlight.

Developments within the field of career counselling continue to occur rapidly. One reason for this trend is the wealth of information already available to researchers that facilitates new inquiries. A second reason is the high interest in career development manifested throughout the life span. A third contributor to the fast-paced nature of this counselling speciality is the ebb and flow of the world economy and the changes within the service and manufacturing sectors of both developed and nondeveloped countries. As advancing technology creates new kinds of jobs almost daily, previously valued skills and entire occupations may diminish. Theories and resources of career counselling will be challenged to keep up with these changes. One theoretical concept of career counselling is gaining increased attention: the constructive-developmentalism perspective. This approach integrates constructivism (people constitute or construct reality) and developmentalism (people evolve through predictable eras) and concludes that what develops during the life-cycle is the activity of meaning-making or making sense of self and situation. This theory is exemplified quite well in the writing of Miller-Tiedeman. She suggests that occupational decision making is, in essence, an opportunity to examine, redefine, and direct one's life. The impetus for decision making is disruption in a person's homeostasis, which motivates people to make new choices to achieve new stability. The theory is particularly compatible with existential and phenomenologically based theories of counselling.

Counselling theories continue to develop, although at a less rapid clip than in the 1950s and 60s. This decline has several causes:

1. A proliferation of theories in the preceding decades that ranged from psychoanalysis to aikido, breathing therapy, soap opera therapy, and past lives therapy
2. A refinement and broadening of already established positions
3. Stringent research requirements that must be met before any novel position will be accepted
4. Current interest in integrating already existing theories, such as cognitive theories with behavioural theories.

The present emphasis in connecting theories instead of creating them is built on the fundamental assumption that no one theoretical viewpoint can provide all of the answers for the clients we see today.

Furthermore, counsellors can be pragmatically flexible in adapting techniques and interventions from different approaches without actually accepting the premises of these points of view. When treating clients, counsellors must consider intrapersonal, interpersonal, and external social systems. Few theories blend all these dimensions together; so, by necessity, many counsellors must weave formerly distinct points of view into a creative, systemic, and eclectic process if they are to be effective and holistic.

Whether one approves or not, individuals choose different sexual life-styles and have distinct social orientations. Gay men and lesbian woman are often stereotyped and discriminated against. Even counsellors are less accepting of members of this population than one might expect. As Rudolph states that ministering to the psychotherapy needs of homosexuals has historically been an exercise in dissatisfaction and discomfort for many clients and counsellors. The majority culture, which professional helpers represent, has a mostly negative view of homosexuals, which can have a detrimental impact on the mental health and well-being of gays and lesbians and may severely disrupt their total development.

In career decision making, gay men often lack role models and are directed too often into socially stereotyped homosexual occupations. In any minority culture that is treated with prejudice, people suffer and the overall culture is negatively affected.

Similar to the growth in multicultural counselling, a current movement is working to sensitize counsellors to issues faced by homosexuals. Now that conservative politics have become stronger in American society and cases of AIDS have risen to new proportions, working with professed homosexuals is bound to be an unpopular activity in many locales but one that can do much good if conducted properly.

Hollis and Wantz mention six major trends in the accreditation of counselling programs. First, counsellor preparation program accreditation has become important to students and graduates. The reasons are linked to the assurance that accreditation provides a tangible measure that students and graduates are receiving a quality education as well as the realization that people are better prepared to complete credentialing procedures when they come out of accredited programs. Second, accreditation standards and criteria are being used to measure the comprehensiveness and quality of counsellor preparation programs. Such standards and criteria are good indicators of the minimum requirements of a quality program and are externally objective. They may also be used to set priorities and validate requests for resources. Third, APA, CACREP, COAMFTE, and CORE have become the recognized bodies for counselling accreditation because all have a proven track record in specific areas of accreditation.

Fourth, counsellor preparation programs are beginning to specialize. The reasons are directly tied to resources: institutions have to decide what kinds of programs they can afford. Fifth, counsellor preparation programs are changing their offerings to meet national accreditation standards. Faculty and administrators understand that accreditation standards are associated with good programs, and standards are a way of determining program priorities. Finally, counsellor preparation programs are moving toward two years of graduate work with more experiential clinical components and faculty/practitioner cooperation. Sixty semester hour programs may soon replace the current 48 semester hour programs.

Counselling programmes have become deeper in course offerings and broader developmentally as a result of accreditation trends. Obtaining certification, licensure, or both is becoming increasingly important in the counselling profession. More than 40 states and the District of Columbia license counsellors, and certification specialities are available from the National Board for Certified Counsellors (NBCC) in school counselling, mental health counselling, career counselling, substance abuse counselling, and gerontological counselling. Credentialed counsellors possess enhanced visibility and credibility. In addition, credentialing through national certification ensures a more unified definition and practice of counselling.

There are four reasons for counsellors to obtain both NBCC certification and state licensure. First, national certification is broader than state licensure and based on a larger population. Second, licensure is more susceptible than national certification to state politics. Third, national certification more readily provides referral sources and networking across state lines. Finally, most state counselling licenses do not recognize speciality areas whereas national certification does.

The juxtaposition of counselling and spirituality was mainly confined to pastoral counsellors, existentialists, and Jungian analysts, until the 1970s. Many counsellors were either indifferent or opposed to exploring openly the spiritual dimensions of life. Some, such as classical Freudian therapists, were quite hostile. Three recent events have had a profound effect on this prevailing attitude. One is the informal spirituality promulgated by Alcoholics Anonymous, Adult Children of Alcoholics, and other 12-step programs.

It is impossible to determine whether the mass attraction of these three events can be credited to the way in which the material is packaged or a widespread hunger for more holistic approaches. There is probably some truth to both views. In the early 1990s, the

Association for Spiritual, Ethical, and Religious Values in Counselling (ASERIV) was one of ACAs fastest growing divisions. There has also been renewed emphasis on the counsellor as a spiritual person and the use of clients' religious or spiritual values to aid progress in counselling. In a comprehensive overview of spirituality, religion, and counselling, Ingersoll points out the importance of defining spirituality and lists seven dimensions that describe it:

— A concept of the divine or a force greater than oneself

— A sense of meaning

— A relationship with the divine

— Openness to mystery

— A sense of playfulness

— Engagement in spiritually enhancing activities

— Systematic use of spiritual forces as an integrator of life

Ingersoll goes on to state that counsellors interested in working well with clients committed to a particular spiritual view can best do so by affirming "the importance of spirituality in the client's life, using language and imagery in problem solving and treatment that is congruent with the client's world view, and consulting with other "healers" in the client's life such as ministers.

AIDS (acquired immunodeficiency syndrome) is the most advanced phase of the human immunodeficiency virus (HIV). AIDS is ultimately fatal, but individuals diagnosed with HIV may live with the virus for a number of years. First identified in the United States and France in 1983-1984, HIV causes a chronic, progressive, immunologic deficiency disorder called HIV disease. Those who contact HIV are often stigmatized and discriminated against, In addition, they usually live with fear and anxiety Their personal crisis with the disease affects not only them but their family members, friends, colleagues, and lovers.

While HIV can be transmitted only by direct exposure to blood or blood derivatives, certain acts of sexual intercourse, or transfer from infected mother to fetus or infant, the spread of the virus in the United States has become an epidemic that has created panic, fear, and hysteria as it spreads to the heterosexual population, affecting persons of all ages, ethnicity and social status. Approximately 1.5 million people have tested positive for HIV, but only a fraction of that number have actually contracted the disease.

It is crucial for counsellors to be aware of the psychological effects of persons who have tested positive for AIDS but have remained asymptomatic. Issues such as feeling infected and infectious; facing death and dying; and ambivalence, uncertainty, and secrecy must be faced and dealt with successfully if counsellors are to help members of this population. Ethical issues surrounding confidentiality also need to be addressed. Cohen proposes a model rule for limiting confidentiality in cases where clients have a contagious and fatal disease such as AIDS and where serious risk to third parties is involved.

There has been an emphasis on positive wellness, since the late 1970s. Such activities include eating natural foods, taking vitamins, going to health spas, meditating, participating in regular exercise, and exploring a variety of humanistic and transpersonal approaches to helping. For the person to be a whole, healthy, functioning organism, one must evaluate the physical, psychological, intellectual, social, emotional, and environmental processes. Signs of the holistic movement toward health and well-being are apparent everywhere as Americans of all ages have become more aware of positive and negative habits. Research backs up the basis for this movement and in some ways leads it. In an extensive review of the literature on the effectiveness of physical fitness on measures of personality, Doan and Scherman found strong support for the idea that regular exercise can have a beneficial effect on people's physical and psychological health. Their review supports counsellors who prescribe health habits to accompany regular counselling practices.

Myers notes the increased need for gerontological counsellors in the 21st century, when more than half the U.S. population will be over 50 years of age. Aging is a time of both positive and negative transitions and transformations. Unfortunately, however, society and counsellors have viewed it primarily as a time of loss. To meet the needs of the aging population and sensitize counsellors to working with this group, Myers, in cooperation with ACA, prepared curriculum guidelines for infusing gerontological counselling into counsellor preparation. She also worked with the Association for Adult Aging and Development to produce video training films to complement the proposed curriculum offerings.

The spectrum from gerontological counselling is counselling in school and college settings. Both areas are expected to grow as counsellor educators and educational personnel give increased attention to the needs of young people. There is a new awareness that passive school counsellors have not and will not work for the good of children and society. School counsellors have the ability to be positive school-change agents, and they will have to implement this role if they want to become part of the mainstream educational process. By emphasizing such a role, school counsellors can become a major part of educational reform that stresses the affective dimensions of school staff and students rather than just academic or cognitive skills. It is significant that NBCC has established a process for certifying school counsellors on the national level.

In college counselling centers, there is also an increased emphasis on outreach and a proactive stance in the delivery of services. These services include consultation, career counselling, crisis management, retention, personalization and humanization of the campus environment, establishment of self-help programs, cooperation with other campus units and professional organizations such as Division 17 of APA, and continuing education. This approach also emphasizes the need for setting limits and maintaining a balance with the campus community.

With the rapid changes in society and counselling, there is an increased need for counselling associations to develop strategic plans and implement leadership training. Both ACA and APA are engaging in these activities, as are their divisions. Strategic planning involves envisioning the future and making preparations to meet anticipated needs.

Similar to the counselling skill of leading, it is usually accomplished in a group and involves hard data as well as anticipations and expectations. Leadership training, on the other hand, includes everything from understanding how leaders envision, plan, and implement ideas to group dynamics and management theory.

The guidance worker needs to develop a sense of unique personal identity, and with it an awareness and appreciation of the meaning of a profession with all the specific guidelines, regulations, and policies that define the practice of the speciality. When one analyses the definition of the term "professional", the importance of the aspects covered in this chapter is clear. The major identifying characteristic of a procession is its knowledge base. Theory and research are organized to guide practice. Guidance, drawing on the disciplines of psychology, sociology, economics, and others, meets this criterion.

A second characteristic is a code of ethical practice. The counselling profession has for many years been concerned with ethical standards, and the American Personnel and Guidance.

Association has formulated a comprehensive and well-designed statement. But it is up to the individual practitioner to observe standards voluntarily. Employers such as school systems may use the APGA's ethical standards as guidelines, but often look to the local standards and ethics of the teaching profession when questions of improper conduct arise. The control of preparation and practice are two further factors that help define a profession. Through establishing admissions standards for preparation programs and specifying what these programs should accomplish, the guidance profession does exercise some control.

A fifth characteristic of professional identity is personal autonomy in the provision of service, the individual counsellor exercises independent judgement, makes decision, and provides help.

Counsellors may have considerable freedom in the way they practice their profession, but little control over allotment of time for specific activities. Even so, there is adequate autonomy for the counsellor to utilize professional expertise. A final professional characteristic involves the function of service to others.

Counselling and guidance qualify as a profession by this criterion more fully than by any other. There is room for improvement in the applications of standards for preparation and practice; but professional status is justified in all crucial respects.

The American Personnel and Guidance Association has taken the lead in formulating standards for preparation for guidance at the elementary and secondary levels. The guidelines are clear-cut, specific, and constitute excellent models. The secondary school standards have been more extensively studied, reviewed, and developed than those for the elementary school, but the current guides cover all counsellors regardless of educational level. Before the most recent standards were adopted in 1973, an earlier set of guidelines had been widely used by counsellor-education institutions and accrediting organizations for self-study and program improvement. A manual was also prepared to help counsellor education staffs prepare for evaluations. The new revision brings together existing guide lines for all levels in a unified and comprehensive report. The Association for Counsellor Education and Supervision carries on the development of standards as a continuous process; new revisions will be forthcoming.

The introduction to the new standards reflects many contemporary trends. First, it spells out the need for students to demonstrate competencies. Second, it assumes differential rates of student progress; some may take longer to acquire proficiency than other. Third, it considers various models that extend graduate preparation beyond a single year; one such program, for example, combines an undergraduate major in guidance with a year of graduate study. The four major sections cover objectives; the program of studies and supervised experience; responsibilities concerning students in the program; and support for the counsellor-education program, administrative relations, and institutional resources.

The opening section on objectives sets the stage for the program. The major emphases are on explicit, cooperatively planned objectives evolving from input of those involved-counsellor educators, students, and practitioners. Objectives show sensitivity to needs, problems, and trends in schools; they are regularly revised and updated.

The program of studies calls for academic and practical work to enable students to move to increasing levels of competence and responsibility. There are opportunities for observation and involvement in guidance. Responsibility for working face-to-face with individuals and groups comes as competence is developed. Along with increasing competence in helping activities, the program fosters a spirit of inquiry, ethical sensitivity, and skill in self-evaluation. The practical-work component is given specific emphasis; in a one-year period, 60 hours should be spent in face-to-face individual or group work.

The third section deals with selection, retention, endorsement, and placement of students. It speaks to student rights, pointing out the need for making clear the criteria and procedures for admitting students, and retaining or separating them from the program. It also indicates the program's responsibility for endorsing and placing graduating students. The final section covers institutional support for programs in guidance. Emphasis is on cooperative relationships with other college or university departments for courses, and with school settings for practical experience. It specifies a minimum full-time staff of three members and spells out the necessary professional qualifications for those working with students. These standards, which describe what the program should provide and define the professional competencies to be mastered, are of great significance to the beginning students.

The APGA standards require preparation to cover all levels of the profession, added emphasis on specialized work settings is to be provided through courses and practical work. For example, students preparing for elementary school counselling would concentrate particularly on courses and practical work designed for this educational level.

Current standards are oriented to competency, as are several contemporary preparation models. The system-based approach and HRD, for example, emphasize specific competencies, systematic means of achieving them, and evaluation in terms of counsellor effect on counselees.

The ACES standards emphasize that programs are to be evaluated in terms of competencies of each student. Such competencies would be illustrated by specific items such as supervised practice in working with groups. Zifferblatt discusses the systems approach, in which specific skills are learned recycled until they reach an acceptable level of competency.

Among other strategies recommended in preparing counsellors is an experiencing-growing-sharing process between counsellor educators and students, which stresses individual development.

Legal status, certification, and licensing are among the must controversial and ambiguous in the counselling profession; they are of major concern to anyone planning to enter the field. Potential legal problems revolve around malpractice, right to privacy, serving as defendant tin criminal action, encouraging an illegal act, or involvement in civil disobedience.

Certification poses fewer potential problems. Your program will probably meet requirements, but you should known not only the standards in your own state,. but also those of any other state you may wish to move to. Licensure is of recent concern. Previously it was critical only for counsellors in some nonschool settings, but it is now emerging as an issue for school counsellors too. Currently the employees of an educational instruction are given sanctions to practice by virtue of their employment status; the institution authorizes their activity and assumes responsibility for performance. This may not be true in the future.

An understanding of legal factors in essential both for day-to-day practice in conventional types of service, and for anticipating problems that may arise with changing conditions. For example a counsellor may feel existing laws and regulations are harmful and ought to be challenged but must know the consequences of disregarding them and share this information with others who might need to know, particularly pupils.

The processes one chooses to bring about changes are to some extent a function of one's political convictions. Counsellors are entitled to their own views, but there are harsh realities to consider when changes involve committing illegal acts. Counselling today has no specific legal status. It has only recently come to be recognized as a formal part of school programs. Few court cases have dealt directly with school counselling, and even fewer statutes specify legal obligations and responsibilities. The status of counsellors must be clarified in the light of the few existing cases and statutes, and on the application of the law to people in general. Enough data are available t spell out some guidelines and to alert counsellor to their responsibilities and limitations.

Increasing professionalising has generated rising concern about legal issues. Counselling today amounts to a service of therapeutic intervention ant he pupils' lives. With the responsibility this implies, it is sometimes uncertain just how the counsellor can offer most help to the counselee without violating civil and criminal law. Counselors have no general immunity from criminal law and are subject to civil law. Moreover, while statutes give some general guidelines, state and local laws vary enormously.

Regardless of national statutes, however, state and local precedents should be examined before assuring counselees of confidentiality. When the counsellor has determined these legal limits, they should be explained to the counselee. In general, these principle are helpful.

1. If the counselee is a clear danger to self or others, the counsellor cannot maintain confidentiality. Steps should be taken to protect others if they are in danger.
2. Generally the counsellor respects the rights of others to confidentiality.
3. If a counselee is the victim of a crime, there is no privileged communication.
4. School counselors in most states do not have privileged communication. Where they do, laws may over only certain types of information.
5. For school use the term "privileged communication" can be defined as information shared with the counsellor by the counselee, which the counsellor cannot release without the approval of the counselee.
6. An individual may subpoena personal case material in college files for use in other actions. In the Bates College case, for example, the court upheld the plaintiff's request to view information he though was hampering his admission to other colleges. The more recent Buckley Amendment deals more completely with the question of access to records.

The counsellor must also be concerned with the right to talk to others about the counselee without danger of legal action for libel and slander. Usually if the counsellor makes comments about pupils, sends reports to parents, etc., believing the reports to be true, acting without malicious intent, and communicating only with individuals entitled to such information, legal action for libel and slander would not be successful.

Civil liability was an issue infrequently raised in past years, but it is a problem causing concern today. There is no sure way to judge what could be construed as counsellor malpractice. If, however, the counsellor follows the ethics and standards of the profession, malpractice liability would likely not be incurred, even if counselling has not been successful. A key requirement is that the counsellor makes a referral when a problem becomes too difficult to handle.

Group counselling involves the same responsibility, except that the probability of malpractice increases-there are more counsellees to observe and understand. Some problems are more likely than others to raise the civil-liability issue, particularly those involving sexual relations and abortion. According to Burgum and Anderson, advice about abortions, including possible medical and psychological complications, are beyond the counsellor's competency. Even so, counselors must deal with these problems every day.

Burgum and Anderson also describe an illustrative case relating to criminal liability in which the school counsellor, who has developed a good relationship with a boy in the custody of the iuvenile court, inadvertently helped him avoid arrest. The boy, with two companions, robbed a service station and then, realizing the gravity of his actions, went to the counsellor for help. The counsellor convinced the boy that he should turn himself, in but it was late at night, and they agreed he would go to the police the following day. Meanwhile, however, the counsellor committed a series of acts that could make him guilty of being an accessory to a felony. He denied to police that the boy was sin his house. He gave the boy money, which was found in the youth's possession when he tried to skip town the next morning rather than reporting to the police. The counsellor would have been well advised to report the matter to the boy's juvenile office, which would have been in his favour in a trial. Another area of local concern to the counsellor relates to the rights of pupils. The Gault case brought about full guarantees of due process for minors. Counselors can help pupils by making them aware of their legal right to due process in education, free speech, and property ownership.

Due process is not satisfied by establishing a standard procedure including such steps as informing the individual of charges and providing for a hearing, but rather it demands protection of pupils' right under the Constitution, just as if they were adults involved in legal charges. Due process should fit the situation and protect the pupil from arbitrary, unfair, and autocratic rules and policies. The Buckley Amendment, already mentioned, deserves special attention. This law restricts the use of information in personal records; enforcement involves the denial of federal funds if violations are allowed to occur. In the past, school records were not treated with respect for the individual's rights of privacy, nor have parents and pupils has access to most of the information contained in them.

The Buckley Amendment has given parents and pupils of legal age the right to inspect records, including letters, comments, and recommen-dations.

Besides opening up records to pupils and parents, the law restricts access of others to these data. In general, parents must give consent for information in records to be released. Nasman discusses the regulations in detail. The complete law appears in the *APGA Ethical Standards Casebook*.

Parts of the Buckley Amendment with specific applicability to counselors' use of student records are as follows:

> Each educational agency or institution except as may be provided by 99.12 shall permit the parent of a student or an eligible student who is or has been in attendance at the agency or institution, to inspect and review the education records of the student.
>
> The parent of a student or an eligible student who believes the information contained in the education record of the student is inaccurate or misleading or violates the privacy or other rights of the student may request that the educational agency or institution which maintains the records amend them.

The legal status of counselling is being established through new laws, statutes, and court decisions. While relatively few cases directly affecting counselling have gone through the courts, more can be expected as counselling achieves greater status and visibility as a helping service. All states regulate the practice of counselling through certification, licensing, or endorsement on a teaching certificate. Certification requirements of counselors in different states are more striking for uniqueness than for similarity, and certification standards are changing both in scope and nature.

The most innovative development is the competency-based program. Dudley and Ruff's survey included only one suggestion of this approach, and only one program of this type was reported in the literature. Now 50 percent of the states have, or are planning a competency-based program, while only about 7 percent are not considering it. Over two thirds of the counsellor preparation programs intent to convert to this approach, even though only about 7 percent have actually done so.

The Washington program started in 1971 is an example. Behavioural objectives were established through input of teachers, pupils, administrators, and counselors. Counselors have been certified at three levels of competency: preparation, initial, and continuing.

The initial-level competencies are the type developed in a masters-level program. Six areas of competency are specified; major ones are counselling, information service, and placement. Deficiencies in any of the competencies must be remedied according to procedures spelled out in guidelines of the certification program. Program accreditation is closely related to certification of individuals; it also gives students an important indication of the quality of a program and enhances job-getting potential If evaluation for accreditation is performed, it conforms to the counsellor preparation standards already discussed.

Licensure is relatively new for counselors, although psychologists have been active in formulating state licensure policies for at least two decades. School counselors have been concerned mainly with certification and have only recently become aware of the potential importance for their work of developments in licensure.

There are important differences between certification and licensure. Each provides a service to the users of counselling by indicating the adequacy of practitioners. Certification laws regulate the use of the title "counsellor" and specify the amount and type of training required for practice. Licensing goes beyond regulating the use of the title and indicates the unique services and practices that fall in the domain of the profession. The term "credentials" is often confused with certification. "Credentials" refers to the degree to other certificate the individual has been awarded; the term is also used to indicate competence for a job.

Up to new, licensure has been a concern of counselors in community settings such as mental health agencies and private practice. To date only one state requires licensing for personnel and guidance workers. But recent licensure laws have alerted counsellors to the potential for state regulation of some or all of their work. In Ohio, for example, licensing laws on the practice of psychology have been interpreted to limit the use of tests by a counsellor in off-duty hours.

In the case, City of Cleveland v. Cook 1975, a counsellor who was not a licensed psychologist was arrested for testing. The court found in favour of the defendant; Ohio counselors are contesting this interpretation of the law. The APGA Model Licensing Law specified the points favoured by he counselling profession, including exemptions for those employed as school counselors. But as the situation now stands, school counselors who plan to enter private practice in states with this type of regulation come under the licensing laws for psychologists.

The implications, however, may of far beyond off-duty activities or future career plans. As Sweeney and Sturdevant point out, the Ohio law and other similar ones specify that helping by licensing. Besides, licensure and privileged communication give school psychologists more freedom and prestige than school counselors. Sweeney and Sturdevant see "the right for school counselors to practice at all as being challenged".

Licensure gives every indication of becoming a major issue. Congress and federal agencies are showing increasing interest in occupational sensing. Present methods of licensure testing can be unfair to qualified persons, some, for example, do not perform well on standardized tests. Licensure can affect employment opportunities, status, and legal bases of counselling. Effective and well-designed licensure laws can enhance the counselling profession, project the public, and open up new work opportunities, restrictive and unfair ones will interfere with the contributions of many potentially well qualified to offer others assistance. Sweeney ad Sturdeant and Cottingham recommend that counselors keep up with what is happening in licensure and support favourable alternatives. Their advice points out a responsibility of all members of the profession.

One mark of a profession is a code of ethics. It serves as a guide for providing services and ensures legality in carrying out these services. The counselling profession has a comprehensive, well-developed code, as well as special guidelines for work in schools. The main points of the section on measurement and evaluation are that the counsellor should understand tests, be particularly cautious about their applicability or minority groups, and present or interpret results in keeping with test validity. The section on ethical standards for research and publishing identified the welfare of the individual as the primary factor to be considered; the counsellor should make every effort to avoid harmful effects of research and should take action to reduce or eliminate such effects if they occur.

The school counsellor code of ethics is uniquely helpful for the elementary and secondary level in that it identified responsibilities to self and those with whom the counsellor works-pupils, parents, faculty, staff, the school, and the community. In all relations the counsellor respects pupils' dignity, individuality, and right to self-direction.

Professional organizations provide counselors with support, facilitate professional development, bring together colleagues with similar interests, offer opportunities for active participation in leadership roles, and provide placement services. Counselors can help themselves by building a strong organization. Representatives of the profession are active at national, state, and local levels to promote favourable legislation and to obtain funds for improved services. Participation can begin during preservice preparation. The American Personnel and Guidance Association, a federation of thirteen divisions, is the most important and best-known organization for counselors. APGA offers student memberships at reduced rates, and students can attend APGA national conventions and take part in programs.

The American School Counsellor Association is the APGA division for school counselors, but others too relate directly to work in public educational settings. These are: National Vocational Guidance Association; Association for Humanistic Education and Development; Association for Measurement and Evaluation in Guidance; Association for Non-White Concerns in Personnel and Guidance; Association for Specialists in Group Work; National Catholic Guidance Conference; and an affiliate, International Association of Counselling Services. The five remaining division deal with particular work settings such as college, university, ad employment service. APGA and each of its division publish newsletters and journals covering current developments in the field, research, practices, legislation, and sources of information and materials.

Students and counselors alike can participate in APGA by contributing to its many professional journals. Editors urge members who have something to say to submit material for publication. Journal staff members give helpful and detailed advice on how to prepare articles for publication, explain common faults that result in rejections, and describe the step-by-step process of editing and publishing a professional journal. Articles that pass the editor are given blind reviews, and evaluators' comments are passed on to the author. At regular intervals each journal prints guidelines for authors specifying length, format number of copies of manuscripts to be submitted, and other such details.

Counselors, like their teaching colleagues, are using collective bargaining, to obtain better salaries, improved working conditions, and other benefits. Humes and Kennedy view the process as a means to gain a power base for achieving professional status in the school ad a full voice in decision making.

Creange believes that building a strong, broad-based national organization is one of the most critical issues facing school counselling today. But the American School Counsellor Association has found little interest among counselors in collective negotiation. Many counselors are concerned with the question of professionalism v. collective negotiations; thus there is a search for a strong organizational base to advance the status of the profession, to protect job security, and to ensure a voice in determining professional roles and responsibilities.

Community agencies and services offer a wide variety of occupational opportunities for counselors.

Interest in these settings and private practice is reflected in the increasing concern about licensure. Counselors work in community mental-health agencies, family-service agencies, crisis-intervention centers, halfway houses, drug-counselling centers, and a host of programmes set up for special populations, such as minorities, the disadvantaged, and the unemployed. Each of these services typically involves some counselling, particularly those that deal with interpersonal conflicts and emotional problems. Those for work problems may put more emphasis on placement and training. Working with older persons is one of the major new opportunities for counselors. The need is apparent. Few services exist. Counsellor-preparation programs have done very litter to develop competencies, but interest is increasing. The reasons for growing concern are not difficult to understand. IT is predicted that by the year 2000 one half of the U.S. population will be over 50 years of age and one third will be over 65. Also, there is increasing emphasis on providing counselling over the entire life span.

Rehabilitation counselors offer assistance to a wide range of handicapped individuals. Typically the master's degree is required. Work is making increasing use of a counselling approach rather than job finding and physical restoration, and its major aim is to increase the effectiveness of rehabilitation and job placement. Preparation is comparable to a school counsellors, with the addition of courses on medical aspects of disability, rehabilitation procedures, and agencies. Since the major emphasis is to get the handicapped individual into a suitable job or preparation program, the assessment of potential through tests and medical examinations is a major function. In helping the handicapped individual move into the new setting successfully, the counsellor must know a great deal about environments and utilize counselling to deal with attitudes that could interfere with success.

Opportunities for counselors are also growing in correctional settings. Penal institutions offer jobs in which counselors serve as links to the community, and work with delinquents. Programs aimed at upgrading the skills of correctional staffs make use of counselling methods and offer a new consultation-training role for counselors in the correctional setting.

6

Teaching Psychology

In a longitudinal view of the teaching of psychology, theoretically we could touch a student's life through two decades. Psychology has been taught in the early school years, at least in the sense of assisting youngsters in problems of human relations, and to some degree in a broader range of topics. At the secondary school level, the teaching of psychology has been growing rapidly since the middle 1960s. In that context, the emphasis is mainly on personal adjustment, but in some high schools a course is offered with a more general, science-oriented approach. Either Fisher or Kasschau and Wertheimer may be consulted for a survey of the teaching of psychology in the secondary schools.

Our present concern is primarily with the teaching of psychology at the post-secondary level. The most striking feature of this endeavour is its tremendous diversity-in the nature of students taught, methods of teaching, theoretical approach, topics covered, and the setting in which the teaching takes place. The heterogeneity is evidenced elsewhere in this book for most of these variables. The 3000 institutions of higher education in the USA also include considerable diversity-in size of student body, primary purpose, academic standards, entrance requirements, faculty quality, and of course geographical locale. These factors contribute in no small way to the manner in which any subject is taught, but more so to a discipline like psychology than to mathematics or languages, for example. An analysis of the impact of each demographic input is beyond the scope of this chapter. Nevertheless, some attention must be given to the major types of academic institutions as a source of influence.

Growth of the two-year college in the USA during the late 1960s was phenomenal. In one year, fifty-two new campuses opened their doors ('one new school each week') and it was estimated conservatively that one in every three students taking introduction to psychology did so at a two-year college. These institutions comprise two types in terms of goals, although both may be represented on a single campus. The older ones, usually known as junior colleges, prepared students for the more rigorous last two years of a regular baccalaureate programme. Rapid expansion of late has been more pronounced in the type known as the community college. In the latter setting, emphasis is upon service to an urban area in terms of assisting the upward mobility of its citizens and providing an employable pool of people for intermediate level occupations. In many of these colleges, awareness and action programmes concerning community social problems are being fostered through training curricula.

Whereas the psychology offerings at a more traditional junior college differ little in kind from those available to a student at a four-year college or university in the underclass years, the community college concept calls for courses with a strong applied emphasis. Programmes leading to the Associate of Arts degree include training as mental health aides, social action managers, and child development specialists, among others. Field work, practicum, or supervised experience in some form is a mainstay of these programmes.

Psychology teachers in two-year colleges typically report an isolation from the mainstream of their profession, frustration with the problem of the heterogeneity of the student body, and lack of opportunity to continue their own training. Yet their task is challenging, their work is satisfying, and their role is firmly established. Preparation of these teachers, by and large, is less thorough than it ought to be. Many of them were trained in a different discipline; a few were overtrained, and the majority hold the traditional masters degree with little or no prior teaching experience or training.

A few universities are beginning to offer specialized masters programmes to provide for the two-year college job market. Perhaps because the community college is not encumbered in tradition, it has been the source of much innovation in the teaching of psychology. Hershey and Lugo have compiled source information on both innovations and problems.

The four-year college is the traditional institution often idealized in American song and story. Many began, and some continue, under the aegis of one or another religious denomination and more than a few 'grew up' to become large universities. Psychology teaching in the four-year college is probably found in its most traditional form. Classes are small to moderate in size; teaching is by lecture, discussion, or seminar format; faculty members are devoted to teaching and are rarely distracted by extensive research efforts; students are capable and accepting of a rigorous programme. Among several surveys the most recent, by Cole and Van Krevelen, shows that in the four-year college there is a low student-faculty ratio a median of forty-five upperclass majors, and a median of 4.2

psychology faculty members. Programmes are primarily designed for those students who plan to continue in graduate school; and it is tacitly assumed that those who do not will also profit from the same curriculum. Many teachers question the validity of that assumption. Quite a few of these college psychology departments have excellent records of placing graduates into post-baccalaureate programmes. An interesting sketch of the activities of a faculty member in a typical small liberal arts college gives insights into the nature of that context.

Another recent trend in US higher education is the transformation of former teacher's colleges into state universities. Typically, psychology departments in these institutions offer a limited graduate programme, and an undergraduate programme not greatly different from that found in the four-year college.

The influence of traditions from the education field still may be found in psychology offerings, or in terms of what is not offered. But here, as elsewhere, much variability is the rule, so that generalizations can be misleading. Little has been reported on teaching problems unique to the state university context. Thornton described a survey study of graduates from six state colleges in Pennsylvania and drew some implications for curriculum emphasis: 'preparation for a well informed life as parent and citizen ... and experiences that employers demand of our graduates'.

Psychology is taught in various professional schools within a context requiring a very different management and structure than one finds in any of the other higher education settings. A comprehensive programme leading to a degree in psychology is not usually offered, although colleges of education may do so in educational psychology, school psychology, or counselling, and some seminaries offer degrees in pastoral counselling.

Psychologists also teach extensively in medical schools, colleges of business administration, child and family development departments of home economics schools, and to a lesser extent in schools of journalism, library science, dentistry and occasionally in others. As one would expect, the work of the psychologist is tailored to the needs of the professional training goal in these specialized settings. Here psychology teachers must bridge the gap between that part of their own field most pertinent to the goal of the host school and the mainstream of that subject. They confront strong competition for student's time and attention and often are not fully accepted as a part of the faculty team, although these identity problems are fading as psychology gradually proves itself useful. Collins and Spiers have made a case for psychology being taught in the seminary, based upon data showing that a large proportion of people who need help in personal problems consult a clergyman.

The university teaching of psychology has been disturbed by the ongoing controversy and conflict between the basic research-teaching mission and the various applied-service missions of the field. When Harvard was facing the splintering of its department President Conant appointed a blue-ribbon commission to advise him on the future of psychology in the university context. The report of that group was widely circulated under the title *The Place of Psychology in the Ideal University*. It set forth prospects for a prosperous psychology era in which we would have 'freedom for change and development' with all psychologists on campus interacting, and centred in a large department staff with a wide variety of specialities represented. That prediction had materialized, more or less, for many universities in the 1960s, with rapidly increasing enrollments, graduate programmes expanding through federal support in both research and training, and the increasing opportunities for psychologists in all of its traditional roles-teaching, research and service.

But the uneasiness between the academic and the applied interests was not quieted. 'Ideal U' was revisited by a special issue of the American Psychologist containing both a look at the recommendations in retrospect and a review of the current scene. Alternate models for psychology's place in the university were described by McQuitty, Webb, Sears, and Coffey. A central theme running through these articles and others in the set was a plea to maintain the unity of all of psychology-a defence of the interdependence of the basic and the applied-for the structure of the discipline and the context in which it is taught. The Harvard report had included a recommendation for the Doctor of Psychology degree for those going into practice, but expected it to be kept in the hands of the arts and sciences department faculty. Whereas the great majority of service-oriented psychologists are still trained in the university context, in the late 1970s we saw the emergence and quickening spread of the professional school of psychology, sometimes affiliated with a university but sometimes not. The impact of this recent trend cannot be fully assessed, yet it is clear that psychology in the USA is suffering appreciable trauma as a result of fundamental differences in the incentives, needs, and interests of the scientifically oriented versus the practice oriented groups of psychologists.

The social-action orientation is emerging, apparently not clearly in alignment with either of the other two groups. A study by Lipsey suggests that there are four ideologically separable groups in psychology: (a) pro-social action, anti-experimental; (b) pro-social action, pro-experimental; (c) anti-social action; anti -experi-mental; and (d) anti-social action, pro-experimental. Because faculty and graduate students studied differed in their distributions across these four classes, the authors draw implications that 'psychology tomorrow' will be more socially concerned and more humanist in orientation. The importance of these issues for our present consideration is clear. Shall the academic context in which psychology is taught remain centralized in the traditional arts and sciences department, as envisioned in the Harvard report, or shall it become divided into two or more separate and independent enterprises. Many departments, ideologically committed to unity, have greatly expanded teaching efforts into the applied areas, but the issue is not thereby resolved. In any case, the contexts for the teaching of psychology are currently in a state of flux.

In the early period of psychology teaching in higher education, courses were taught within the department of philosophy. By the 1880s, courses under the title psychology were being offered at Cornell, Amherst and Brown, but some historians credit James's laboratory at Harvard in 1875 as marking the first true recognition of the discipline in the USA. Academic organizational and course patterns emerged and changed slowly, being 'handed down' from mentor to student who carried them into the next generation.

The first significant attempt to influence the pattern of undergraduate programmes was apparently the report of a conference at Cornell in 1951. A group of six distinguished teachers of psychology met for eight weeks to exercise their collective judgement 'to develop a better undergraduate curriculum' than was typical at that time.

The recommended curriculum plan consisted of a broad, science-based in introductory course leading laterally to special interest and applied courses, and vertically to a set of intermediate core courses, thence to upper level specialized and integrative courses. Considerable detail was provided for each course to be included, as well as a defence of the exclusion of some other courses. The programme was science- based throughout, and avoided the vocational or self-help type of course. Whatever direct impact this report may have had on programmes was never assessed systematically, but if one allows some variations in detail, it does seem to characterize a great many departments in the period that followed. A second, conference was held at Mighigan nearly ten years later. As in the Wolfle report, the emphasis was on designing the curriculum for liberal education and avoiding different tracks for different goals. However, instead of a single structure, the Michigan report offered three acceptable designs: the inverted pyramid, the hourglass, and the flexible. In any case, the suggestion was made that a department define a core of courses required for every major. As this summary suggests, the Michigan report favoured more flexibility and innovation than had the Wolfle report.

Again after about a decade, the report of a project of the American Psychological Association appeared following a three-year study funded by the National Science Foundation. This time, it was a data-based investigation 'to describe undergraduate education in psychology nationwide and to report on innovative approaches that may point the way to the future'. The task was accomplished by extensive mailed survey and case study, interview methods.

A selected few of the impressive number of demographic quantifications which were made from the survey; these data are based upon a sampling and overall 31 per cent representation of all institutions in the USA. Surprisingly, more than 500,000 students were in attendance at schools which did not offer a major in psychology, not counting two-year colleges, but nearly 4,000,000 students did have the psychology major option available. Such data would seem to suggest that the development of a full curriculum in many institutions is still a frontier for the teaching of psychology. Only about one fourth of the total psychology enrollment was filled by psychology majors, but 25 to 35 per cent of those majors entered graduate school in psychology. This figure has been obtained in a number of other studies over a period of years, but one might expect it to decrease as employment opportunities for psychologists have become tighter in the late 1970s. The mean faculty size ranged from 4.36 in two-year colleges to 24.44 in public universities, and the 4.81 mean given for four-year colleges compares favourably with the previously cited figure of 4.2 from the Cole and Van Krevelen study. The mix of courses offered provides an interesting contrast with patterns found twenty-two years earlier. Where the major was offered, 6 per cent of the courses were introductory, 11 per cent methodology, 19 per cent natural science, 32 per cent social science oriented, 7 per cent history and systems, 15 per cent applied and 10 per cent other, according to the authors classification scheme. This distribution differs from that for 1947 in that there is heavier emphasis on natural science processes and less on applied work in 1969.

Incidence of particular courses declined across the three types in the order just mentioned. The authors made historical comparison based upon three previous studies and examined shifts to verify Kulik's finding, for colleges and universities of: (a) an increase in field work experience and human services courses; (b) an increase in natural science type courses; (c) a less, but still pronounced, increase in social science oriented courses; and (d) decrease in the traditional applied course. Two-year colleges showed the greatest increase in categories (a) and (c).

Kulik reports that the variety of plans to satisfy the major requirements was to defy reduction to a summary quantification or description. The observation suggests that the fairly tight plans recommended in the earlier had little impact by 1969. He goes on to describe a hos+ of innovations that have been integrated into requirements by a significant portion of his respondents. These innovations: (a) student participation in curriculum plan field experience; (c) independent study; (d) extensive use; (e) programmed approaches; (f) encounter groups; (g) team teaching; (h) grading innovations; (i) interdisciplinary, social issues, or humanistic courses; and 0) multi-track programmes for students with different goals.

The typical undergraduate electing to major in psychology has an academic smorgasbord to choose from, will probably encounter modern techniques of teaching in one or more of his courses, has an opportunity for some exposure to human services training, but still gets a strong natural science base in his education. Students who transfer from one institution to another are likely to encounter a new set of requirements and curriculum structure, with the exception of junior college transfers where the programme is coordinated with a college or university.

Departmental faculties must continuously monitor themselves and their programmes and they must maintain flexibility in order to respond to shifting needs of students and society. Although academia is notoriously slow to respond to change, information culled from the literature and summarized in the previous section of this chapter would suggest that psychology is a rather fluid discipline, with many of its problems being tackled if not resolved. I shall not discuss current problems which psychologists share with other faculties. But, there are a few critical within-the-field problems deserving of more attention and investigation—problems which, in part, establish the context of teaching psychology.

Students are bewildered with the variety of material, roles, and models they encounter in courses. Some are turned away by the confusion. Psychology is variously classified in academic organization charts, and our courses may be used to satisfy many different college requirements. We relate to biology, sociology, anthropology, physics, philosophy, education, medicine, law, child development, speech and other disciplines-who are we? How do we clarify our identity to the student? We are often confused ourselves. The identity of psychology is clearly shifting at the professional and national association level and we would be less than honest to represent ourselves otherwise to students. The traditional three role functions: (a) generation of knowledge; (b) communication of knowledge; and (c) application of knowledge, is shifting from emphasis on (a) and (b) to (c), and (c) seems to be expanding from service to people and institutions into the social action arena. McKeachie has analysed the problem of the emerging social action concern, and made proposals for embracing it with minimal trauma. Unless and until these shifts stabilize, or we become fragmented and separately identified at a professional level, we must be prepared to tolerate ambiguity ourselves and avoid the excessive foisting of confusion on our students. The problem of multiple role representation to the student is more intense in the large-faculty situation of the university department. Few such departments have escaped the emergence at some time of intrafaculty conflicts. When these are known by students, and especially when a teacher~ exposes students to stabs at other specialities, the department has an identity problem at best and a problem of ethics at worst.

One promising arrangement for a proper representation of psychology's identity is the 'fields of psychology' course, described most recently by Gottleib and Bluestein . Introductory texts include at least a brief introduction to the topic, but that exposure requires extension and clarification by the teacher. After all, the mass of one-course-in- psychology students represent a tremendously important segment of educated citizens. They deserve to have as clear an image of the discipline as is possible to give them. The public image of psychology is not as accurate or fair as it ought to be-the first course offers a splendid opportunity to improve it.

What is the psychology department mission within the college and campus of which it is a part? I have an uneasy feeling about our tendency to become too insular, especially in the university -exactly where there are multiple opportunities to interact profitably. Expansion of psychology's base through broader campus involvement could add stability to the context of teaching. Interdisciplinary courses appear to be a barely tapped means of counteracting parochialism. Recent literature includes descriptions of such courses for introductory psychology experimental psychology with physics, a course in creativity, and psycho-biology. Even greater co-operation and cross fertilization can be had from joint programmes such as one at the University of Washington to produce AB level para-professional psychologists or one for social psychology.

A second mission problem is one teachers are not discussing much in recent years-should we mount a major's programme to produce psychologists or to produce scholarly educated citizens in the liberal arts tradition? There are sometimes subtle, but very real differences between the two, and the second alternative has greater compatibility with the objective of embedding psychology more deeply in the college programme.

Harper in reporting a conference on this subject, conveys the words of Dashiell that a well-educated person has the ability to generalize soundly, to insist upon evidence, and to judge objectively. If these are prime goals, then our academic context should feature sampling over a wide range of content material, be directed to needs of the individual, develop and exercise intellectual processes, and use a problem solving approach. For the most part, our psychology courses fall short of these characteristics. In contrast, they put undue emphasis upon learning facts and methods; or at least many of us so believe. In a fictional 'annual report to the president', Lichtenstein developed nicely how a psychology department might mount a science-oriented programme within the liberal arts tradition. Stress was to be placed upon values, problems, and issues rather than on facts, vocational techniques, or mere knowledge. Psychology, like some other disciplines, has moved away from the liberal arts tradition or simply assumed that the student will be able to bridge the gap.

A third mission problem is a corollary of the second: do we design pro grammes for all of our majors or primarily for the graduate-school bound? It has become trite to point out that if N students on campus take general psychology, 0.25N will take additional courses, 0.04N will become majors, and 0.008N will go on to graduate school. Yet we ask ourselves, are we not usually addressing that small 0.8 per cent in our teaching? The issue has been with us for many years, it is resolved in some departments, but certainly not in all of them. This problem has been subjected to considerable examination and action in recent years, at least in terms of some thought for the employability of bachelor graduates. In fact there is a growing literature on the placement of graduates.

An increasing number of departments are adding field work experience for credit in an effort to give graduates marketable skills; others have introduced field work without expressly planning for vocational preparation; or as expressly intending only educational enrichment; and some have attempted to integrate practical training into a liberal arts programme. To what extent can practical experience or technical course work be added to the liberal arts curriculum without degrading or redirecting its intent? Should we be planning an undergraduate professional school as an alternative? Should we give up the general education tradition altogether? Before we move too far and too fast toward professionalisation of the AB degree, perhaps we should consider some alternatives, at least as transition measures. A strategy not yet tried is the utilization of intersessions and summer periods to build up credit hours in applied work beyond the traditional 120, then award an appropriate certificate along with the AB degree.

The fourth mission problem to be discussed involves the distinction between courses for the major student and service courses offered to others. I believe this area provides another opportunity for a psychology department to strengthen its role on the campus in contributing to the education of a wider range of students than most of us do now. Individual faculty members too often treat service courses as a necessary evil, to be tolerated only because it helps hold up enrollment. This attitude is incompatible with Miller's now famous 'giving psychology away' concept. Unless or until a sister department builds up enough of a need to justify appointing its own psychologist, we have responsibility to teach other students just as we send our own majors to other departments for support courses. Unless psychology takes pains to integrate itself into the collegiate mainstream, it will stagnate.

Finally, support a position Brown clarified in his discussion of the Kulik book. A mission of the psychology department should be to structure its programme in terms of the needs of its own campus—perhaps even at the expense of emulating an admired department in another school, or a hypothetical norm. There is no standard department programme, nor is there any standardization board for establishing one. Much of the literature in this subject speaks to the need for innovation, exploration, and adaptation. As Professor Brown put it, each department 'must make a concentrated effort to determine the place of our science within the context of institutional goals, strengths, resources and the current needs of students.'

Simon has made an earnest and convincing plea for teachers not only to listen to students, but to actively seek their concerns; then to pay attention to them by modifying our curricula to satisfy those needs. Many departments have added graduate and undergraduate students to important committees. Others have conducted opinion surveys of graduates, some of which have been published and have specifically influenced the modification of programmes. There are, of course, two sides to this responsibility coin. The general practice of admitting students to faculty committees, an outcome of the activist 1960s, has not always worked out as well as had been hoped. Faculty members may take the position that students cannot be expected to know what is best for their intellectual diet. Yet the practice of student evaluations of teachers and classes as input for assessing quality and relevance is now widespread. No doubt, the wisest posture is effected through close and frequent interaction of faculty and students on the issues. The ethical and liability implications of innovations we introduce must also be accepted as a responsibility.

First, there are the academic concerns-will the academic programme be enhanced? Will the student make a contribution to the agency? How should assessment and grading be handled? How much and what kind of student selection is proper? Second, there are supervision concerns.

A department embarking on field work opportunities for the first time is likely to underestimate the faculty time requirements for a programme of acceptable quality. Lastly, and most often overlooked, is the question of who is responsible if there is a malpractice claim against a student intern.

We must accept the responsibility of assessing our innovations. Do they prove the level of achievement, ease or speed of learning, or the attitudinal aspects of the teaching/learning process? Classroom research, in common with their research outside of the laboratory, is difficult to manage with rigour, but can be done. A 1973 APA convention symposium was devoted strategies applicable to the assessment of teaching innovations. Unfortunately, teachers often plan a new approach with care, but fail to follow through with a demonstration of its value. As we move into a greater concern for the employability of our graduates,

As we move into greater concern for the employability of our graduates. We must recognize that there are adjunct responsibilities which cannot be separated from employment preparation: advisement and placement.

Academic advisement is very familiar to psychologists, but many of us worry that it is too often not done with the thoroughness it deserves, and it is the subject of frequent complaint of students. We tend to toss off the problem by noting that e administration does not credit faculty for advisement time or quality. If we undertake training for AB careers, we must also assume responsibility for more advisement of students into career types, career ladders, and planning for shifting job demands. To the scholar or practitioner in any mature discipline, it seems normal and inevitable that the discipline should exist in its current form. But disciplines, like persons, have their own individual histories, and current status reflects accumulated experience for both categories. Psychology and education have origins lost in the mists of history; education in some form is as old as civilization. Here we describe some of the social and academic circumstances of psychology and education that led to the emergence of a new discipline, educational psychology.

Psychology grew out of philosophy and physiology, attempting to answer questions that neither discipline could answer alone. As psychology emerged, some of the practitioners felt that their knowledge and skill would be useful to education, and began to carry out research and to offer practical advice to the often-beleaguered schools. For our history, then, we need to examine the activities of early psychologists who involved themselves in the problems of education. The scholarly world in which educational psychology grew did not emerge in the late 19th century fully developed but evolved from antecedents appearing in much earlier centuries.

Psychology is ancient in origin. We find psychological concepts and concerns in the work of Aristotle, Bacon, Descartes, and other ancients. Juan Vives whose work clearly and directly related to the questions that psychology began to deal with 350 years later. Vives employed "a self-conscious emphasis on induction as a method of inquiry and discovery in philosophical and particularly psychological questions, according to his translator and biographer, F. Watson.

The first work of relevance is his De Anima et Vita, he considered manifestations of reality, not what is but what could be observed. This is a psychology that is introspective and empirical, dependent on the association of ideas in an attempt to discover laws. He presents a twofold nature of memory, an apprehending function and a maintaining function, plus fourfold laws of forgetfulness. Two more books followed to complete his psychology, one on intellectual faculties and another on emotions.

Educational psychology, in the form he gave it, is set forth in De Tradendis Disciplinus, apparently written earlier than the books described above, despite the later publication date.

A teacher or educational psychologist would find little to quarrel with in these conclusions. Vives addressed not only teachers, but also physicians, politicians, historians, and economists on the grounds that all of these professionals dealt with other persons, and thus had need for psychology. Closer in time were two turn-of-the-century thinkers, Pestalozzi and Herbart. Although quite unlike each other in experience and character, both wanted to ground education in psychology as that philosphically-based discipline was understood at the time. Johan Pestalozzi planned to enter the ministry, but a failed sermon changed his aim. After reading Rousseau's Emile he was attracted to pedagogy.

Eventually he became a teacher, and he created the first modem elementary school. He soon distilled his experience into a book, How Gertrude Teaches Her Children and developed a new school that prospered for 20 years. His attempt to psychologize education was based on an inadequate understanding of the faculty psychology of the day, but somehow it succeeded and his school and ideas were stimulating to educators for the rest of the century. His influence on the development of educational psychology lay primarily in his emphasis on the centrality of the child, rather than the content of the school, and on the role of observation in learning rather than the rote memory then extant in the classroom. One of the visitors to the school was Johann Herbart, who was to organize and systematize education in a scholarly fashion beyond the capacities of his forerunner. He worked at Konigsberg where he occupied the chair once held by Immanuel Kant. He was a prodigious worker.

Those of interest here include a Manual of Psychology as a Science, and General Metaphysics. His psychology rested on the idea that learning was powered by interest, both self-generated and manufactured by the teacher. The catchword for Herbart's notion was apperception. Interest and apperception were combined and worked to form his teaching method, called the Formal Steps, of which there were eventually five. By the last quarter of the 19th century this notion had reached its summit, according to Mayer. Translations and commentaries spread his ideas to American educators well into the 20th century. The growth of what became behaviour science in the 20th century, of course did not occur in a social vacuum. In the 19th century in the United States especially, suggests Silver, the luster of science was such that academic respectability was secured in part by labelling a discipline accordingly; thus there was political science, economic science, historical science, and the like. So the new pedagogical science, based on psychology, emerged from the moral philosophy that preceded it.

Wilhelm Wundt did not invent psychology, any more than Henry Ford invented the automobile, but like Ford he turned his vision into something new. Wundt stated in the preface to his Principles of Physiological Psychology that he was presenting work that would "mark out a new domain of science." Watson comments that "Wilhelm Wundt was the first man one can call a psychologist without qualifying the statement by reference to another, perhaps stronger, interest.

Wundt's immediate predecessors of psychological note were the psychophysiologist Gustav Fechner and the neural physiologist Hermann von Helmholtz Wundt described Fechner as having made the first conquest of experimental psychology. Helmholtz, interested in physics, was too poor to study it at a university, so instead he took up tuition-free medical training, and eventually became an army surgeon. But he studied physics on his own and began to experiment; in time he was able to hold rank as professor of anatomy and physiology in a number of German universities. He, like Fechner, was an experimenter and an empiricist, and used measurement techniques to specify results. It was, if not inevitable, entirely logical and reasonable that the problems and methods generated by these scientists would evolve into experimental psychology.

Wundt advanced and modified both the methods and the orientation of his predecessors. His method was introspection, an ancient process he tried to change from meditation to a precise, experimental approach emphasizing discrimination responses, reaction time, emotional responses, and the like. He had arrived at his eminence by way of medical and physiological training. At Heidelberg he published the previously mentioned Principles; the first half in 1873, the second half the next year. His last revision was published in 1911. His growing fame brought him to Leipzig, where he established his famous laboratory in 1879.

James had little interest in laboratory work, however, and his venture languished whereas Wundt's flourished and attracted worldwide academic attention. A scholar almost anywhere in the world had few choices of places to go to learn about psychology. There was an absence of almost anything resembling graduate education in American colleges and universities. Thus it was that anyone who had a serious interest in scholarship, especially in the developing discipline of psychology, pretty much had to go to Europe to pursue the interest, and Wundt's laboratory was a magnet for many Americans who made up the early cadre of psychologists in this country.

Among the founders and shapers of early American psychology who worked and studied with Wundt were G. Stanley Hall (Clark), J. McKeen Cattell (Columbia), Edward Scripture (Yale), Lightner Witmer (Pennsylvania), and Charles Judd (Chicago). Although Wundt expanded his work to include social or cultural psychology, he was most influential in work with sensation and perception, reaction time, attention, and feeling and association. But it was the stimulation students received experiencing his laboratory that had the greatest impact on American psychology. Evans observes that Wundt's philosophical orientation, "mind-as-contents" did not survive the ocean voyage his students made in returning to America. At the universities to which they dispersed, they were soon talking about "mind-in-use," but trying to study it with methods they learned in Germany.

Another strong influence on what became American psychology was not a psychologist at all, but a wealthy and somewhat eccentric Briton named Francis Galton. Stimulated by his cousin Charles Darwin's new evolutionary ideas, he pursued interests that led to the field of eugenics. Specifically, he published a book called Hereditary Genius in which he considered the whole range of human ability, and offered as evidence of the hereditary nature of intelligence the disproportionate number of eminent relatives possessed by men of importance. He also made some twin comparisons. However shaky the assumptions on which his hereditarian concepts were based, his work was sufficient to set off what continues to be one of the enduring controversies in psychology, the primacy of "nature or nurture." His anthropological concerns led to the collection of large amounts of quantitative data; the distribution of human measures in what came to be known as the "normal curve" fascinated him, as did the relationship of one set of measures with another.

In order to look at relationships of these data in human subjects, he developed a primitive kind of correlation technique, later refined by his associate Karl Pearson, into the product-moment coefficient of correlation, a tool much used by psychologists. He dabbled also in memory and association, mental tests, and other psychologically related topics, but his major contribution to the development of psychology was the work and stimulation on the inheritance of psychological traits in human beings, and the development of statistical ways of making sense of quantities of data from human subjects. Galton did not, like Wundt, attract students. Although he was visited by a number of Americans, only J. McKeen Cattell acknowledged Galton's profound influence.

The idea of a science of the mind appealed to educators, and through various routes and by various names, psychology began to enter the teacher-training curriculum. Apparently the first educational psychology in America was in a course at Lexington, Massachusetts; in 1839 a course was offered in Mental Philosophy, a name for the new psychology. The Oswego, New York normal school offered a course in child study as early as 1863. The Normal Department of Iowa University offered a mental philosophy course in 1866, and the University of Missouri in 1869. In 1870, the Bridgewater, Massachusetts Normal School required psychology of all its students. Educational psychology was offered as Applied Psychology in 1886 by the Department of Pedagogics at Indiana, and in the same year the University of North Carolina offered a Methods of Culture course for teacher trainees. The University of Minnesota had a course in 1893 called The Development of Child Mind. A course described as Educational Psychology was taught at Illinois in 1890 by Charles DeGarmo, and was later taught by an early psychological clinician, a Professor Krohn. The text used by Krohn was Sully's 1887 Handbook of Psychology.

Psychology was widespread enough in normal schools to stimulate people to try to define the discipline and its role in education. In 1887 two speakers commented on educational psychology in addresses to the National Education Association convention. One was S. S. Parr on "The Normal School Problems": "Educational psychology is commonly interpreted to mean the study of general psychology, with stray observations about children's minds." Joseph Baldwin noted that "Educational psychology is made the basis of distinctive normal-school work. Through self the normal student studies the race, and thus becomes familiar with the laws of mental activity and mental growth." The presence, nature, and content of textbooks of this period tell something about the nature of the discipline. Apparently, the first to be called "Educational Psychology" was a booklet published by Louisa Hopkins in 1886. Bain published Education as Science in 1884, and Claparede, a book on experimental pedagogy in 1905 in French, later translated and revised. Shortly before and after 1900, a number of American texts appeared: one was Baldwin's Elementary Psychology and Education.

Baldwin espoused the faculty psychology widely accepted at the time, commenting that "it is evident that psychology can make no progress whatever without introspection". The divisions of Baldwin's book include six sections. Another representative text was written by Dexter and Garlick and published in 1908. Their point of view was expressed in the phrase, "Psychology is the science of consciousness... there is a connection between mind and body."

American psychology was beginning to form itself into a discipline in the years on either side of 1900. Whereas most of the early departments or programs were being developed by psychologists who had experience in Wundt's laboratory, the tone, orientation, philosophy, and continuity stemmed largely from the influence of William James.

William James was a member of a distinguished New England family. After dabbling in many areas of interest, James eventually took a degree in medicine at Harvard, but interested himself primarily in philosophy. He was invited to teach physiology at Harvard in 1872, and by 1875 had offered his first course in psychology. As he later put it, the first lecture on psychology he ever heard, he gave himself! In the same year, he founded the laboratory mentioned earlier, a laboratory little used except for student demonstrations. James described Herbert Spencer as an "ignoramus," and Wundt was dismissed with the comment that he was "The finished example of how much mere education can do for a man". European psychologists with whom he was friendly and whose ideas he responded to included James Sully, James Ward, Theodore Flournoy, and Carl Stumpf. He was no follower, but worked out his own concepts.

These concepts were presented in papers published from time to time and eventually were presented in a more organized fashion in his Principles of Psychology, which had been under contract to Henry Holt for 12 years at the time of publication. His ideas were appealing to the American mind, and the book was widely read and used; it helped determine the direction of American psychology. In his view, mind is not a passive adapter to circumstances, but is active, spontaneous, and selective. Habit is central to his views, and is his way of explaining the workings of the nervous system; his chapter begins, "Habit is thus the enormous flywheel of society, its most precious conservative agent". Although he was not an associationist, because of his rejection of its atomism and elementarism, he did recognize the role of association or contiguity on memory; in this context he rejected the then popular faculty psychology, later demolished by Thornlike and others. In total, his psychology was functional and pragmatic, and so American psychology became. Gardner Murphy observed that James' "central importance" was due to his I rich, beautiful and very modem concept of how the will actually operates".

But his influence was greater and more focused than such generalizations suggest. Woodward has identified Jamesian concepts in the work of the succeeding generation of psychologists. These include work in learning concepts, habits, and ideo-motor action by Edward Thorndike, which led to the "law of exercise"; the motivational theory of volition developed by R. S. Woodworth; Mary Calkins developed James' will, faith, and belief concepts into a personality theory following his volitional ideas; Gordon Allport, also a personality theorist, took from James traits, functional autonomy, and a unifying philosophy of life; John Dewey, Josiah Royce, William Macdougal, Floyd Allport, and George H. Mead were other borrowers in the social sciences.

The influence of James on educational psychology can be identified at this period in terms of his influence on the whole fabric of American psychology, in which educational psychology was embedded. But James also had a more direct hand in psychology applied to education; he both lectured and wrote for teachers and teacher trainees specifically, and adapted his theoretical system to applications in the classroom. It would be tempting to say that education, in the public school sense, was one of his central interests, but there is no evidence that is so.

James had a large family and needed money, and he earned it where he could. In 1892 he was invited, for a fee, to discuss education with the teachers of Cambridge, The lectures were well received, and next he took them on the Chatauqua circuit. James did not find association with teachers stimulating or rewarding. His lack of enthusiasm for the activity was expressed in a letter commenting on the female teachers in his audience: "I have never seen more women and less beauty, heard more voices and less sweetness, perceived more earnestness and less triumph than I ever supposed possible." In another letter to his wife, he further commented on his teacher audiences: "Meeting minds so earnest and helpless that it takes them half an hour to get from one idea to its immediately adjacent next neighbour, and then they lie down on it... like a cow on a doormat, so that you can get neither in nor out with them. " Despite his distaste for the process, the lectures prospered, and 1889 they were published as Talks to Teachers on Psychology and to Students on Some of Life's Ideals.

James' psychology for teachers was functional: the child was seen as an active organism and it was education's obligation to be consistent with the child's instincts and yet fit him for life in society. Although the instinct notion was abandoned, his position made inroads into the existing faculty psychology, and the success of what he attempted in lectures and in his book-practical, concrete application of psychology for teachers-helped bring the attention of later psychologists to the child in the classroom. James had many students in his classes, but not many advisees and he supervised few doctoral dissertations. Among his students who did go on to make names for themselves in psychology were Mary Calkins, William Healy, Edward Thorndike and Robert S. Woodworth.

Hall was a contemporary of James, but very different temperamentally and intellectually. After an abortive start at the ministry, Hall went to Europe to study, first at Bonn and then at Berlin. In 3 years he returned to the United States without a degree, and then worked at Harvard long enough to earn a Ph.D. in psychology by way of philosophy. He worked as a tutor, read Wundt and returned to Germany to work with Wundt briefly and also with Helmholtz. Back in America, he somehow got the opportunity to give Saturday lectures on education at Harvard. These lectures went well, and led to an invitation to repeat them at Johns Hopkins. Again they were successful, and he joined the faculty there. Later he became first president and developer of Clark University. Hall's influence was more that of enthusiast and promoter than that of scientist or researcher. He founded the American Journal of Psychology and later the Pedagogical Seminary, founded and was first president of the American Psychological Association, encouraged the study of psychoanalysis and later taught psychoanalysis himself.

Hall was fascinated by children and their development, and consequently, their education. It was his ambition for educators to study children, learn what children were trying to accomplish, and then help children reach their own goals. He described his approach as "scholiocentric" rather than the existing "pedocentric" orientation to education by advising educators:

> The guardians of the young should strive first of all to keep out of nature's way and to prevent harm... they should feel profoundly that childhood... is not corrupt... there is nothing else so worthy of love, reverence, and service as the body and soul of the growing child.

Somewhat later he expressed his interest in adolescence in his two-volume work on the subject, Adolescence. After these developmental books, he pulled together his child and education ideas in a volume called Educational Problems. All during this period, of course, the journal he founded, now called Journal of Genetic Psychology, was publishing research and analytical pieces on children and on education; this was important because up until Hall, all the psychological journals were German and would not have published this kind of material. As observed earlier, Hall had many students who distinguished themselves, unlike James, who towers over him intellectually. Hall was described recently by Mortimer Appley as a sometimes "Mean, vain and self-serving man, Hall could also be generous and supportive of others".

His students form a roster that is almost a "Who's Who" of early century psychology: James McKeen Cattell, John Dewey, Joseph Jastrow, William H. Burnham, Edmund C. Sanford, and others who attended his seminar at Clark, including Lewis Terman. Cattell and Dewey, however, did little work with him. When Hall moved to Clark, he brought Burnham with him to teach pedagogics, which in this setting was educational psychology and mental hygiene. Many of his students found him stimulating and supportive: Lewis Terman, who later developed the Stanford-Binet scales, studied gifted children, and in general led the investigation of intelligence in America, commented in his autobiography that "For me, Clark University meant briefly three things: freedom to work as I pleased, unlimited library facilities, and Hall's Monday evening seminar". The secret of Hall's extraordinary influence on American psychology is revealed in Terman's further discussion of that famous seminar; he observes that "it was unique in character and about the most important single educational influence that ever entered their lives".

Cattell was ambitious and enterprising, beginning his graduate study by appointing himself the assistant Wundt did not know he needed. Although he worked productively with Wundt, he found greater stimulation with Francis Galton, "The greatest man whom I have known," as he described his mentor. He became, in 1888, not only the first psychology professor in America, but in the world. He advanced rapidly: at 28, professor at Pennsylvania, at 31 chairman of the department at Columbia, at 35 president of the American Psychological Association, and at 40 elected to the National Academy of Sciences.

Cattell, like Hall, was something of a promotor, although he did considerable scientific work. He began studying reading with Wundt, attempting to measure various components of the process. He went on to study words, time needed for impression on the retina, and the legibility of type. He had no love for G. S. Hall or his journals, and in 1894 founded the first of what became several competing journals, the Psychological Review. At Columbia Cattell was associated for many years with Robert S. Woodworth, and of course Edward Thorndike. Although Thorndike came as a student, it can hardly be said that he was influenced a great deal by Cattell: Thorndike was always a loner, and made his own way intellectually. But perhaps it is more than accidental that he emphasized and developed individual differences and measurement, two of Cattell's special concerns.

Functionalism. Men like James, Hall, and Cattell had their own theoretical orientations and numerous followers, but none founded a school or movement like functionalism, which emerged at the turn of the century. Any brief description of a philosophical or psychological view will be oversimplified and somewhat misleading, but we need to be aware of it because the attitude or orientation of functionalism was essential for the development of American psychology, and especially for the emergence of educational psychology. Functionalism concerned itself with the mind as it acted or functioned. From this orientation it becomes possible to consider—and then realize—application of psychology to a host of real-life problems and situations. John Dewey and J. R. Angell, both familiar names in education, were among the leading figures of the new movement; indeed, Dewey might be called the first psychologist to be identified with functionalism as a separate school or theory of psychology.

John Dewey was a major figure in the development of functionalism, and its role in the emergence of educational psychology. As was reported earlier, Dewey took his Ph.D. at Johns Hopkins when Hall was there, but except for a stint in Hall's laboratory was little influenced by him. He taught psychology and philosophy at Michigan after his graduation, and published a general psychology text during his tenure there, but his influence began to rise after his move to Chicago in 1894. During the years he spent at Chicago his psychological work peaked and here he was instrumental in the development of the orientation that made educational psychology possible in its American form. Dewey, and Angell after him, were influenced by James' conviction that consciousness was a causal factor in life and biological survival; thus consciousness is related to the environment on both sensory and motor sides. He therefore taught at Chicago a James-like philosophy of wholeness of activity and adjustment. Adaptation to the environment was Dewey's psychological interest and orientation. He had a high level of concern for the adjustment of human beings-physical, mental, and moral-these concerns, coupled with functional psychology, appealed to educators and were factors in the development of educational psychology. Dewey's pioneering work in progressive education grew out of his adaptation-to-the-environment orientation, and out of his belief that education should be based on an understanding of the child's needs as they develop. In 1904, Dewey left Chicago for Columbia where he appeared to abandon psychological work and gained greater fame as a philosopher.

James R. Angell replaced Dewey at Chicago within a year of Dewey's departure. Angell had studied under James at Harvard and after the customary contact with European psychologists-in his case, Ebbinghaus and Helmholtz-he became Dewey's assistant at Michigan. The James-Dewey exposure impelled him towards functionalism, which he further developed. In 1906, Angell's American Psychological Association presidential address provided a definition of functionalism: it is concerned with the how and why of consciousness, mind-consciousness—mediates between the needs of the organism and the environment and this helps to solve problems and finally it is psychophysiological and thus requires that mind-body relations be considered. A somewhat earlier text also presented his views in a fashion set forth by the subtitle: An introductory Study of the structure and function of human consciousness.

Under his guidance, the University of Chicago became the leader of the functionalist movement and a center of psychological, philosophical, and intellectual stimulation. Angell stayed at Chicago until 1919 and supervised 50 doctoral dissertations during those years, including those of John B. Watson, the founder of the behaviourist movement, Walter Hunter, a leading experimentalist of succeeding decades, and Walter Van Dyke Bingham, who became a leader in applied psychology and aptitude testing. After leaving Chicago, he was for 16 years president of Yale University. Harvey Carr replaced Angell, his former teacher, and remained head of the department until 1938. About 150 students received Ph.D.s during this time, and of course brought their Chicago orientation with them to various parts of the United States.

Although Carr continued Angell's functionalist orientation, it gradually lost importance as a movement. This occurred in part because of the rise of behaviourism, but also in part because all movements in American-and other-psychology have had a period of development and enthusiastic reception, followed by a period when much of the new orientation is absorbed into the mass of what everybody knows in the field, and the lesser peculiarities of the position fade into history. But the residual effect of functionalism on American psychology was a desire to make psychology useful.

Robert S. Woodworth of Columbia was not a functionalist like the foregoing-he was independent and eschewed all "schools" but he was making his contributions during the period discussed. Although not accepting the label or agrecing in all the dimensions he was in the broadest sense of the term a major American functionalist. He collaborated in his early work at Columbia with Thorndike on research on transfer of training, a concept contrary to the then current faculty psychology. Thorndike, of course, continued at various times in his career to work in the transfer area, and it became an important part of the developing educational psychology. Along the way

Woodworth assisted the anthropologist Franz Boas in a study of individual differences in primitive peoples. At various times he developed psychological tests, produced a stream of books on experimental and physiological psychology, edited the Archives of Psychology from 1906 to 1948, developed an orientation that he called dynamic psychology, and through his teaching-his real love-helped to integrate and organize psychological knowledge, and helped shape the destiny of scientific psychology.

Although it is difficult, as we shall see, to pin down just when specific institutions defined educational psychology as a separate discipline, it is not difficult to determine who defined educational psychology through his own research and writing: it was, of course, Edward L. Thorndike of whom Travers said, "No psychologist has ever had a greater impact on education than Edward L. Thorndike". Travers goes on to point out that this was in part a product of the general rise to fame of Teachers College, Columbia early in the century. What became Teachers College was created in 1887 with a faculty of three; it expanded rapidly and eventually offered degrees of Bachelor of Pedagogy, Master of Pedagogy, and Doctor of Pedagogy. In 1894, a reorganized college appeared in a new building across the street from and tied to Columbia College; eventually the aggregate became Columbia University. For more than four decades, Thorndike and Teachers College together led American education into a science-based age of teacher education and pupil instruction.

Thorndike was one of several scholarly children of a Methodist minister. After education at Wesleyan, he attended Harvard for a year. It was James' lectures that turned Thorndike to psychology. Although he never became a Jamesian, he was intellectually excited by James' presentation of ideas, and James in turn let

Thorndike raise his experimental laboratory chickens in the basement field to enter of the family home; the James children were reportedly fascinated by these feathered subjects. Thorndike did not go to Europe to study but, on the advice and recommendation of James, went to Columbia to work with J. McKeen Cattell. Cattell gave him an assistantship and space in the psychology department's building attic for his chicken research, but not much direction or help. This was satisfying to Thorndike, who liked to work alone. He already had some thesis ideas when he arrived, and soon settled on a learning study with his birds. The thesis, Animal Intelligence, quickly became a classic in psychology as his biographer describes it.

The study was published as a monograph in 1898, as one of the early Columbia Contributions to Education, and later revised and expanded as a book. The thesis focused on learning that occurs as the animal forms and strengthens associations. Later he would call these connections; his theory of connectionism was descended from the work of the British empiricists Locke, Bain, and Berkeley. The work excited the psychological community. John B. Watson cited this work frequently as part of the background for his own new behaviourism, and the work also played a role in developing the ideas of Yerkes at Harvard, and later B. F. Skinner. His emphasis on motivation and the learning process helped orient American psychology of succeeding decades up to the present. Thorndike taught briefly at Western Reserve College for Women as a Special Lecturer in Education. At this time, however, Thorndike had little use for pedagogy and psychology's role in it, finding it neither "profuse nor profound," as his biographer put it. Psychology had no division in the National Education Association at that time, and although there was talk of using psychological data in education, little was actually done by way of gathering data through experimentation. Charles Judd recalls asking William James, whose Talks to Teachers had just been published, what he thought of educational psychology. James' reply: "Educational psychology? I think there are about six weeks of it". Thus, despite James' writing and Hall's more educationally oriented work, educational psychology did not have much status as a scientific discipline, or as an interesting

In 1899, Thorndike succeeded in getting what he wanted: an appointment in psychology at Teachers College, Columbia, where he could do research. The research, of course, was to be done only after he had completed his principal duties, teaching 15 hours per term.

Thorndike became a compulsive and tremendously productive worker. As mentioned earlier, he began studying transfer of training with Woodworth and continued this line of research for years. All his course outlines turned into books. In child psychology, he rejected the questionnaire method of the Child Study Movement, and advised them to observe, using objective methods only. In teacher training, he emphasized attention, memory, habit, mental training, and experimental approaches in general. In applied psychology, he put his students to work analysing teaching materials to determine how they conformed to psychological principles. His mind and work habits enabled him to produce, by 1940, more than 500 publications, a majority of them research based. The early and continuing transfer of training studies are especially important, because the question of how learning topic A affects learning topic B is central to almost every major question in education, including curriculum. The data accumulated, and Thorndike summarized his early work in Educational Psychology; the book was successful, Thorndike was promoted, and he continued his efforts. This book succeeded in killing formal discipline, which had dominated education for decades. With accumulated research, Thorndike in 1913-1924 published his three-volume Educational Psychology. Thorndike carried out the first scientific study of animal intelligence and learning, helped demolish faculty theory and the theory of formal discipline, developed laws of learning that marked the end of the mental-process approach in psychology, formulated the laws of readiness and law of effect, introduced statistical methods in education and psychology and invented a performance scale, stimulated the achievement test, developed group methods of intelligence testing, explored heredity and environment as causes of behaviour, explored individual differences, did pioneer research in adult learning, developed methods and materials for many school subjects, studied children's vocabulary-the list goes on and on to include the development of modern learning curves, the importance of feedback and reinforcement, the effect of massed versus distributed learning, and the nature of forgetting. His work was "one of the great milestones of education".

Charles Judd was a contemporary of Thorndike and Terman, and was another Wundt Ph.D. of the period. He commented that he tried to mold himself after the master. He taught at Wesleyan, New York University, Cincinnati, and Yale before his final move to Chicago. Although he had an enormous range of interests, he began to publish in education, beginning at Yale, and is remembered for his contributions to that field. In 1903 he published Genetic Psychology for Teachers. This was a Darwinian attempt to explain how the teacher perceives the classroom, and included advice on discipline, an emphasis on imitation, discussion of the origins of reading and other topics, all with a very different orientation than Thorndike's, whose work did not impress him. He also had little admiration for James or Hall.

In 1907 he moved to Chicago, where he became head of the School of Education. Chicago was in decline, according to Travers and Judd tried to raise standards to the level of the Arts and Science faculty. He developed several journals, published Psychology of School-Subjects, Introduction to Scientific Study of Education, Psychology of Secondary Education, and Educational Psychology in 1939, after his retirement. He was opposed to the concept of transfer that Thorndike espoused and usually ignored it, but did confront the idea in his education text: his explanation for the phenomenon was not identical elements (Thorndike's view), but rather the degree to which generalizations were taught. Among his students were William S. Gray, Guy Buswell, and Karl Holzinger.

From the foregoing description of the views and work of a number of psychologists, it is apparent that from the turn of the century to the post World War I period, educational psychology had become identified as a scientific discipline, complete with theoretical orientations, methods and procedures, several areas of focus, and an accumulated body of knowledge. The areas of study generally were learning, tests and measurements, human development, child clinical, including the study of exceptional children, and in general, a focus on the scientific study of the child in school.

In the first decade of the century, the American Psychological Association appointed a committee to study the teaching of psychology in colleges. The committee, chaired by Carl Seashore, included Guy Whipple whose assignment was normal schools. Whipple was a Clark product, a student of G. S. Hall. He sent a 33-item questionnaire to 259 normal schools listed by the Commissioner of Education in 1907. The questionnaire concerned content, techniques, and the like, and also included questions about the training of the instructor. Replies were received from 100 institutions. The source of instructors' degrees was also reported. Thus, a list of institutions training educational psychology instructors was generated and reported. These instructors were educational psychologists only in that they were teaching psychology in teacher-training institutions, of course.

In 1927, Clara Robertson, in pursuit of a doctorate at Columbia Teachers College, replicated the Whipple study for her dissertation. She sent out her questionnaire to 195 institutions: I 10 normal schools and 85 teachers colleges, with a response from 91 schools. Not all schools contacted replied to Robinson, but her list seems to offer a reasonable description of faculty teaching psychology for teacher trainees in institutions of the 1920s, at which time the discipline was developing rapidly. The Robinson list provided the starting point for finding out more about the way in which educational psychology was handled by institutions early in the century. The writer contacted schools that had produced more than one instructor of psychology for teacher trainees—21 in all—and queried them about the organization of educational psychology in their early days. Specifically, they were asked if a separate department of educational psychology was organized in the institution, and if so, when, and if the teaching was not done in a separate department, how it was handled.

They were asked further for any general information about the role of educational psychology in their school. Heads of appropriate departments were addressed first, and when they were unable to provide information, other channels were used. Of the 21 institutions, one made no reply to repeated queries, and another could not provide any historical information. The remaining 19 provided a variety of kinds of information: printed material from department files, recollections of emeritus professors, references to published documents, and in more than one case, a book or monograph. Because the information received takes many forms, it does not lend itself well to any kind of neat tabular ordering, so each institution's early way of handling educational psychology will be presented in brief narrative form.

The School of Education goes back to 1892. Its title was changed in 1901 to Department of Education and in 1916 to School of Education. The first Ph.D. in Education was awarded to Millicent Shinn in 1898; her dissertation, a baby biography, was widely studied and remains readable and interesting today. In the late 1890s the departments of Pedagogy and Philosophy cooperated in offering Philosophy 2, described as a "valuable" prerequisite to education; in 1898 it became a degree requirement, and by 1903 students were expected to take it prior to admission, for it was a prerequisite to all undergraduate courses in the Department of Education. Additional courses appeared by the 1920s: tests and measurements educational psychology, educational statistics. Later, Giles Ruch, Noel Keys, and Luther Gilbert worked in educational psychology, Edna Bailey and Anita Laton taught growth and development of the child, and Richard French taught a course on atypical children. During the first 20 years, the faculty of the School of Education functioned as a common faculty rather than as a group of departments in a school. In time, a divisional identity emerged, with Psychology of Education as a field for the doctorate, probably the first such specialization in the school. By 1930, more than a dozen dissertations had been produced on topics of an educational psychology nature.

The development of educational psychology in this institution has been discussed earlier in considering the work of Dewey, Angell, and Carr. The special field of educational psychology was founded in 1892 as part of the Department of Philosophy. In 1896, Education became a formal part of the Department of Philosophy; the new name reflected the change, for it was subsequently called the Department of Philosophy and Education.

In 1900, Education was separated and thereafter remained alone. During all this time, educational psychology was a specialization with the departments.

Some aspects of Columbia's role in the field can be inferred from the earlier discussion of Edward L. Thorndike, who was employed by Teachers College, Columbia, in 1899 as Instructor in Genetic Psychology. In 1902, his title was changed to Adjunct Professor of Educational Psychology. This title reflected a change in the college structure, when Dean James Russell broke the Division of Education into five administrative departments, of which Educational Psychology was one. In 1921, the college embarked on an extensive program of research. Administratively, there were three divisions: Educational Psychology School Experimentation, and Field Studies. In the next few years the educational psychology enterprise developed College Board examinations, carried out a study of intelligence measurement, and did a study of exceptional children.

The intertwining of education and psychology at Clark can be inferred from G. S. Hall's work there. Although they never had a separate department of educational psychology 'there was never a time when education did not include psychology. By Hall's second year there as president, 1890-1891, and with the appointment of his former Johns Hopkins student William Burnham, development began and by 1893 education was made a subdepartment within the psychology department—by 1904-1905, education gained full departmental status. The first course in educational psychology per se appears to have been offered in 1894-1895, although the content was always present to some extent in Hall's work. In an 1899 report, Burnham commented that "pedagogy is based upon psychology and owes to it the inspiration and stimulus to scientific work, and psychology owes to pedagogy the suggestion of some of its most fruitful fields of education". He comments favourably on lectures in educational psychology in the institution, and discusses desirable qualities of a training program for producing professors of pedagogy, one of these being "an acquaintance with elementary psychology". In a footnote to the paper he also comments, "Many of the papers mentioned in this list are quite as much products of the department of psychology as of that of pedagogy; and, on the other hand, the pedagogical department has contributed to many of the psychological studies mentioned above".

Cornell responded to the late 19th-century work of psychologists in laying the foundation for a scientific basis of education by emphasizing education in the Arts and Science College, and by development of a Department of Education in the Agriculture College. A geologist early offered courses in teaching, and was succeeded by Charles DeGarmo. DeGarmo was joined by Guy Whipple, a Clark product who was a pioneer in the testing movement. In 1907 a School of Education was formed, whereas Arts and Science and Agriculture continued to offer courses in education. The School offered work in principles of education, educational psychology, methods of teaching and mental tests. In 1914 the first Professor of Educational Psychology, P. Kruse, was appointed, and in time four faculty positions were created. Educational psychology was presented under the aegis of the Department of Education, and was also allied with other psychology units on campus.

Harvard University has never had a program officially named educational psychology, but educational psychology has been taught as a course there since early in the century, and as White notes, "a good number of psychologists on the faculty have addressed themselves to education in one way or another". By 1906 a separate Division of Education existed and by 1909 enough expansion had occurred so that the Board felt justified in endowing a graduate school of education. James and Royce were on the faculty, but neither they nor any other members encouraged interest in research in education; this attitude encouraged forward-looking graduate students to go to Columbia or Clark rather than Harvard. In 1910, Robert Yerkes was dragooned into teaching a course in educational psychology, an assignment he resisted and tried to turn over to someone else when he could. Although the subject was taught, it was not included among the four basic fields required for a Ph.D. in Education. In the course of time, psychological science, and especially measurement, became a matter of concern to President Lowell, and he offered a post to Edward Thorndike, who rejected it, and then to Walter Dearborn of Chicago, who also turned it down, but later was induced to accept. Dearborn's eventual acceptance filled the position, but his interests evolved away from classroom learning, and educational psychology never became an area of emphasis.

Psychology per se was a part of philosophy at Harvard as at most schools in the early 1900s, with James, of course, the great name in American psychology. James was followed by Munsterberg, whose work had no discernible effect on education. Psychology did not separate from philosophy until 1934. Educational psychology has had no role in these arrangements. Although there has been no institutional commitment to educational psychology, individual psychologists in the Education School have taught the coursework of the discipline. Besides Yerkes, these include Walter Dearborn, Truman Kelley, Philip J. Rulon, O. Hobart Mowrer, Robert R. Sears, and John B. Carroll. In addition, besides James, Jerome Bruner and B. F. Skinner have contributed to educational theory and practice.

Indiana was very early in the field, having some educational psychology instruction before 1900, mainly in child study. A three-term course was offered in 1911 by the School of Education. Indiana's president from 1902 to 1937, William Lowe Bryan, was a Hall student from Clark and had become a well-known researcher. He established a psychological laboratory in the philosophy department in the 1890s, described by Lynch as "the oldest continuous center of experimental psychology in the United States." Sidney Pressey, who had worked with Munsterberg and Yerkes at Harvard, was a research associate in this laboratory from 1917 to 1922, when he went to Ohio State. Lewis Terman received his BA and AM at Indiana and went to Clark in part at Bryan's urging.

By 1913, educational psychology offered three courses and was listed as a unit in the Graduate School. All courses were taught by W. F. Book, the major figure in educational psychology there from 1912 to 1934. He too was from Clark, and taught learning, mental development, intelligence measurement, and general educational psychology courses; he also directed the laboratory during most of his tenure, and carried out his own experiments, especially in acquisition of typing skill. He also published a number of volumes relevant to the field during this period. Other early faculty in the area, besides Book and Pressey, included Herman Young, Grover Somers, and Douglas Scates. Through the 1920s and 1930s, the program consisted of one elementary course and more advanced courses for upper-level undergraduates and graduate students; these courses included work in individual differences, mental measurements, individual mental testing, psychology of elementary school subjects, psychology of exceptional children, diagnostic teaching, and other advanced educational and research-oriented courses. Many of the courses were cross-listed between Education and Psychology and some faculty had appointments in either or both of the areas. By 1913 educational psychology was a regular part of the training of teachers at Indiana, and the possibility of a Ph.D. specifically in educational psychology has existed there since 1913.

In 1879, a chair in the Science and Art of Teaching was established at Michigan, "the first permanent chair in any American College or university devoted exclusively to the preparation of teachers". In 1899, Allen Whitney introduced a course in child study and social education, but the first course labelled educational psychology was offered by Irving King in 1906, and more advanced work began with Charles Johnston's "seminary," "Psychological Investigations of Educational Processes" in 1909. By 1910 a general advanced course in educational psychology was offered by Fredrick Breed, and was repeated occasionally thereafter. Arthur Irion, a visiting instructor in the summer of 1925, gave the first course in the psychology of learning, and from 1926 on, William Clark Trow continued this course for many years.

Clark Trow was a major figure in the field at Michigan and in the nation. His career spanned the years from the World War I period to the 1970s. He was an innovator in concerning educational psychology with the real problems teachers faced in the classroom, the teaching of specific subject matters, and with social behaviour and values. He had a lifelong concern with methodology and with technologies. He was instrumental in establishing school psychology as a discipline in Michigan, and, in general, strove to integrate technology from psychology with applied education. As educational psychology expanded, the Michigan work also diversified. Social education, later called social learning, was offered nearly from the beginning.

Exceptional child work began in 1911, and continued with considerable involvement with other schools and institutions. Psychology of elementary subjects was introduced in 1912, and a reading clinic was established along the way.

Mental measurements, emphasizing statistics, appeared in 1912 and evolved into more statistics and measurement courses, and other aspects of educational measurement began to be an important part of the curriculum. Research and experimentation was always important. As early as 1910 Experimental Education was offered; by 1914 it became Experimental Educational Psychology, and was expanded by Guy Whipple in 1921, and by Howard McClusky in 1924.

In 1905, a formal college of education was established in the university. Educational psychology courses were offered as early as 1915, and such courses became the backbone of teacher training. Beck observed that "Underlying all... programs was of course educational psychology". The early courses included a general educational psychology course, mental testing with laboratory, mental diagnosis, and an educational psychology seminar.

From 1924 to 1928, the department had a 4-year undergraduate program for the training of school psychologists; the term is not defined in available material, so it is not clear what they were trained to do, or actually did in the schools. From 1925 on, the Institute of Child Welfare carried out research and clinical work with children. A number of psychologists were attached to the Institute, and although it did not join the College of Education administratively for some years, there was a good bit of interaction between the academic educational psychologists and the Institute staff. By 1919, 10 credits were required in psychology for all teacher trainees, at least five of which had to come from educational psychology.

A Normal College was established shortly after the Civil War, but this institution was short-lived. In 1883, education reappeared in the university, under the Department of English. By 1903, it had become a separate department and in 1904 one of the dozen or so areas offered was educational psychology, taught by the department head, A. Ross Hill.

Under the aegis of the Graduate College, both AM and Ph.D. degrees were offered in education, including educational psychology; the first Ph.D. was granted in 1916. The institutional name changed again, to School of Education during this period. Viles reports that the functional psychology of John Dewey was the dominant orientation of the school at this time. The education college, and especially educational psychology, flourished through the 1920s.

In 1901-1902, the Regents of the University of Nebraska established a College of Education. In the listing of departments of the new college was a department named Educational Psychology. About a year or two later, the phrase "and Measurements" was added to the title; early in the century, in the eyes of many educators, psychology was primarily measurement. In another year or two, the Regents removed the addition.

During the early years, the Arts and Science College had been the parent of Education, and was the degree-granting authority, but in March 1921, Teachers

College was freed from this tie, and was granted authority to grant its own degrees. By 1924 eight departments existed in the College, including Educational Psychology and Measurements, headed by Charles Fordyce.

The School of Pedagogy was founded in 1890 at New York University. Educational Psychology of the time was a part of the program from the beginning: when the school opened, a course was offered called "The Practical Applications of the Psychology of Expressional Activities." By 1910, 25% of the school's program was made up of psychology courses. By 1915 the catalogue listed Child and Adolescent Psychology, Physiological and Experimental Psychology, and Elementary and Advanced Psychoanalysis.

As early as 1920, references to "special education" appeared in course offerings. The faculty in these early years consisted of James E. Lough and Robert MacDougall. In 1921, the school was renamed as noted above, and the traditional academic degrees-BS, MA, and Ph.D. were authorized. In 1919, the Department of Educational Psychology was established, with Charles E. Benson as Chairman. Charles E. Skinner and Paul V. West were early faculty members in the department.

In 1926, Benson, Lough, Skinner, and West published Psychology for Teachers. Some special programs introduced before 1940 included training for school psychologists, research experts in educational psychology, teachers of mentally retarded children, and introduction to clinical psychology.

Educational psychology has not been a separate department at Ohio State, but many courses that could be considered educational psychology have been taught in the College of Social and Behavioural Sciences, which has had a specially area in educational psychology as one of its subareas. Educational psychology content first appeared at Ohio State in a course taught by John Short; this was in the department of philosophy. The course was later taught sequentially by two university presidents, and a laboratory existed as early as 1900.

A psychology department, for many years administered by the College of Education, was established in 1907, primarily as a universitywide undergraduate service department. Between 1913 and 1920, graduate work began with the first MA in 1915 and the first Ph.D. in 1917.

By the middle 1920s, the department was considerably larger and began to distinguish itself. Several familiar names appeared during this period: Pressey, Williams, Toops, Warfield, and Renshaw, and for a brief time Luella Cole and Edgar A. Doll.

By 1927, the date of the survey reported earlier, 67 MAs had graduated, and 30 Ph.D.s. In educational psychology alone, 39 MAs and 21 Ph.D.s had been granted under Sidney Pressey's direction by 1937. Pressey was a sometimes eccentric but creative and productive educational psychologist, who kept the discipline stirred up in a variety of ways for decades.

Peabody began its psychological work in education early in the century. In 1915, the college dedicated Jesup Psychological Laboratory: according to E. K. Strong, the first Professor of Psychology at Peabody, "Never before, in any institution in this country or in Europe has there been a building called a psychological building, and devoted and dedicated to psychology". Both psychology and educational psychology were housed in the building. A few years later it was reported of faculty members Joseph Peterson in Psychology and S. C. Garrison in Educational Psychology that "Both hold to the experimental type of psychology rather than the old philosophical theories".

S. C. Garrison, the faculty member mentioned earlier, had received the first Ph.D. from the Department in 1919. He later became president of the college. Other faculty members, and visiting professors over the years, included Edgar James Swift, E. L. Thorndike, Truman Lee Kelley, Robert Morris Ogden, Henry Woodburn Chase, William McCall, Arthur 1. Gates, Charles E. Spearman, Karl Garrison, A. S. Edwards, Paul. Boynton, Joseph Moore, Norman Munn, Lyle H. Lanier, and others. Besides S. C. Garrison, several of these names are' of Peabody graduates: Karl Garrison, Paul Boynton, Joseph Moore, and Lyle Lanier.

No formal program in the content areas of educational psychology appeared at Pennsylvania until the 1960s, but the psychology department is one of the very old ones in the United States.

In 1888, James McKeen Cattell was appointed to a Chair in Psychology, the first such in the world. In the previous year, he had established at Penn the first psychological laboratory, one of the very early ones in America. During these early years, teachers took some courses in the psychology department.

In 1895—1896, Lightner Witmer, Cattell's successor, gave a course on child psychology to a class composed primarily of teachers. One of these teachers brought to class a bright boy who had been unable to learn to read. Witmer and the class were interested and worked with the boy. Other such experiences occurred. In the summer of 1896, in an extension class, a horde of problem youngsters were brought in for help, and parents also began to bring in their own children who had various difficulties-usually school problems. Out of this demand came the establishment of the Psychological Clinic, the first in America, if not in the world. By 1909, the department had been reorganized and university appropriations were granted to the clinic. A professional staff was built up, and thus a link was forged between academic psychology and the needs of children.

Stanford opened in 1891, and presumably worked in teacher training from the beginning, but not until 1897-1898 was there any statement in the catalogue on education. The earliest information concerns Earl Barnes, who studied child psychology in this department.

Before training psychologists were appointed, Cubberly included some psychology in his introductory course: one of his lectures was entitled "Apperception—Principles of Psychology Applied," and he spoke on James' "Talks to Teachers." Lewis Terman later observed that although Cubberly had no training in psychology, he obviously had a good general grasp of the discipline. One of Cubberly's appointees was Lewis Terman, in 1910. Terman, a Clark product, had been teaching at Los Angeles Normal School with his friend Arnold Gesell, of later developmental psychology fame at Yale. E. B. Huey was an old friend of Terman from graduate school, and it was Huey who stimulated Terman to begin thinking about mental testing and clinical work with children.

A position in education at Stanford was first offered to Huey, who did not want to leave his work at Johns Hopkins. He in turn recommended Terman, who accepted. Other psychologists were added later, including Truman L. Kelley in 1919. In addition to Terman and Kelley, Reginald Bell, a graduate student there at one time, became Assistant Professor of Education and Assistant Director of Citizenship; he taught child psychology. Only nine master's degrees were granted in the first 17 years by the Education. As the staff and student body expanded, courses were added in educational psychology, mental testing, educational measurement, statistics, guidance, and in other aspects of educational psychology.

Terman began developing new courses at once. Among his first courses were those in child and adolescent psychology, for example, "Social and Moral Education," and "The Literature of Child Psychology. " He moved next to school health and hygiene, and then to clinical aspects of child psychology and a special course in mental tests. Next he added educational psychology through courses in experimental pedagogy, educational psychology, and educational problems. Finally he worked in teacher training and supervision of teachers. But eventually, of course, his interest in individual differences and intelligence dominated his work.

By 1916 he had published his version of the Binet test, was a full Professor and was becoming widely known. A few years later, he began his Genetic Studies of Genius, the landmark longitudinal study of the gifted. In 1922, he was appointed to succeed Frank Angell as head of the Psychology Department, which he quickly expanded and upgraded. In 1923 he was elected president of the American Psychological Association. The School of Education has never had departments as such, but functions with an area committee system.

Psychology instruction began very early at Tufts, but until 1932, when a separate department was established, courses appeared under a variety of titles, and in often confusing combination with other subjects, usually theology and philosophy. A course was offered to juniors in 1854 in Moral Science, with text by Alexander, and taught by President Ballou, followed in the second semester by Intellectual Philosophy, with text by Wayland. The first course listed as psychology was offered in 1869-1870, with a text by Porter; the course was called Human Intellect; by 1875 a text by Bain was being used. For the next three decades, psychology continued to appear in philosophy and theology under a variety of titles. In 1892, psychology was listed as a Department of Instruction, offering but one course.

In the late 1890s physiological psychology appeared, and James' text began to be used in some courses. In 1899, Robert Cushman became philosophy chairman, and psychology was no longer primarily a preparatory area for philosophy. In 1910-1911, psychology was temporarily removed from philosophy; a new Department of Education and Psychology was created with Dr. Colin A. Scott as Chairman. In succeeding years, however, courses still appeared in philosophy, including a course in experimental psychology with a 9-hour laboratory requirement. This was taught by Professor Schmidt of philosophy. Educational psychology was taught in the Department of Education, by the same Professor Schmidt, who was also listed as a mathematics instructor.

Things continued in this fashion for several years. More courses were added in the 1920s; Leonard Carmichael was by this time a member of the faculty. In 1925-1926, the department was renamed the Department of Philosophy and Psychology, and eight courses were listed, though not all were taught, and a major was possible. Fred Keller was an instructor during this period. As noted earlier, in 1932 psychology was made a separate department, and a straight major was possible, without philosophy or education involvement.

University of Wisconsin

In addition to training teachers in the middle of the 19th century, Wisconsin forced improvement of education in the state through the structure of their entrance requirements. In earliest times, teachers were trained in a Normal Department, but were later cast into a ghetto called the Female College. But with changes in administration, teacher trainees came to be awarded the same degrees as other students of the university in 1869, and by 1873 the Female College had disappeared.

Psychology was a regular part of teacher training. A Professor was appointed in 1849 and assigned to deal with mental philosophy logic, rhetoric, and English literature; this was the Normal Professor. One of the early enthusiasts for psychology was the president, John Bascom, who published several psychology texts between 1869 and 188 1. During these years, he regularly taught a course in psychology, one that "baffled and intrigued" students.

In 1884, a Chair of Pedagogy was established, and in 1888 a Chair of Psychology. The appointee to this Chair was Joseph Jastrow from Johns Hopkins; he was hired to establish a psychology laboratory and organize an active experimental psychology program. Jastrow and the University were not always happy together. His interests in experimental psychology declined, whereas his interest in education increased. However, the department progressed. Clark Hull, who took his Ph.D. in 1918, began to attract attention before he left for Yale in 1929. Daniel Starch, a 1906 graduate from Iowa under Carl Seashore, published Experiments in Educational Psychology in 1911; this book was described as being objective in a fashion similar to Thomdike's. Starch later moved to advertising as a major interest. V.A.C. Henmon was a Columbia product of Cattell and Thorndike, and came in 1910 to represent educational psychology on the faculty. During World War I he worked at aviation psychology, taught briefly at Yale, and then returned to Wisconsin.

Prior to 1891, occasional courses in psychology were offered by George T. Ladd and others, but in this year the Graduate School came into being. Professors Hershey Sneath and E. F. Buchner taught Pedagogics and included Bain and Herbart in their readings, but in 1894 Edward Scripture, with a Ph.D. from Leipzig, began to teach what he called "Research work in Pedagogy"; he had earlier been appointed director of the Yale Psychological Laboratory. At about the turn of the century, Carl Seashore was on the staff, as well as other trained psychologists. The administration unit under which this work was offered was called at various times The Department of Philosophy, The Department of Philosophy and Psychology, and The Department of Philosophy, Psychology, and Education.

New faculty appeared and offerings were expanded. Charles H. Judd joined the faculty in 1902, taught psychology, and inaugurated a summer session aimed primarily at teachers in 1905. From 1908 to 1910, however, only a single course in educational psychology was taught, by Edward H. Cameron. Judd was discouraged at the lack of support he found at Yale, and moved to Chicago to carry out a distinguished career there. When the doctoral program in education matured in the late 1920s and early 1930s, the general background required of all Ph.D. candidates included the history and philosophy of education, educational psychology, and basic educational issues. Educational psychology was one of the nine specialization areas most frequently chosen by candidates. It was not until 1920 that psychology was freed from its bondage to philosophy and became a department in its own right. New appointments, expansion, and a growing reputation followed quickly.

It would be unrealistic to assume that the schools described in the latter part of this chapter constituted all the important producers of psychologists working in teacher education early in the century. Other institutions of consequence in the field may have failed to respond to the 1927 queries of Robinson and so escaped notice as preparers of psychologists working in education during the period. However, the listed schools certainly were among the primary producers of such professionals and would seem representative of the rest. Who should be included as an early educational psychologist is very much a matter of judgment. A high proportion of all psychologists from the turn of the century onward saw their discipline as a potentially useful one, and were eager to apply it. In part, of course, this was an aspect of the zeitgeist, the optimistic assumption pervading Western culture in the late 1800s and early 1900s that science and technology of all kinds had the capacity to alleviate or solve many of the problems of society, and to improve nearly every aspect of life.

The school seemed a particularly appropriate locus for application of the developing science of behaviour. Need was high because the schools were burgeoning, expanding rapidly in number and size, and increasingly responsible for new kinds of students and were seeking help wherever promise seemed to exist. Thus many psychologists who had little intrinsic interest in education or the schools became involved in the process through professional obligation or perceived opportunity. Searching for early manifestations of psychology or educational psychology requires some ingenuity because the nomenclature is not clear. Early in the century, psychology was likely to appear in departments of philosophy, where it lingered in some institutions until well into the 1930s or beyond. Courses carried a variety of innovative labels: Educational applications of psychology often emerged in schools or departments of education, with traditional psychology remaining in the philosophy department. In at least one institution, work in education was administered by the College of Agriculture.

It should be clear that psychologists were not just trying to hawk their product to the education enterprise: many educators were actively seeking and supporting psychology because of their perceptions of its value. A good example of this attitude was that of Elwood P. Cubberley, a figure of considerable importance in early 20th-century education. He acquired a good basic understanding of psychology on his own, attracted Lewis Terman to his school, Stanford, and encouraged and supported Terman's work in intelligence, and that of other psychologists.

Who were the major figures in the emergence of educational psychology as a discipline? William James must be included because his views established a direction and orientation for generations of American psychologists, an orientation that made use and application of the discipline not only possible, but probable. James' own work in education is interesting to observe, but had little long-term effect other than to reduce the influence of faculty psychology. G. S. Hall was of major importance for two reasons. One was his emphasis on the centrality of the child in the educational process, relegating content to second place. This emphasis had long-term effects because of the second reason for his importance: his roster of distinguished students, including Jastrow, Burnham, Sanford, Terman and to a lesser degree Cattell and Dewey. These men realized in their life work what Hall suggested in his teaching. Edward L. Thorndike is the dominant figure in the emergence of educational psychology as a discipline.

In his Columbia laboratory, for the first time, all the scientific rigor and sophisticated measurement emerging in the field was applied to the child, and specifically to the child as learner in school. If one wishes to review the literature of the major aspects of educational psychology today, one usually starts with Thorndike, or encounters his work as a major early exploration of the matter under consideration. James

Angell at Chicago resembles G. S. Hall in that the Chicago students were influential for years in American education. They carried with them a clear orientation to a useful psychology and a devotion to learning and learning theory; the work of their teacher was important in its own right, but the students spread out to institutions all over America, bringing with them the Chicago orientation. Dewey of course had preceded Angell at Chicago and set the tone for the movement that followed, but his own psychological work had less impact than his theoretical orientation. James, Hall, Thorndike, and the Chicago group then seem to be leaders without whose influence the discipline would not have emerged, or would have taken a very different form than it did. To delineate the emergence of educational psychology as a discipline, this chapter has necessarily focused on ways in which individuals and institutions taught, applied, or promoted educational psychology as a source of help for education.

7

Vocational and Personal Guidance

There has been considerable attention to the formation of guidance teams, and to the use of team work techniques to help overcome the communication problems in big establishments, and to deal with the wide diversity of problems encountered. These developments, as Moore emphasised in his study of five such systems, have taken place response to immediate problems, and, judging by the growing importance attached to them, seem to have met with a good deal of success. Movements of this kind tend to call for role-differentiation, and specialists of the kind or another tend to appear in the teamwork, leading naturally to the question of appointing a personal counsellor, or counsellors, for the pupils. The tradition of guidance, as employment-centered vocational guidance, was of course inadequate to meet the need, and hence the importation wholesale of the American theories and practices of counselling.

But the solutions worked out from the 1950's onwards, and increasingly throughout the 1960's, were in terms of how to develop and integrate *new areas* of guidance to meet the peculiar problems of big schools, and not generally in terms of deeping thinking about the existing concepts-especially, of vocational guidance. The goals were seen in terms of the solution of immediate problems. Thus it happens that we can only say that vocational guidance in Britain has evolved during the last two decades, if by 'evolution' we mean the expansion and refinement of provision, not of concepts. In some such patterns the careers teacher actually appears as an additional specialist *outside* the main guidance team, itself organised around a system of personal counselling. Again, in some schools, counselling is dominated by a concept of vocational guidance crudely centred on helping the adolescent to make a happy 'first-job' choice, which of course means that the emphasis is on the early leavers rather than over the whole school population. Again, some at least of the confusion that exists about the difference between 'counselling' and 'guidance' stems from the fact that there has been a continuous development of provision in this semi-specialist area, but as a result of the failure of the concept to evolve, there is now a spilt between a concept which began in Britain, and a similar one, which evolved in a totally different fashion in North America, and was then imported into Britain in its matured form, as counselling, in the 1960's. As an example of this difficulty, an authoritative article in *New Era* in 1968 stated that vocational guidance was essentially *informative*, and should be handled by careers teachers, whereas personal guidance was essentially *problem centred*, and constituted the main role of the counsellor in secondary schools. Likewise, vocational guidance is still seen by the Youth Employment Service in terms of employment-guidance. In this however the Service is not to blame, being hamstrung by its terms of reference.

Underlying all these questions about the relationship of vocational guidance to counselling are of course big questions about the relationship between the individual and his society, and about social duties. While we shall touch on some of these issues in the second part of this book, we can immediately turn to look at the institutional framework within which the various guidance functions take place, and by which they are also partly shaped and limited.

One of the most satisfying experiences in human life is that of creativity; the creative process is essentially that of a search, and this search is inseparable from a process of work as we have so far defined it.

It is impossible to avoid the suggestions of sexuality in this: to create is to give birth, whether physically in woman after her labour; or to new ideas after a period of creative disturbance; or to an object after mental and physical labour on it. It is also associated with the release of aggression and even with the concept of war: to gain victory after struggle and after sustaining intermittent defeats in which the individual may have felt not only his self-confidence, but his personal integrity, threatened. A successful outcome to a creative struggle is in fact the outward projection of part of the individual's life force; in the newly born child, the completed boat, the beautiful garden, the individual sees a material assurance of his own identity, and even at times a kind of immortality.

Just as work is central to the creative process, so this in turn provides the context within which work takes on its deepest significance. Boris Pasternak once wrote: 'the fabulous is never anything but the commonplace by the hand of genius,' and genius itself has been described as an capacity for taking pains. Even at its highest level, the transformation of the mundane involves a process of work. These thoughts give us the possibility of refining our definition of work: in its most significant from, work is the sustaining of tensions, or risks, and intermittent failures, inseparable from the process of forming new ideas and giving them material reality.

The idea, sometimes heard, that a child passes in adolescence from a phantasy view of the world of work, to a reality view of it, seems to miss the fact that human development is normally a continuous, unfolding pattern in which the past can never be dismissed or neglected.

When an individual is required to work for long periods of time, usually out of economic or social necessity, at tasks which afford him to opportunity whatever for any expression of his personality, both the concept of work and the individual are thereby degraded, and the destructive effects are no doubt proportional to the length of time over which such a situation continues. Much, but not all, of peoples' work takes place in the context of earning a living, or following a career, and for ease of discussion let us call this 'employment'.

A man's employment of course includes its social setting: the people he meets in the course of his employment, and the social recognition which his employment affords, both of which are important influences on his attitude towards it. Employment roles usually require a fairly massive commitment of work, and this is a good point at which to examine some of the broad possible consequences of this.

The most satisfying employment is one which presents challenges that we can meet by a deep and creative personal involvement. This is usually seen as a good thing, and we are apt to forget some negative sides of it. Success here, as elsewhere in behaviour patterns generally, is likely to be followed by a deeper involvement. This can usually be justified, if the need arises, but the requirements of 'earning a living' or 'following a career.' If progressive improvements is accompanied by increasing success, the employment may begin to draw in too much available energy, and insidiously to attenuate the private life, which may become correspondingly shallow. Too much work now take place in one setting only-the employment role-and is not sufficiently distributed over the broad spectrum of life. Whether this is seen as a good or a bad thing depends greatly on the social values that are accorded to private life, the family, religion, and so on. These may well vary from one society to another.

One specific aspect of a deepening involvement with a employment role is, however, worth a special mention: a tendency to use it to compensate for failures in private life, and to evade the need for more effort there. Work-especially creative work-can take the mind off other things, and release the tension generated by frustration elsewhere. Persistent evasions of this sort may well amount to a rejection of life itself, impossible to justify except by rare creative genius in the employment role. At the other extreme are employments which are potentially creative, but in which the individual has failed in the sense that the cannot involve his deeper life with the work, whose functions he discharges in a mechanical way; and employments which are basically sterile, such as many forms of factory labour.

In the first of these we may find the imitator-the individual who conforms over-closely to the style of clothing, the turns of speech, the ways of thought, the patterns of activity appropriate to his employment role, as a compensation for a deeper failure there. 'Action', wrote Canard, 'is consolatory. It is the enemy of thought and the friend of flattering illusions.' This over-identification with the trivia of the employment stereotype may extend into many distant and apparently irrelevant areas of life, so that in extreme cases we may say with the scathing words of Volatire about an acquaintance: 'he was born a man, and died a grocer.'

If, on the other hand, the work offered by the employment role is both demanding and boring, the concept of work itself may be rejected wholesale, leading to the use of non-creative, non-demanding leisure activities upgraded out of all proportion to their value. Harold Entwhistle has emphasised the high likelihood that boring employment leads to the dull and unimaginative use of leisure: a man whose brain has been dulled by eight hours of monotonous toil can hardly be expected to burst into creative leisure activity: in short his ability to work has been damaged. It is perhaps significant that throughout history we see examples of those sections of the population engaged in the dullest, most routine work, putting a high value on non-demanding 'viewing' activities, from the circuses of ancient Rome to the football stadiums of today.

How far does vocational guidance, as practised in our schools, stand up to examination from this viewpoint? Nearly everywhere, in the practice of vocational guidance, it is assumed that work means employment, and this is particularly clear in the description of the various offices and activities in this field, such as 'careers officers,' 'careers teachers,' 'careers convention,' 'careers literature,' and 'work experience'. The over-emphasis on this association of work with employment reflects a general failure to think deeply enough about the meaning of work; and implies an acceptance of the popular idea that work and leisure are different things. Perhaps this is partly the price of an empirical approach to guidance generally, with its unwillingness to explore concepts at the abstract level. The idea of a clear distinction between work and leisure certainly needs to be broken down, perhaps by more attention in training programmes and conferences in counselling, to the definition and discussion of goals and assumptions. If it is not, there may be some future danger of the spread of courses and programmes of 'education for leisure', carrying further the artificial distinction already present in the terms we looked at earlier. Where pupils can be encouraged to relate ideas which they find personally exciting, to those which they associate with work, the basis of a new approach exists, meaning, in effect, the marriage of vocational guidance to counselling.

However, the question of how far children should be encouraged to express their creative energies through employment *alone* is very complex, and illustrates the impossibility separating vocational guidance from the need an overall philosophy of life. At one extreme is a certain view of employment as a 'job' void of anything worthwhile; a daily interruption of life; at the other extreme is the obsessively employment-dedicated man to whom nothing but a career matters.

Proponents of the first viewpoint sometimes take a 'realistic' or 'tough-minded' approach to the formation of employment-attitudes, and hence to vocational guidance. They argue that at the present time, and in the foreseeable future, many forms of industry will require large reserves of manpower for the dullest and most routine jobs. For such people education should concentrate on the creative use of leisure; and in any case, not encourage a false view of the world of work, among those most likely to fall into routine employments. Such unimaginative attitudes ignore the onrush of automation, the increasing geographical mobility of urbanised societies, and the whole background pattern of change, and which, however materialist its methods and aims, is swiftly changing the approach of many young people towards their vocational futures.

The question which adolescents increasingly ask, is not how to find a good job, or to make a career, but whether to bother about such things. I have little sympathy with those who dismiss such young people as being simply lazy: their problems seem to me to arise out of a deeply sincere questioning of the worth of modern urban civilization.

The spread of cynicism about accepted values, the rejection of the 'establishment,' of authority, seem to me to go wider than the characteristic and temporary rebellion in adolescent development against the older generations; and as we shall see later, even in communist countries there is some evidence of a similar trend, masked by lip-service to stereotype ideals. The drift of this wind through our societies further illustrates the change of separating vocational guidance from counselling. Why in fact has the development of guidance in semi-specialised from in British schools, been so closely identified in the past with careers work? Why have these simple and essential ideas about the relationship between work, leisure, and personal development not been sufficiently considered to lead guidance away from a narrow pre-occupation with employment, to a wider view of life goals? The answers probably lie in the tendency in British society, which we have looked at, to concentrate on processes rather than on concepts; on immediate problems rather than on long term goals. Thus the earliest government intervention, represented by the Employment Acts of 1909 and 1910, set up juvenile departments in some Employment Exchange to help place boys and girls in jobs, and to allow Local Education Authorities to do this also. To be fair, the wording of the Acts and official memoranda at this time indicate a recognition of the need for guidance on a wider basis; but in practice the provision become one of job-placement, predominantly for the children of the poor.

The excessive concentration on job-placement has remained as part of the official attitude towards vocational guidance, in spite of various attempts at improvement, and in spite of being drawn much more closely into the frame work of L.E.A supervision since 1948. Why did the concept not evolve faster? There are several possibilities.

One is the fact that guidance structures existed outside and independently of the schools: the contact between Youth Employment Officers and school staff was too fleeting for serious discussion of deeper issues in guidance. The fact that an organised structure existed outside the schools; and school heads, often tending to think of the successful pupil as one who made the ascent into a university or teacher-training college, may, as we have suggested earlier, have thought of an early leaver looking for a job, as an educational failure. Also, for many years, the use of psychological tests was almost totally unknown among teachers, so that no independent pointer to the relationships between personal, educational, and vocational needs of children was available.

But the main reason why for so long the idea of guidance lay at the level of job-placement in Britain is almost certainly to be found in the social stratification of education. The acceptance of new ideas in guidance and the rise in the numbers of careers teachers, and the emergence of the counsellor as a new figure in schools, co-incide closely with the rise of comprehensive secondary schools.

We have already emphasised the tendency of grammar and public school heads to judge success in terms of educational attainment. This limited the development of the concept in those areas.

In the secondary modern schools which emerged after the 1944 Education Act, a large number were situated in industrial slum areas, where the prospects, career or otherwise, were too grim to think about. Here there was little or no incentive to start thinking along sophisticated lines about guidance. But the comprehensive schools which emerged a few years later were in a different position: they offered a diversity of educational opportunity at the secondary level unknown in the other kinds of school, and extended deep into adolescence the problems of educational, vocational, and personal choice. In such circumstance, especially in the larger schools, sense of uncertainty, even of being lost, can easily emerge, and for the young pupil soon grow to formidable proportions among so many new faces, both of pupils and staff, most of them stranger. In such a situation, the development of an effective guidance system, able to make contact with such pupils is completely necessary if the main aims of the school are to achieved: one can go further and say that it is the presence of such a system, and its efficient functioning, that largely holds the balance between a comprehensive school approaching its ideals, and an 'education processing factory' of the kind described by opponents of the comprehensive school principle.

In fact, the sort of situation we have suggested here has involved fairly specific problems, and their solution has here has involved fairly specific problems, and their solution has encouraged the emergence of techniques.

The newcomer has to be introduced to the school; at its simplest this means making certain that the pupil understands what opportunities are open to him, and how to use the main lines of communication. Pupil records have to be developed beyond the simple report-card stage, in order to record as much as possible of the kind of information which, in a smaller community, would be casually picked up by teachers in getting to know their pupils.

The advantages of using psychological tests as a short-cut to objective information have begun to be recognised, and teachers involved in guidance work in comprehensive schools frequently seek courses at which they can build up their knowledge and experience with such instruments, and so improve the quality of the record system.

Personal guidance

Personal guidance is the assistance given to any individual to solve his emotional problems and to assist him to control his emotions. Controlled emotion is the most significant characteristic of a mentally healthy individual. An individual having control over his emotions when threatened with conflicts and frustrations is able the maintain a mental balance by working against stress. Polytechnic students who are in the adolescent period of their growth and development exhibit heightened emotionality. Anxiety and frustration in students also result in emotional tension. These may be accompanied by irritability and tendency for emotional outbursts. Their hightened emotionality may be due to environmental and social factors. Students at this stage feel the urgency of breaking down old habits of thought and action. They are upset during the period of adjustment. Once they explore certain coping mechanisms of adjustment, the excessive emotionality usually disappears.

Students greatly need assistance in understanding the various coping mechanisms of adjustment.

When the individual is confronted with a succession of frustrating situations, the immediate reaction maybe one of anger or hostility. In many respects anger and hostility are difficult emotions to deal with. Both involve tension which demands discharge. But the conditions of civilized living permit only a few direct outlets. The hostile behaviour is expressed through intolerance, aggression, impatience, over excitement and the like, which may be observed in adolescents.

Fear is one of the emotions which may be related to material objects, social relationships or to self. The thing we fear are actual or potential sources of frustration. Specific dangers tend to arouse fear. Ordinarily, fear elicits a withdrawal or flight reaction. In the face of intense fear, the individual may panic or freeze and become unable to function in any organised manner.

Many situations give rise to anxiety. Situations causing worry is generally accompanied by anxiety. Stress situations inducing anxiety are often difficult to cope with. This is because, the nature of the threat is usually unclear to the individual. Adolescents quite often express this motion.

Jealousy is one of the emotions which is social in origin. In its extreme form it may take the form of violence. Jealousy and annoyance may arise together. The causes of annoyance have a broader canwas than jealousy. The emotional types discussed above generally have adverse effects on the individual. But like biological drives, emotions may arouse, sustain and direct activity and as such play an energizing role in behaviour. Emotions also may serve as emergency sources of power.

For example, in stress situations which habitual reaction patterns are not adequate, strong emotions make maximum energy resources available and thus help the organism for meeting such emergencies.

The emotions like joy, pleasure delight affection etc., are mostly helpful in overcoming the stress situation and thus protect the self from crisis and frustration. These emotions also dominate during the adolescence period. Emotional disequilibrium produces conflict within a individual. When emotional conflicts are unresolved, he becomes emotionally problematic. Emotional conflict is a painful mental state in which opposing and contrary wishes and thoughts are ranged against each other and pull the individual in opposite directions. Conflicts arising out of emotions may vary greatly in their kind and intensity. Frustration is a feeling of inadequacy and tension caused by blocking of desires or pathways to a goal. This may happen consciously or unconsciously.

The manifestation of an emotional problem may be observed in such behaviours as fear of meeting people, psychological withdrawal, upset in minor happenings, angry, hostility, aggressiveness, criticising of everybody and everything. There may be several causes of frustration which is one of the major emotional problems of students. These include disappointment in love, loss of comfort and stability, complicated situation, lack of personality traits, loneliness, rejection by peers, and lack of mental abilities.

Anxiety is frustrated fear. Students suffering from anxiety exhibit feelings of insecurity, lack of self-confidence, fear about their ability to achieve their goals and meet difficulties of life and world. A number of causes for emotional problems have been identified. These are favouritism by teachers, heavy load of home work, lack of concentration, threat of self due to bias, insult, contradiction, being teased, sarcastic comments etc. Emotional insecurity is also one of the major causes of anxiety reaction. Nervousness means a large variety of reaction. The nervous students are restless, unable to concentrate on studies get upset at the slightest defeat or threat.

On the surface, such a student may show behaviour like biting his nails, playing with his handkerchief or buttons, moping the forehead again and again etc. These meaningless activities help him to get over from the tension. It has been observed that students who suffer from nervousness have gone through great insecurity in their life time. This feeling of insecurity may be due to poverty, neglect, loss of parents, occasional threats and dangers. In some cases the students may acquire this insecurity from their Parents. "Psychological stress is the state of an organism where the student perceives that his well-being (or integrity) is endangered and that he must devote all of his energies to its, protection".

In Psychological stress the integrity of the organism is involved and he cannot find a normal adjustive response. Frustration and anxiety produce tension within the individual and prolonged tension causes stress. Almost all behaviour manifesting stress are similar to anxiety. But in stress their degree of intensity may be more. In the ever changing environment every individual must change his behaviour to maintain emotional stability. Adjustment to change is a conscious process involving reasoning, imagination and learning new behaviour.

Emotional conflict may arise out of a stressful situation, the degree of which depends the individual's personality structure. Emotional conflict produces anxiety and tension within the individual and when all the coping mechanisms fail to adjust the individual undergoes stress. Neurosis is a milder form of mental ailment which generally originates from prolonged emotional strain and emotional conflict. It gives a lot of trouble to the individual in the form of anxiety and causes a number of adjustment problems.

The neurotics are unhappy, anxious' inefficient and ineffective. They are over sensitive, lack maturity, self-centered and always complain of physical ailments like tiredness, indigestion, headaches and sleeplessness. Neurotics believe that they are the victims of misfortunes over which they don't have any control. They are highly suggestible-and obstinate.

Case histories of neurotic students reveal the underlying causes such as violent emotional conflicts, distressing emotional experiences, loss and disappoint-ment in life, violent discord in social relationships or some frightening happenings.

Unfavourable early training, noncongenial environment also cause neuroticism. If the life at home and institution are full of tensions, annoyances, fears and anxieties students are likely to develop a neurotic personality. Several strategies depending on the nature of the problem and the purpose can be used for emotional guidance.

Cooperative counselling "is a blend of the direct guidance and authority typical of directive counselling and the non judgmental, active listening behaviour typical of nondirective techniques". In co-operative counselling the following phases of activities are followed: The data and time of counselling session is fixed by the counsellor with the consent of the counsellee. The counselling session is to start with self introduction. The counsellor tries to stimulate clients' thinking by asking questions.

When the counsellee remains silent, the counsellor waits for the response.

The counsellor restates the counsellees feelings and message. The counsellor assists the counsellee to choose appropriate coping mechanism. The counselling traits as per prefixed date and time. The counsellor introduces himself with his brief professional expertise. The student who comes for help also introduces himself.

In the bringing of the session the counsellor asks a few questions to the counsellee. These questions are asked in a nonthreatening manner. The purpose of asking these questions is to stimulate the clients' thinking. These questions are specific and related to counsellees' emotions and attitude. Thus, the client is encouraged to express his thoughts. When non-threatening questions work, these stimulate deep communication.

8

Counselling Techniques

Counselling is as old as society itself. In every day life, we find, counselling goes on at many levels-in a family setup, parents counsel their children, in society doctors counsel patients, lawyers clients, teachers students. In other words, there is no limit to the problems on which counselling can be offered nor to the type of persons who can render this help. Professional counselling, in its present form, is a recent development. Colleges and universities, industries an business establishments are becoming increasingly interested in counselling and its potential for improving interpersonal relationships. It is believed, where no counsel is, the people fall; but in the multitude of counsellors, there is safety. No wonder, counselling is being recognised as an important technique of guidance here, there are everywhere!

Before we discuss the how of his technique, let us try to know what counselling is? Counselling has been understood and defined in a number of ways:

i. Webster's dictionary defines counselling as "Consultation, mutual interchange of opinions, deliberating together."

ii. Wren says, "Counselling is a dynamic and purposeful relationship between two people who approach to mutually defined problems with mutual consideration of each other to the end that the younger or less mature, or more troubled of the two is aide to a self-determined resolution of his problem."

iii. James Michael Lee and Nathaniel J. Pattan say, "Counselling is the relationship between two persons in which one of them attempts to assist the other in so organising himself as to attain a particular form of happiness, adjustment to a life-situation, or in short, self-actualisation. Counselling always involves a one-to-one relationship, that is one client and one guidance worker in a formal or an informal interview situation."

iv. Merle M. Ohlsen writes, "Counselling is an accepting, trusting an safe relationship in which clients learn to discuss openly what worries and upsets them, to define precise behaviour goals, to acquire the essential social skills, and to develop the courage and self-confidence to implement desired new behaviours."

v. According to Arbuckle, "Counselling is helping a person to come to see who he really is, what he has and does not have; what he can do easily, what he can do with difficulty and what he probably cannot do at all...(It) is a close sharing of a human relationship with one who has form him a high regard; one who can offer him unconditional acceptance, but own who has no guarantees, no answers."

vi. Pepinsky and Pepinsky feel, "Counselling relationship refers to the interaction which (i) occurs between two individual called "counsellor" and "client", (ii) takes place within a professional setting and (iii) is initiated and maintained as a means of facilitating changes in the behaviour of the client. The Counselling relationship develops from the interaction between two individuals, one a professionally trained worker and the other a person who seeks his services."

vii. Hahn and Maclean define "Counselling as a process which takes place in a one-to-one relationship between an individual beset by problems with which he cannot cope alone and a professional worker whose training and experience have qualified him to help others reach solutions to various types of personal difficulties."

viii. Blocker explains it as "helping an individual became aware of himself an the ways in which he is reacting to the behavioural influences of his environment. It further helps him to establish some personal meaning for this behaviour and to develop and clarify a set of goals and values for future behaviour."

An analysis of the above viewpoints will reveal the major elements of counselling.

(a) Counselling involves two individuals-one seeking help and the other, a professionally trained person who can help the first.

(b) There should be a relationship of mutual respect between the two individuals. The counsellor should be friendly and co-operative and the counsellee should have trust and confidence in the counsellor.

(c) The aim of counselling is to help a student to form a decision, make a choice or find a direction at some important fork in the road such as that of planning a life career, a programme in college or university, or a campaign to obtain employment.

(d) It helps the counsellee acquire independence and develop a sense of responsibility. It helps him explore and fully utilise his potentialities and actualise himself.

(e) It is more than advice-giving. Progress comes through the thinking that a person with a problem does for himself rather than through solutions suggested by the counsellors.

(f) It involves something more than the solution to an immediate problem. Its function is to produce changes in the individual that will enable him to extricate himself from his immediate difficulties.

(g) It concerns itself with attitudes as well as action.

(h) Emotional rather than purely intellectual attitudes are the raw material of the counselling process. Information and intellectual understanding have their place in the counselling process. But it is the emotionalized feelings which are most important.

Counselling is a generic service of student personnel work having a wide range of activities and includes faculty advising, counselling in psychological clinics, mental hygiene and other specialised types of counselling. It is a body of techniques which helps young individuals to grow up normally through guided learning.

Counselling has proved to be very useful wherever the development of an individual student is cared for. It helps an individual to know himself better, gives him confidence, encourages his self-directiveness and provides him with new vision to grow.

What counselling is not

1. Counselling is not giving information though information may be given.

2. Counselling is not giving advice, making suggestions and recommendations.
3. Counselling is not influencing the client's values, attitudes, beliefs, interests, decisions, etc. with or without any threat or admonition.

The main objective of counselling is to bring about a *voluntary* change in the client. For this purpose, the counsellor provides facilities to help achieve the desired change or make the suitable choice. The client alone is responsible for the decisions or the choices he make, though that counsellor may assist in this process by his warmth and understanding relationship.

Counselling and psychotherapy are different. Although the psychotherapist uses counselling as one of the techniques of treatment, psychotherapy is concerned mostly with individuals whose behaviours are neurotic. It deals with repressed individuals but counselling is concerned mostly with normal anxieties. Psychotherapy operates in a medical setting whereas counselling operates in an educational setting. Psychotherapist uses play therapy, psychodrama, socio-drama, etc. as techniques; in counselling, such techniques are used as can be employed in educational institutions, industrial establishments etc. Psychotechnics is deeper in scope whereas counselling is broader in scope. A counsellor cannot be a psychotherapist, a psychotherapist can be a counsellor, being better and specially qualified.

Dunsmoor and Miller are of the view that the core of student counselling is to help the student to help himself. From this point of view they describe the following purposes of student counselling:

1. To give the student information on matters important to success.

2. To get information about student which will be of help in solving his problems.
3. To establish a feeling of mutual understanding between student and teacher.
4. To help the student work out a plan for solving his difficulties.
5. To help the student know himself better-his interests, abilities, aptitudes and opportunities.
6. To encourage and develop special abilities and right attitudes.
7. To inspire successful endeavour toward attainment.
8. To assist the student in planning for educational and vocational choices.

It is obvious that the goal of counselling is problem clarification and self-directed needs. The counselling officer helps the student to understand the problems and helps the student to help himself. In this process, the role or the student is objective self-assessment of the situation and the role of counselling officer is to formulate the decision making process and to act as the stimulator of insights and sensitivities of the student. Counselling does not solve the problems but helps in solving and if solution is not possible to help face challenges and to live with them.

The fact is so well brought out in Hannah's Green-book. Here, the girl bitterly accuses her psychiatrist after an unpleasant incident-what good is your reality when justice fails and dishonesty is glossed over and the ones who keep faith suffer—what good is you reality then?

The response is "..I never promised you a rose garden, I never promised you perfect justice...and I never promised you peace or happiness. My help is so that you can be free to fight for all of these things. The only reality I offer is challenge and being well is being free to accept is or not at whatever level you are capable. I never promise lies and the rose garden world of perfection is a lie and a bore too."

Counselling has a vast scope. According to Williamson, "The techniques of counselling individual students may be observed in greatly modified form, in the individualized service; granting loans and scholarships; handling discipline cases; assignment of rooms and selection of room-mates in dormitories; advising on student activities and programmes; helping students choose vocational objectives; selecting optional courses of study; learning to read at college rate and comprehension." Concerns about educational progress, course programme planning financial and health matters, and problems of family, social and emotional adjustment are commonly expressed in the context of counselling. Very often, many of these are closely intertwined in experience of the same student. In such instances, terms such as 'vocational problem' and 'emotional problem' are nothing more than convenient labels which serve as tentative and approximate methods of classifying counselling cases. It often happens that a problem which is initially expressed by the student as simply one of learning how to study better or of making a suitable vocational choice turns out to be much more complex than that.

Counselling is a term that is used quite loosely for face-to-face interviews in which the counsellor attempts non-coercively to help the counsellee or client, or a group of clients, to make personal decisions.

It may be helpful to differentiate three levels of activity related to training:

1. *Informal counselling*: It is any helping relationship by responsible person who may have little or no

training for the work. For instance, ladies helping patients in hospitals through friendly conversation with them.

2. *Non-Specialist counselling by professionals*: It is the help provided by physicians, lawyers, teachers, ministers, and others who do a great deal of face-to-face work with psychological problems in the course of their other work. Sometimes, special titles are used like "religious counselling" or "financial counselling".

3. *Professional counselling*: It is helping another person with decision and life-plans, whether personal or educational vocational, by a person specially trained for this work. Professional counsellors are usually psychologists, or educational psychologists. 'Professional' means among other things the possession of master's or doctor's degree with at least a year of supervision by a trained professional and the acceptance of a professional code of ethics. Training for psychologists, among other things, emphasises test interpretation, research, the psychology of personality, occupational information and experience with a variety of clients.

Counselling can be classified according to the nature of the problem, the complexity of treatment, and the competence of the counsellor.

Some writers classify counselling in terms of several factors. Lloyd Jones and Smith, for example, describe various levels of counselling with respect to the depth of the problem, length of contact, degree of need, and the skill of the counsellor.

At the Surface level is the counselling offered when the student wishes only some item of information. The counselling given may be casual; it is brief, and it may be superficial inn that it is not extensive or intensive.

The need for help is important even though slight, and the relationship maintained through the brief contact should not be less than that maintained during the long counselling session.

Counselling at the next level requires a more prolonged contact because the counsellee needs more and complicated information. He may, for example, wish assistance in planning a programme of study for a two or four year period. As the problems became more complicated and as more intensive study of the case is required, and more specialised help is needed, counselling at deeper levels becomes necessary.

When the student is seriously disturbed, therapeutic counselling may be needed. Williamson feels that counselling is needed not only for helping individuals to gain insight into their emotional conflicts but also for helping them with problems stemming from lack of information, such as information about vocational aptitudes and interests or about work opportunities, so that they may conduct their future adjustments in such a way, that 'minimum of maladaptive repressions' occur.

The following are some of the situations in which counselling is needed:

i. When the student needs not only reliable information but an interested interpretation of such information as meets his own personal difficulties.

ii. When the students needs a wide, sympathetic listener with border experience than his own, to whom he can recount his difficulties and from whom he may gain suggestions regarding his own proposed plan of action.

iii. When the counsellor has access to facilities for helping in the solution of a students' problem to which the student does not have easy access.

iv. When the student is unaware that he has a certain problem but of his best development, must be around to a consciousness of that problem.

v. When the student is aware of a problem and of the strain and difficulty it is causing, but is unable to define and understand it, and is unable to cope with it independently.

Who should be counselled?

The following type of students are in urgent need of counselling:

i. Students who have a consistent record of under-achievement.

ii. Students whose scholastic achievement drops suddenly.

iii. Students who need financial aid in order to continue their studies.

iv. Students who find it difficult to participate in class and extra-class activities.

v. Students who use exhibitionism for gaining recognition or attention in class.

vi. Students who find it difficult to adjust to the college/university.

vii. Students who suddenly decide to drop out of college/university.

viii. Students who display unusual ability in any direction intellectual, artistic, musical, etc.

ix. Students who have behaviour problems such as drug addiction, aggressiveness, bullying, stealing, shyness, timidity, etc.

There techniques are used for counselling. These are divided on the basis of the nature of the counselling process an the part of the counsellor.

1. Directive or Prescriptive or Counsellor-centered counselling.
2. Non-directive or Permissive of Client-centered counselling.
3. Eclectic counselling.

E.G. Williamson is the chief exponent of this viewpoint. Such type of counselling involves six essential steps:

— *Analysis*—Collection from a variety of sources the data needed for a adequate understanding of the student.

— *Synthesis*—Summarising and organising the data so that they reveal the students' assets, liabilities, adjustments and maladjustments.

— *Diagnosis*—Formulating conclusions regarding the nature and the cause of the problems exhibited by the student.

— *Prognosis*—Predicting the future development of the student's problems.

— *Counselling*—The counsellor's taking steps with the student to bring about adjustment and readjustment for the student.

— *Follow-up*—Helping the student with new problems or with recurrence of the original problem and determining the effectiveness of the counselling provided to him.

Here the counsellor plays the major role; he does all that he can to get the counsellee to make a decision in keeping with his diagnosis. He tired to direct the thinking of the consellee by informing, explaining, interpreting and advising.

A considerably use of interpretations and direction by the counsellor has led to this type of counselling being described as directive or counsellor-centered or active approach technique.

Car R. Rogers is the chief exponent of this viewpoint. In this type of counselling, it is the client-the counsellee-who is the pivot. He takes an active part in the process of therapy. He gains insight into his problem with the help of the counsellor. It is he who takes decisions as to the action to be taken. The counsellor's role is passive. This type of counselling is a growth experience.

The goal is the independence and integration of the client rather than the solution of particular problem. The principal function of the counsellor is not to cultivate self-understanding in the client but instead, to create an atmosphere in which the client can work out his own understanding.

The emotional elements or the feeling aspects are stressed rather than the intellectual aspects and the counselling leads to a voluntary choice of action. In this type of counselling, we make use of few or no diagnostic instruments, except in typical situations when the individual is handicapped due to certain limitations.

Some psychologists like Bordin believe that Rogers and Williamson are towards opposite ends of the pole and the counselling methods may be evaluated along a continuum from non-directive to directive. When a counsellor deliberately tries to incorporate in his practice both directive and non-directive techniques, the result is eclecticism. F.C. Thorne, who is the exponent of this view, finds that it is possible for a counsellor to alternate between directive and non-directive methods even in the same interview without disrupting the non-directive permissive relationship with the client.

Here, the counsellor first studies the personality and needs of the individual. He then selects the technique that would be most helpful for the individual. He can start with the directive one but when the situation demands, the counsellor may switch over to the non-directive and vice-versa.

The attempt is made to adjust the techniques to the requirements of the situation and the individual. Even techniques like reassurance, merely giving information, case history, testing, etc. can be used to achieve the purpose. The counsellor must be competent and proficient in the use of all available methods. The validity of the results is determined by the skill with which any method is used with reference to etiologic diagnosis and the indications of each individual case. The critical factor is not what method is used but rater the skill with which it is used.

The process of eclectic counselling proceeds somewhat along the following lines:

i. Counselling may be preceded by an intake interview.

ii. During the opening phase of counselling, the counsellor tries to establish rapport and may have to do structuring so that the client understands what to expect of counselling.

iii. Often a tentative diagnosis is made which may include the collection of a case history and a plan for counselling is formulated.

iv. To enhance the client's self-understanding, information, about him and his background may be gathered form various sources. The client needs to be helped to assimilate this information.

v. Educational, occupational and social information, if needed by the client, may be supplied to him.

vi. The client achieves emotional release and insights, alters his perceptions and attitudes about himself and his situations.

vii. During the closing phase, the client makes decisions and plans, modifies behaviour, solves his problems.

vii. There may be follow-up contact, if needed.

No matter what method or view-point-directive, non-directive or eclectic is employed in the practice of interviewing and counselling, counselling should have developmental preventive and remedial values.

It is obvious that counselling process is viewed differently by different approaches, But in spite of the diversity in approaches to counselling, there are common factors which are:

i. All counsellors accept the importance of ideal counselling relationship.

ii. Interview is the basic tool of counselling.

iii. The counselling relationship is built during interviews.

iv. All counsellors realise the importance of acceptance of and respect for the counsellee.

v. "Honesty", "sincerity", or "Openness" of the counsellor is another common element with all counselling approaches. How the counsellee perceives the counsellor is more important than even the skills and the knowledge of the counsellor.

Counselling can be:

1. Individual, and
2. Group.

1. Individual counselling tools

Individual counselling can be done through Interviews of different types.

Interview is a give and take of views between the interviewer and the interviewee. It consists of consultation, mutual interchange of opinions and deliberating together. It can be used to get information, to give information and to change behaviour. Its purpose, thus is three-fold-it involves gathering all available pertinent facts, making a diagnosis on the basis of all the evidence and formulating an appropriate plan of action. All problems may no be settled in the interview but to be successful, it should lead to some plan of action. Its aim should be to serve the individual even though the counsellor may do no more than present the facts in a more objective light, thus enabling the student to see himself, his asses, his liabilities and his opportunities more clearly than he cult see them unaided.

The interview may be used for any of several purposes, but a purpose it must have. It may be introductory, fact finding, informative, evaluative, therapeutic in nature and its use for any of these purposes should be clearly recognised by the counselling officer and his subject.

What are some of the specific practical questions which are likely to come up for consideration during an interview? There are a great many such questions of course and they are as varied and as individually coloured as the interviewee who seeks answers them. The student who feels a need to be better informed about his scholastic and vocational prospects may want estimates of his aptitude for college work, his intellectual promise for special fields of training, his disposition to favour or avoid various spheres of activity, and his emotional adjustment tendencies. He may wish to consider with his counsellor the questions as whether he should remain in college, how much additional training he should take, what course he should take and whether he should transfer to another institution. He may decide to ask about the duties and services performed by workers in a particular occupation and about employment requirements and opportunities in that field of work. There might be some difficulties at home or harassment by other students or he might find difficulty in his a adjustment with room-mates in the hostel.

It is obvious there is no simple answer to the question 'what problems should be discussed in an interview?' Perhaps the best rule of thumb is the any personal problem that generally concerns the interviewee or any question that bears upon his personal planning ad decision making activities is a legitimate matter for interview. What is a proper counselling topic for one student may not be suitable for another. There are a number of problems of the students-academic, disciplinary, economic, educational, emotional, residential, social, etc. which necessitate the use of this tool. Here is a suggestive list of problems on which students may seek interview:

Change of subjects
Guidance at bifurcating stage
Courses where available
Courses where available
Co-curricular activities
Free studentship, fee concessions, etc.
Unfair means case
Difficulties at home
Harassment by other students
Misunderstanding with some teachers
Love affair
Prospects after completion of studies
Living in the hostels
How to study?

How to prepare for examinations?

The fact that a student comes to a teacher occasions a meeting and may result into an interview. For some problems , interview may have to be arranged and the interviewee may have to the called for, as stated earlier, under the heading 'Who should be counselled?'

Types of interviews

The first interview with a subject should be designed for the purpose of getting mutually acquainted and building rapport, so that follow-up conference and procedures sill be welcomed and appreciated. The counsellor may introduce himself, state the purpose of the interview and advise the subject about the procedures that will be used later. The short ten-to-fifteen minute introductory interview may end with an invitation to the subject to drop in at any time, with making a second appointment, with informing him about the time of the next conference, or with setting the data of the first administration of tests or of any other procedures that are to follow.

Expending of whatever time is necessary to establish happy relationship in this introductory interview, is justified. In the part of the counsellee, it involves developing a feeling of ease, born of growing confidence in the counsellors' competence, interest, knowledge, and skill, and a feeling of freedom to reveal both facts and emotions. On the part of the counsellor, it entails treating the student as a responsible adult, being considerate of all attitudes and feelings.

The introductory interview should be held very soon after the students enters the college. If the first interview is delayed until the student runs into difficulty, fails in some subjects, breaks a rule, has trouble with other students or, the like, the counselling officer may not find it easy or possible to establish good relations with the students.

The counselling officer should make notes about this introductory interview after the subject has left the conference room. It is not advisable to take or recommend any action on the basis of data obtained in the introductory interview, as there will usually be little information to justify action.

Fact-finding interviews may be designed to discover the intensity of a counsellee's attitudes towards persons and situations which he cannot or will not reveal in writing or in response to formalised questions which do not allow for indication of strong feelings. Thus interview may reveal interests that had no previously been noted, and it may allow the counsellor to determine their strength and their source. It can be used to obtain information concerning relationships with other persons and about activities that are carried out with them.

Informative interview may be interviews for the purpose of informing him about data that have been obtained form other sources, for providing information to answer question that he has raised or of passing on some decision that has been made about him by a person in a position of authority. The counselling officer may also inform a student about such matters as his performance in tests and their interpretation; the acceptance or rejection f an application for a position or for permission to a change in courses, the decision of the principal/head of the department concerning his success in an examination.

Many educational-vocational problems of the students are solved by acquisition of new and accurate information about themselves and the world of work or by discovering a different orientation to information which they already possess.

Interview may be used for therapeutic purposes. All of us like to discuss our problems, dreams and aspirations with others in whom we have confidence ad with whom we have rapport. Interview gives a chance to the counsellee to talk about himself, his past, his wishes and fears, his hopes and aspirations.

The process of talking things over bring new clarity of thought, relief from over-tension, and a new objectivity. We can know a lot from what the counsellee says, from how he behaves in the interview situation, by noting what the student is not inclined to talk about, what he speaks of with the most satisfaction and the most distress, what are the topics which when mentioned cause him the most embarrassment or inhibition.

In other words, it often happens that how a thing is said, seems just as important as what is said and it is only in the interview that this aspect of the counsellee's revelations can be appraised. When through interview the counsellee is permitted to "think aloud" in the presence of a sympathetic listener, it can give a clue to a number of problems of the counsellee.

Interviewing is an art that requires careful planning and preparation for satisfactory performance and good results. Before the interview, the counselling officer needs to work out the entire interview procedure. He needs to be sure as to how is the going to initiate it, what responses are possible to his opening statement, which one of these responses does he want, how he can eliminate the unwanted responses and achieve definite objective.

i. Decide what is to be a accomplished:

The interviewer knows the problem, when the interviewee comes for the interview, he has his own expectations and objectives. It is, therefore, important for the interviewer to be clear about what is to be accomplished. It will be desirable to write them down.

ii. Know the interviewee:

It is necessary to know the interviewee before he comes for the interview. This could be done from college records, test records, cumulative records, activity reports, from his friends and, if necessary, form his parents/guardians, etc. This will help in two-ways-in giving a good start to the interviewer and in establishing rapport and in solving the problem. Such data can furnish a framework within which the students' problem can be advantageously surveyed.

iii. Make appointments:

When appointments are made, both the interviewer and the interviewee are prepared. It saves time.

iv. Provide for privacy:

Privacy is an essentials condition of interviewing. It is necessary that the student is in a proper frame of mind induced by privacy and respect for the counselling officer's competence. Interruptions during the course of the interview should not be there.

v. Practice taking the interviewee's point of view:

The interviewer must learn to step in the shoes of the interviewee. He must be able to see the interviewee's point of view, how he looks at the problem, how he reacts to the interviewing.

vi. Know your own personality:

The interviewer needs to be objective. He must be able to introspect, overcome or at least control his opinions, convictions, attitudes, preconceptions, prejudices, notions, etc.

The process

The interviewer should make all out efforts for establishing rapport relationship of confidence, trust and mutual appreciation which helps the counsellee to express himself without inhibitions and resistance. Building of this relationships helped by the atmosphere of the counselling officer's room, his attitude and the initial reception he gives to the counsellee. The room should be attractive and pleasing. The general atmosphere should convey an impression of friendliness and informality. By rising to meet the student as an expected guest, the interviewer may give an impression that he is welcome. By giving him full attention and avoiding a preoccupied manner, he can give to the student the impression that the conference is the most important thing he could be doing at the moment.

The interviewer should being with topics which are easy to talk about and thus warm up the interviewee. After getting on the main topic, the counselling officer should make the interviewee talk freely. It is essential that the interviewee feels free to express his own ideas unhampered by the ideals, values and preconceptions of the interviewer. He should give advice only sparingly. Even when advice is sought, it would be better to avoid assuming responsibility for the decision which rightly should rest on the student himself.

The interviewer should be alert to catch the change of expressions which may drop after the interview has ended when the tension has been released and he is off guard, he may say things which he may have wanted to say earlier but which seemed to him irrelevant or too trivial to mention. The interviewer must always remember that the interview has not yet closed even when he has asked all his questions.

What the interviewee says is often a mixture of facts, his view of the situation as he sees it, and his feelings. Unless the interviewer has information from other sources, he is often unable to distinguish between fact and fiction. There is another difficulty arising out of the interviewer himself-his tendency to project his ideas and attitudes upon the interviewee. Without interpretation the counsellee may remain on a superficial level of self-understanding. The interpretation to students of the varied aspects of their emotional life is essential and it requires great skill and understanding.

The process of clarifying and gaining insight naturally leads to the making of decisions and the planning of courses of action. The successful interviewer is resourceful in making the counsellee reach his decisions and put them into practice.

There should be an efficient system of recording and maintaining the interview notes. If a complete record is desired, it may ;be necessary to keep a taper-recorder in the room. In cases, where good rapport has been established, the necessary notes can be taken without disturbing the subject. In general, however, the interview will proceed better if no notes are taken. A summary must, however, be written, immediately after the interview, to make sure nothing of importance is forgotten.

The following are the limitations:

i. The validity of data obtained from interviews is always suspect because the results are contained in judgments made by one person.

ii. The validity and reliability of this technique varies with how well and skilfully the interview has been structured and who is conducting it.

iii. Interviewer's bias is another limitation of this technique. Researchers have pointed out the fact that the interviewers report a particular phenomenon according to their own interpretations, understandings, beliefs and attitudes. The validity studies of interviews have revealed very low statistical measures of validity when interview predictions have been compared n the principle of learning. The most important contribution to behavioural counselling has been made by. Pavlov, Skinner, Wolpe and John D. Kumhboltz who believed that neurotic behaviour is acquired and is subject to the established laws of learning.

Goal

The goal of behavioural counselling is to change particular behaviour efficiently and specifically.

Blackhom and Silverman have suggested the following steps of behavioural counselling:

i *Problem definition*: The counsellor should specifically define the problem-all the circumstances regarding the inappropriate behaviour should be identified.

ii Development and socials history of the problem should be prepared.

iii. *Specification of the Counselling goals*: The client and the counsellor should come to an agreement as to what the problem actually is. It is the counsellor's responsibility to decide if the goal is within his realm of expertise and in accordance with ethical behaviour.

iv *Selection of methods*: The techniques used in the counselling, consistent with the client's goals, need to be selected.

Behaviourists use a variety of techniques to build new habits:

i. *Operant conditioning*: It is based on the idea that

a person will learn to behave in a different way if the new behaviour is rewarded and the old behaviour is ignored.

ii. *Aversive conditioning*: It is technique for eliminating specific behaviour patterns. The therapist teaches the person to associate pain and discomfort with the response he wants to unlearn. This form of behaviour therapy has been used successfully to treat alcoholism, homosexuality, obesity and smoking. Dent treated alcoholics by giving them a drug that produces extreme nausea when mixed with alcohol in the stomach. The people were encouraged, infact, instructed to drink, and each time they did they became violently sick. Gradually they began to feel sick everytime they even saw a bottle of whisky.

Desensitization—It is another technique for reducing irrational behaviour. In this technique if a client has described several anxiety producing situations, those situations are ranked from the lowest to the highest in terms of disturbance. The client is instructed in relaxation technique. When this is accomplished each anxious situation is presented starting with the one that produces the least anxiety. As the situation is recalled by the client he is reinforced by the relaxation process until there is no anxiety. Behaviourists have used desensitization to cure phobias about snakes, heights, closed rooms and sex.

Reciprocal Inhibition—There are individuals who feel anxious and unhappy most of the time. Wolpe feels behaviourists can treat diffused anxiety. Here the therapist establishes a hierarchy, from the least to the most anxiety, provoking situations. Next he teachers the client to clear his mind, release tense muscles and relax. In some cases, he may use drugs or mild hypnosis to produce relaxation. Once the client has mastered the technique of deep relaxation, they begin at the bottom of his anxiety hierarchy. The therapist asks the person to imagine the least threatening scene and to signals when he begins to feel tense. At the signal, the therapist tells him to forget the scene and concentrate on relaxing. After a short period, he instructs him to return to the scene. This process is repeated until the person feels completely relaxed. Gradually they move up the list until the client is able to imagine the situation he most learn to inhibit anxiety responses with incompatible, deep muscle relaxation.

It is obvious that the success of behavioural counselling depends upon the following:

i. establishing a valid hierarchy by ;the client and the therapist;

ii. discovering and adequate reinforcer (cooperant conditioning) by the therapist; and

iii. lack of counter conditioning outside the therapy sessions.

Some psychologists are critical of behavioural counselling. They feel that by concentrating only on behaviour, it presents an over-simplified version of human psychology. These psychologists feel that an individual's mental behaviour is just as important in therapy as his overt behaviour. It is also felt that the behavioural counselling is symptom oriented. Effort is made to smother the neurotic symptoms, no effort is made to remove the conflict that caused them. There is always a danger of the client relapsing intuit to be educated about invite each student for an individual counselling interview, particularly so in case of freshmen, as TDC I year and MA/MSc First year students, who besides their educational and vocational problems, have their peculiar problems of personal and social adjustment as they are passing through the difficult and social adjustment as they are passing through the difficult phase of adolescence. What technique of counselling-directive or non-directive or a combination of both-would be suitable under our cultural set-up is a point that deserves careful consideration at the hands of counselling officers.

Group guidance is an important part of the guidance programme. It is true that the most important objectives in the guidance process are to help the individual achieve self-direction, self-knowledge and self-realisation-these objectives cannot be achieved in a cultural vacuum. Many important experiences must take place in a group setting, since it is the only way they can be learned realistically. Group guidance is that relationship in which a guidance worker attempts to assist a number of students to attain for themselves satisfactory development or adjustment to their respective individual or collective life situations. It occurs in a setting in which one or more guidance workers encounter students as a group.

Group are best suited for discussing educational and vocational plans, problems relating to adjustment to college and social situations, problems relating to choice of options and choosing a career, economic and occupational problems, personality adjustment problems, etc.

A number of techniques can be used for imparting group guidance:

i. *Informal Discussions* - Informal discussions, if done under the able and skillful leaders, can prove very helpful. These discussions should centre around desirable objectives and should be so guided as to result in conclusions that may be helpful to he group as whole.

ii. *Group Reports*- If the students are divided into groups which have certain specific problems to tackle and later these reports are presented in larger groups. They can help all the members of the group in gaining awareness of a number of problems and their solution.

iii. *Lectures* - Lectures delivered by experts on certain problems too can impart group guidance in an effective way.

iv. *Dramatics* This is another good techniqued of group guidance. If certain interesting topics are dramatised, the students can be given guidance in an interesting way. How to appear for an interview, how to prepare for an examination, how to prepare notes-all these can be dramatised land guidelines suggested to the students in an interesting way.

v. *Question box* - "Question-box" says Jones, "If carefully organised and not too frequently used, is also a desirable technique, for it gives the shy and retiring pupil and opportunity to propose a question that is bothering him without revealing that it is his question". Most of the times, we find the shy student remains buried with his problems as he is not vocal. It is also possible that there are quite a few students having the same problem. So if the question could be proposed in a silent way, the same could be discussed in a group and valuable guidance provided to the students.

vi. *The case conference*- Here the problem faced by the majority of the group is stated concretely by way of a case. Each member of the group reviews his own experience in a similar situation. The group is guided away from the more immediate and temporary advantages to be gained toward more remote and temporary values. Then the effect of the exceptions may be discussed. Some other conditions that should be considered in deciding a plan of action are also gone through. Some generalisations are also formulated which may prove helpful another situations. According to

Jones, the entire process of the case conference is an experience in social thinking and it has positive and unique values in the group guidance program.

Various types of groups may be utilised for group guidance like;

i. Regular subject classes

ii. Special Groups organised for the consideration of special topics

iii Tutorial groups

iv. Advises under a particular adviser

v. Conferences such as career and educational conferences

vi. Clubs or other groups organised around some common interest

vii. Students with common adjustment problem and use all pertinent tools and techniques in its solution.

Theoretical approaches

Counselling is in many way a synthesis of approaches from related movements such as social casework, psychometrics, clinical psychology, and psychotherapy. Although human difficulties appear to lie in specific areas, for example vocational, personal or marital difficulties, it is people who need help. Consequently the person, not the problem, is the maintain focus of the counselling process. This applies even when the counsellor is using a behavioural approach, which is specifically problem centered.

To work effectively to help a person it is important that the counsellor should analyse what is happening in the counselling sessions. The theories upon which her approach to counselling are based offer the conceptual tools and provide a frame work for this thinking. Although theories provide a framework, this does not imply that they are rigid and inflexible; they are working assumptions which offer provisional ways of analysing and organizing evidence in a search for something better. Theory helps to explain, predict, evaluate and improve what happens in the counselling relationship and to answer questions such as 'What is happening now?' 'What accounts for this?' Using her particular theoretical orientation with its underlying philosophical implications, each counsellor attempts to answer these questions with her own unique yet limited perception. Work on a satisfactory general theory of counselling is being done by Egan and by Carkhuff in his work on helping through human relationships.

Theories of counselling are drawn from a number of schools or approaches and although they differ in emphases, they all acknowledge acceptance, rapport, the need for support, some limits and the professional status of the counsellor.

It is possible to trace two historical bases for counselling theory, one depending on psychoanalytic principles and emphasizing the emotional 'feeling' aspects of personality, and the other on learning theory, concentrating on re-learning some adaptive ways of behaviour in response to the demands of life. Some writers such as Barclay trace learning theory back to psychoanalytic thinking.

It has been suggested that there are three elements which are either explicit or implied in all systems of psychotherapy or counselling: a theory of personality, a social philosophy concerning the relationship of individuals to society and a body of therapeutic skills which influence behaviour.

American writers vary in their approach to the problem of delineating the differences between counselling and psychotherapy. Some suggest that they are viewed as overlapping areas of professional competence, counselling being characteristically short term, educational, supportive, situational, problem-solving, with emphasis on conscious awareness and normal people, while psychotherapy is long term, supportive and reconstructive; it has a focus on the unconscious, and an emphasis on 'neurotics' or other severe emotional problems. The scope of both counselling and psychotherapy and be subsumed under the framework of therapeutic psychology, and the distinctions between them often seem to be quantitative as opposed to qualitative.

In the area of personal problems counselling and psychotherapy are most nearly synonymous.

> What is most likely to trigger the request for a counselling appointment is unhappiness or dissatisfaction with the course one's life is taking. Thee may be problems in relationships to other people. There may be feelings of boredom and general meaninglessness. There is likely to be anxiety, along with vague or well-defined fears about the soundness of one's own personality. The treatment given to persons in such states of mind has frequently been labelled psychotherapy: it is in such cases that therapy and counselling are indistinguishable. Most of he controversy that has arisen..over whether there is or is not such a distinction can be resolved if we think in terms of what a counsellor is eligible to do.
>
> What a counsellor should be equipped with, if he is to serve clients of this sort well, is some tools that will enable him to make visible in its main outlines the present patterns of a person's

> life and the possibilities this pattern provides for future development. Whether members of the professions giving such assistance decide to label such tools 'counselling; or 'therapy' is not really a very important matter.

The theoretical orientation of the counsellor may well have some influence on whether she calls her work counselling or psychotherapy. Some people working in student counselling base their approach on an analytically oriented theory, and frequently refer to their work in the Student Counselling Service as psychotherapy.

A thought-provoking comment suggests that

> It may be, however, that we no longer need to worry about what counselling is, or what psychotherapy is, or if and how they differ. There has been increasingly recognition that counselling or psychotherapy is not enough. It will not solve all our social problems. It is not applicable to many people, at least as presently practised or, more accurately, in the hands of our present practitioners.

There are several personality theories which have useful implications for counselling.

1. Psychoanalytic theory.
2. Self theory.
3. Trait theory.
4. Field theory.
5. Behaviouristic learning theory.

Not all these are applicable to the present approaches to counselling in this country, but 4 they are worth a mention, since no theory has been found as yet to explain completely the process of counselling. Some of the main points of each theory are suggested below.

The 'talking cure', first used extensively by Freud, forms the basis of the counselling relationship for all the approaches, although they vary in the way in which they use it.

The psychoanalytic concepts of levels of awareness are significant for the 'dynamic' approaches to counselling, though not for the behaviourist or learning theory approaches which place no value on the concept of 'depth' of the unconscious. Both use the conscious level of awareness consisting of those ideas of which the person is at present aware, and both utilize the preconscious ideas which, although not in the individual's present awareness, can be recalled. Although Freud regarded the unconscious level of awareness as having a powerful influence on behaviour, the behaviourists prefer to think that the explanations of and solutions to human problems are to be found within the perceptual capabilities of the individual without recourse to the depths of personality.

The Neo-Freudian theorists, Adler, Horney, From and Harry Stack Sullivan in American have moved away from traditional Freudian theory in so far as it postulates a personality based on a biological drive concept, mainly sexual in nature, the satisfaction of which is the goal to which all behaviour is directed. For the Neo-Freudians personality is a social product 'processing needs which arise as much from the individual's society as from his biology'. Whilst the American approach is sociological in the sense of approaching human problems and conflicts as social ones, European practice seems to have retained the biological individual approach: 'in Europe.. the approach is not only predominantly biological, but, under the influence of Melanie Klein and others, increasingly so'. The scientist's social background and his culture influence psychological theories but although the American approach is having an increasingly active influence on European psychology, the interest is selective rather than complete. For example, Britain has been interested in behaviourist theory but accepted it from Pavlov rather than from Watson; the Neo-Freudians Horney and From have proved to be almost scientific best-sellers here-but were read by the intelligent layman rather than the analyst or psychiatrist.

The American approach to counselling in education may be added to this list of increasingly active interests from across the Atlantic, for 'the general acceptability of a scientific theory is not wholly dependent upon its validity as a science, because history shows that its relevance to the contemporary situation and the degree to which it conforms to the contemporary approach are equally important. In a world which increasingly sees all human problems as social problems, psychoanalysis as a method of treatment may well fall into desuetude, not because it does not work, but simply because it is inapplicable to the problems of the day'.

The use of a modern analytical approach to counselling in England is well described by Ellen Noonan in a recent book on different counselling styles.

Self theory

Self theories are much newer in counselling and psychotherapy than analytic theories. Carl Rogers is credited with having collected the most systematic assumptions and constructs on self theory and is recognized for his application of the theory to counselling ad psychotherapy in his client-centered or non-directive therapy, recently re-named experimental therapy. This is one of the main theories taught in the departments of counsellor education in American universities and it is one of the main approaches to counselling in American schools. It also has a strong emphasis in several such courses in English universities, although it is only one of the theories which are studied. It seems particularly appropriate for counselling in education because it was initially developed whilst Rogers, a psychologist, was Director of the Child Guidance Clinic at Rochester, Psychologist, was Director of the Child Guidance Clinic at Rochester, in New York State. He observed that certain administrative structures and policies in schools and colleges prevent maladjustment, while others contribute to it. It is important to know how to prevent maladjustment in school sand homes, in addition to knowing how to treat it. Rogers stressed the need for more concern with the teaching of reading to prevent the costly effects of reading disability, as well as emphasizing the psychological, social and economic loss which results from wrong vocational choices, and the consequent need for education about vocations and course choice.

Client-centered counselling derives from its time and its cultural setting, but Rogers acknowledges its debt to the appreciation of unconscious striving and the complex emotional nature of man contributed by Freud; to the therapy of Otto Rank; to the scientific method of psychology, which submits all hypotheses to a process of objective verification or disproof; and to Gestalt psychology for its relationship of the cluster, or various phenomena which make up the individual, to the whole. Rogers suggests that this approach is rooted in the educational, social and political philosophy of American culture, though he does believe that behaviour in the counselling relationship transcends to some extent the limitations of influences of a specific culture. To this list, Barclay adds the antecedents of liberal Christian theology, existentialism and phenomenology. Carl Rogers is in some ways the Martin Luther of psychotherapy, not philosophically or temperamentally, but in the sense that he has challenged the dogma and extended the scope of participation in the work to make it available to a much wider range of people. Counselling is not the appropriate approach to the problems of all children or all parents, but it is one significant method of dealing with adjustment problems.

Adjustment begs the question 'adjustment to what?' but used in the context of self-theory is signified a person who is acting in accord with his self-concept, which is learned progressively form birth. When a person's awareness and experience are closely matched his behaviour may be described as congruent. Where there is incongruence between a person's awareness and his experience, if he is aware of trying to communicate a feeling of love but experiences hostility his communication is defensively distorted. The implication for counselling is that the communications of both counsellor and client should aim at a state of congruence.

A further assumption of client-centered counselling is that the individual's reality is that which he perceives, and external events are only significant in so far as the person experiences them as meaningful. Thus the counsellor must try to work from the client's 'internal frame of reference' if she is to accept his feelings and attitudes. The most significant therapeutic element in this view of counselling is the emotional quality of the relationship. Information, diagnosis, historical understanding are all secondary to the climate created by the counsellor through her sincerity, warmth, acceptance and sensitive empathic understanding. The client is believed to have the capacity and motivation to solve his own problems and it is suggested that these will emerge in the freedom and safety of the counselling relationship.

Although Roger's early work was with children, adolescents and families he later moved from the Child

Guidance field into the academic world, constantly researching the results of his counselling and revising his theory. Since then the scope of client-centered work has extended into hospitals and Rogers's present position is probably to be found in this comment on schizophrenia.

> What does the word schizophrenic mean to me? To the extent that it has any definite meaning at all, it means that there is a person who is highly sensitive to his own inner experience and also to interpersonal relationships with others, who has been so defeated and traumatised in endeavouring to make use of his sensitivities that he has retreated both from his own experiencing ad from any real contact with others. In addition to his fairly basic understanding, the work schizophrenic also means to me that anyone whose behaviour is deviant and who cannot easily be understood is tossed in this all encompassing basket. Subsequently Rogers concentrated his attention on encounter group work and then on relationships between couples. His latest work, Carl Rogers on Personal Power, focuses on the power residing in individuals rather than in traditional areas and the effect that people who are aware of their own power can have politically, in systems, institutions and societies.

Trait theory

The trait and factor theorists see personality as a collection of interdependent factors, abilities, attitudes, interests and values an temperament together with social traits. This approaches mainly used by counsellors working with educational and vocational problems, in which some prediction of success in school or job is of value, rather than by the therapeutic counsellor concerned more with feelings which have become debilitating. It is in this theory that the influence of psychometrics on counselling is greatest. Williamson regards it as equally unfortunate to underemphasize the rational aspects of the counselling situation as it is to understress the emotional, for he believes that counselling should help people to learn to think logically and constructively about themselves, their relationships and their situation. He is an exponent of the directive counselling approach, which because of its emphasis on learning, the collection of information, diagnosis, prognosis, counselling and follow-up within a caring relationship, and his view that counselling follow-up within a caring relationship, and his view that counselling and discipline are not incompatible seems to offer a way of counselling appropriate to the dual role or teacher/counsellor, which other approaches do not offer so readily.

Cattell's factorial work on the organization of personality, and Allport's psychology of the individual have both contributed to this approach to counselling; indeed it is perhaps more appropriate term this an approach to counselling rather than a theory of personality.

Field theory

Any theory of personality wide enough to encompass the vital aspects of man's behaviour was recognized by Kurt Lewin as one which would be multidimensional. Field theory revived the concept of man as a complex energy field, a set of forces operating in conjunction with an environment which is also a set of forces. Lewin's work on group dynamics, social conflicts and re-education has particular relevance for counselling. Gestalt psychology, another approach to field theory, has made two main contributions to counselling theory through Gestalt therapy which applied the principles of Gestalt psychology to psychotherapy. One contribution is the principle of the organization of perception and the other is the 'phenomenon of insightful learning'.

The implications of these principles are that a person in a dis-organized state will organize his perceptions as completely as possible to reduce the tension. Behaviour is construed as a primary function of the person's present perceptions and it is therefore important first to understand a person in terms of his own unique perception or his phenomenological field, not in terms of his past history, as in the psychoanalytic approach, nor in terms of past learning, as in the behavioural approach. Insightful learning is achieved in counselling by a 'reconstructing of the field', or a review of past experiences with a loosing of the rigidity of former thinking through re-experiencing past or present feelings and ideas, so that over a period of time the reorganization and freeing of perception which results in insight may take place. This is important for the self-theorists and the psychoanalytic orientation which lean heavily on insight. In Counselling Shop, Gaie Houston gives an indigenous view of Gestalt therapy.

The learning theorist is characterized by his assumption that most human behaviour is learned and can be modified. The stimulus response model is an important explanation of behaviour, and this approach is sometimes known as the stimulus-response theory of personality. Stated simply, in order to learn, a person must want something, notice something, do something and get something. It is the reward which acts as the reinforcement, so that the S-R pattern tends to be repeated under similar circumstances. A response which is not repeated and rewarded or reinforced from time to time tends to disappear, or be extinguished. Substituting one stimulus for another to get the same response is known as reconditioning or, when used in therapeutic terms, re-education. This emphasis on how behaviour was acquired and how it can be changed offers a way of helping students with some practical difficulties, such as study problems. Whilst some students cannot study because other things worry them, there are students who cannot study well because in the past they learned to study badly.

Krumboltz is another theorist who sees behavioural counselling as the application of learning theory to counselling. He defines counselling somewhat broadly as 'whatever ethical activities a counsellor undertakes in an effort to help the client engage in those types of behaviours which will lead to a resolution of the client's problems'. Krumboltz considers that the goals of behavioural counselling can be achieved by the use of several approaches including the operant learning process, the use of imitative learning, classical conditioning and emotional and cognitive learning. He views the counsellor as an active helper in the learning process working towards specific and precise kinds of behaviour change through the use of techniques and procedures which are experimentally tested to determine their usefulness. The goals of counselling must be defined in terms of specific behaviour so that these behaviours may be recognized and reinforced when they occur. The counsellor is seen as one who arranges conditions so that the student may learn more adaptive ways of coping with his difficulties within the setting of a warn, friendly and secure counselling relationship. Michael and Myerson relate the experimental analysis of behaviour to counselling an suggest that the phenomenon with which counsellors deal is behaviour and that the independent variable which controls that behaviour is the environment. They accept that behaviour derives from the interaction of hereditary and environmental variables, but point out that a behavioural approach attempts to specify those conditions and process by which the environment controls human behaviour. The example of students who discontinue their studies is used to illustrate that by their behaviour such students are showing that they are not being 'reinforced' by those influences which keep other students at college, or that the educational reinforcement they are receiving is weaker than reinforcement coming from other sources. In such a case, it is the job of the counsellor to discover what reinforces student 'drop-outs' and to make these reinforcements contingent upon learning. They make he provocative claim that 'Under appropriate environmental conditions, which man can create, almost anyone can be motivated to do anything'.

It is perhaps unfortunate that the vocabulary of behavioural theorists often appears to be so technical, and so removed from the experience which most of us have of human interaction. The behavioural approach has much to offer to guidance ad counselling. Behaviour therapy as evolved in this country in opposition to psychotherapy. Hans Eysenck, Head of the Department of Psychology of the Institute of Psychiatry, London University, has written critically of the ineffectiveness of psychotherapy and has claimed successful outcomes for behaviour therapy.

New ways of helping people in difficulty have recently been developed in America. They are not new theories of personality and tend to be derivatives of some of the older approaches. However, there is no longer just a triadic conflict of psychoanalytic versus client-centered, versus behaviour therapy, but a series of new developments which have arisen in part because of a disaffection with existing methods and in part as a result of renewed efforts to provide help for the poor and the disadvantaged. Role playing, psychodrama, sociotherapy and reality therapy-which seems to have been particularly effective amongst delinquents and in schools-are some of these newer approaches. There has been a change, too, in the range of people offering this therapeutic help. Whereas formerly the therapeutic role was held primarily by the psychiatrist, therapist, psychologist, counsellor or social worker, an increasing number of lay therapists or 'paraprofessionals' are working in hospitals, schools and in the local communities with heartening success: 'this burgeoning of new practitioners has presumably terminated the search for the "one" most effective way of helping troubled people'.

It is now possible to find an introduction to the theories and techniques of ten of the styles of counselling currently in use in this country in one volume. Brigid proctor's book Counselling Shop contains the comments of then practitioners working in England, each of whom represents a different approach to counselling. I think it will be helpful to note these in the detail.

Psychoanalytic/object relations	Ellen Noonan
Rogerian counselling	Pat Milner
Behavioural counselling	Dougal Mackay
Developmental counselling	Francesca Inskip
Transactional analysis	Michael Reddy
Gestalt therapy	Gaie Houston
Reality therapy	David Wilmot
Social functioning	Eugene Heimler
co-counselling	John Heron
A radical respective	Tom Osborn

Below is a brief routine of three of the newer American approaches which may be quite helpful in educational settings.

Developmental counselling is an approach which aims to change behaviour in order to facilitate human development and is based on the assumption that students are capable of choosing the desired direction of their own development. Blocher has suggested a number of basic assumptions about the nature of developmental counselling which are summarized as follows:

1. Students are not considered to be 'mentally ill', but capable of choosing goals, making decisions and generally assuming responsibility for their own behaviour and future development.
2. Developmental counselling is focused on the present and the future and is primarily concerned with where the client is going not where he has been.
3. The student is a client, not a patient. The counsellor is not an authority figure, she is a partner of the student as they move toward mutually defined goals.
4. The counsellor is not morally neutral or amoral, but has values, feelings ad standards of her own. She does not necessarily impose these on students, nor does she attempt to hide them.
5. The counsellor focuses on changing behaviour not merely creating insight. She is a helping person, a teacher, a consultant and a confidante as these functions are seen to be appropriate in meeting mutually defined goals.

Developmental counselling is educational and is based on the assumption that human personality develops in terms of a mainly healthy interaction between the growing person and the environment. It aims to maximize human freedom, whilst recognizing that such freedom is sometimes severely limited by reality, and that few people are prepared to exercise the freedom which they do have. It also aims to maximize human effectiveness and suggests that the effective human being strives for control over those aspects of his environment which he can manipulate and also for control over his effective responses to those aspects of his environment which he cannot change.

Blocher admits that the psychology of human effectiveness is a relatively neglected area and acknowledges that psychology knows little about the behaviours which thousands of people employ to lead satisfying and effective lives. Despite the poverty of knowledge about human effectiveness, this approach to counselling may have particular appeal to counsellors working in educational settings.

Leona Tyler points out that the dominant personality theories of our time have grown out of the intensive study of abnormal individuals. Analytic theories offer useful conceptual tools to consider what is wrong with a student and how it might be set right, but not consider what this person might do. Learning theories are useful when there is an identifiable behaviour which needs to be changed, but are perhaps not as helpful to the student who is not seeking obvious change so much as to plan his future. The increasingly popular counselling characteristic of promoting full potential ignores the closed so that a few may be actualized. None of us use our full potential and such an objective is in many way illusory.

Developmental counsellors may also help those who are not troubled by confusion or anxiety but who might benefit from doing some serious thinking before taking important steps in their lives such as choosing a college course or a career.

A theory made up of what we know about the way in which individuals use human possibilities leads to a definition of counselling as a process of helping an individual to make his choices in such a way as to maximize the probability that his future development will be satisfying to himself and useful to those around him. A counsellor is seen as a specialist in developmental possibilities.

The personal qualities of the group leader are important determinants of group outcomes. Certainly the personality of the counsellor influences strongly the whole therapeutic process, regardless of attempts to be a neutral, therapeutic instrument. The counsellor's reactions and interventions are coloured by his or her values, personality, and personal needs. Likewise, the character and personal qualities, even the philosophy of life of the leader, are potentially as important as any specific technique in facilitating the group process.

Napier and Gershenfeld point out that many individuals subconsciously form a mental picture of what a group leader looks like. They suggest, for instance, that in the T-group sensitivity track, the image is one of a handsome, sexy, six-foot, blue-eyed man with an "ingratiating smile and an even more ingratiating manner". This individual is dressed informally, wearing an assortment of chains around the neck and probably a mustache or beard. Charisma oozes from the individual as his nontraditional, nonauthoritarian style commands attention. Speaking with confidence, but without using big words or getting overly cognitive, this leader is a cross between "Robert Redford and Carl Rogers." They further describe the organization development image as being a leader who is tall and lean, dressed in the Ivy League tradition, with book-lined walls and an important degree.

Such an individual is comfortable with survey data, computer printouts, and research analysis. However, Napier and Gershenfeld go on to suggest that various fantasies tend to have a consistency in that the successful group leader is "male, attractive in his style, has instantaneous charisma, has a natural sense of what to do and how to do it, and leads a group effortlessly—and always successfully". Unfortunately, such an image is all too common, held not only by romantic teenagers, but by all kinds of intelligent, educated individuals. The reality, of course, is that effective group leaders come in all styles and types-male and female, tall and short, black and white, old and young, and charismatic and just normal.

The question of the kinds of personal characteristics and qualities that enable the individual to be most effective has been given as much attention as any other question in the field of counselling. Belkin points out that such an emphasis is justified. First, he believes that such an emphasis enables counsellors to understand the importance of various subtle factors that contribute to counselling success. Second, counsellor educators gain important information in helping them make crucial decisions regarding selection and training of potential counsellors. Third, aspiring counsellors are encouraged to find within themselves, and to strengthen, those qualities that have been indicated as predictors of successful counselling. Finally, trainers and researchers arc aided in their attempts to determine the likely outcome of specific counselling interactions, based on tested criteria of counsellor effectiveness. Still, after a number of years and a vast amount of research, theorists are uncertain as to the exact qualities that distinguish an effective counsellor from an ineffective one. Often this difficulty is one of semantics, in that words to identify clearly the specific human traits essential in effective counselling intervention are sometimes polluted by their everyday use and thus convey a large variety of meanings.

Words such as *accepting, open, warm, genuine,* and *sincere* no longer have specific meanings, but often overlap and are ambiguous. Despite these problems, a great deal is known about these general qualities that significantly contribute to counsellor effectiveness. In 1964, the Association for Counsellor Education and Supervision indicated that the counsellor should have six basic qualities: belief in each individual, commitment to individual human values, alertness to the world, openmindedness, understanding of self, and professional commitment. Such a position partially resulted from Rogers' position that the effective counsellor had to be an attractive, friendly person, who inspired confidence and trust.

Combs and Soper had concluded from a study of effective and ineffective counsellors that effective counsellors perceived their clients as capable, dependable, friendly, and worthy, and perceived themselves as altruistic and nondominating. Further studies by Combs and his coworkers led Combs to conclude that the major "technique" of counselling was the " self- as- instrument"; that is, that the self, or personal characteristics, of the counsellor and the basic beliefs that counsellors had concerning people were major factors in facilitating positive growth in clients. Combs found that effective counsellors perceived other people as able rather than unable to solve their own problems and to manage their own lives. Effective counsellors also perceived people as *dependable, friendly,* and *worthy.* They were also more likely to identify with *people* than things, to see people as having an adequate *capacity to cope* with problems, and to be more *self-revealing* than self-concealing.

Any analysis of personal characteristics of effective *counsellors* must begin with an analysis of the characteristics of effective *persons.* A number of models of human effectiveness have been presented over the years, many of them in the 1962 yearbook of the Association for Supervision and Curriculum Development, entitled *Perceiving, Behaving, Becoming.* In this yearbook, Rogers listed three characteristics of the "fully functioning" person, presenting them as trends and goals toward which the individual strives. He suggested that the fully functioning person:

(a) has an increasing openness to experience, as opposed to defensive reactions to experiences perceived as being incongruent with his or her self-image;

(b) is continually moving toward being a process, constantly in change, but fully living each moment in the "here and now"; and

(c) has an increasing trust in his own organism.

Combs provided his description of "adequate, self-actualizing" persons in the same yearbook. Combs described adequate persons as individuals who saw themselves as being liked, wanted, acceptable, and able; as possessing a capacity for identification with others; and as having perceptual fields that are maximally open to experience. George and Cristiani present a composite model of human effectiveness that includes the following personal characteristics:

1. Effective counsellors are open to, and accepting of, their own experiences.
2. Effective counsellors are aware of their own values and beliefs.
3. Effective counsellors are able to develop warm and deep relationships with i others.
4. Effective counsellors are able to allow themselves to be seen by others as they actually are.
5. Effective counsellors accept personal responsibility for their own behaviours.
6. Effective counsellors have developed realistic levels of aspiration.

Some writers about group counselling have also

attempted to list personal traits of effective group counsellors or leaders. Dinkmeyer and Muro list eight such traits. First, members of the group perceive that the group leader is with them and for them as individuals. Second, the leader is aware of group phases and has the ability to facilitate those phases, knowing when to offer acceptance, confrontation, or cognitive input. Third, the leader has a positive outlook on life. Fourth, the leader is able to help each group member feel that he or she is an important part of the group. Fifth, the leader is professionally knowledgeable and creative. Sixth, the leader's perception of the group is influenced by the relationships that he or she has with the group itself. Seventh, the leader permits participants extensive autonomy. Eighth, their leader's style and work level matches that of the group members.

Corey and Corey identify some characteristics that they consider to be important elements of the group leader's personhood. Their list includes courage, a willingness to model, a sense of presence, good will and caring, a belief in group process, openness, an ability to cope with attacks, personal power, stamina, a willingness to seck new experiences, self-awareness, a sense of humour, and inventiveness.

Kottler presents his model for the group leader as being one in which counsellors are busy, concerned with the well-being of others and selves, "action-oriented truth seekers" who take risks, and in an ongoing condition of positive change. He describes the effective group leader as being open to self-understanding as the issues of group members unfold, so that in being better able to solve his own personal conflicts, the group leader would become better at working with the problems of the group members.

There is general agreement as to the characteristics of an effective leader. Honesty and openness are important in that they imply a willingness to accept feedback and a willingness for the leader to self-examine needs and values to determine their impact on the group. These qualities suggest the leader's interest in personal and professional growth as well as the personal growth of the group members. Such a leader can be nonjudgmental and accepting, can value personal relationships, and can have positive relationships. Without narrow or rigid behaviour patterns the effective group counsellor takes risks, is flexible and spontaneous, and has a healthy degree of self-confidence and enthusiasm. However, a more thorough look at these qualities is important, so that potential group leaders can evaluate their own personal characteristics in terms of effective and ineffective group leadership.

One of the most important traits of effective group leaders is self-awareness. Permitting oneself to be aware of one's experiencing is often a difficult thing for the group leader to do. Paying attention to oneself includes being aware of the emotional reactions that one is having during the group experience. Thus, awareness implies a quality of openness, that is accepting one's feelings as they are, rather than trying to control those emotional reactions. This quality is difficult to achieve because of the pressure of previous experiences, which teach individuals to deny their feelings. Pressures are applied not to feel depressed or not to be angry or not to be frustrated.

Effective group leaders are able to accept within themselves feelings of sadness, anger, frustration, resentment, and other feelings ordinarily considered negative. By being aware of and accepting those feelings as they are, without denying or distorting them, group leaders have greater control over their own behaviour.

This awareness of their emotional reactions allows leaders to choose how they wish to act, rather than permitting their feelings to affect their behaviour without their conscious awareness.

Certainly the effective group leader becomes involved with the experiencing of the group members to the extent that the leader is emotionally touched by the pain, struggles, and joys of others. Some group members may elicit anger in the group leader; while others may evoke pain, sadness, guilt, frustration, or even happiness. When the group leader is afraid of the kinds of emotional reactions that he or she may have during the group setting, there is a tendency to emotionally detach from the experiencing of the group members as an attempt to prevent undesirable reactions. However, effective group leaders recognize that by being aware of their own feelings they can allow themselves to experience those feelings, even for just a few moments.

Fully experiencing emotions gives leaders the ability to be compassionate and empathic with the members, while remaining separate persons with their own experiencing. Group leaders must also be aware of the ways in which group members conform or fail to conform to the leaders' values and beliefs, whether these concern education, morals, or hobbies. When group leaders are aware of their own values and beliefs they are more likely to be tolerant of group members whose life values differ significantly from their own. Also, group leaders must be aware of their own values and beliefs in order to determine to what degree they will expose those values and in what way they will influence the group members.

In our opinion, no other personal quality is more important than that of genuineness. The leader who is authentic, real, congruent, and honest is able to establish a special relationship with group members who recognize that the group leader is not playing a role or hiding behind a facade. Such leaders do not live by pretenses, but are willing to appropriately disclose self and share feelings and reactions to what is going on in the group.

Genuine individuals are willing to be themselves and to express, in their words and their behaviour, the various feelings and attitudes they hold. They do not need to present an outward appearance of one attitude while holding another attitude at a deeper level. They do not pretend to know the answers when they do not. They do not act like loving persons at moments when they feel hostile. They do not act as though they are confident and full of assurance when they are actually frightened and unsure. On a simpler level, they do not act well when they feel ill.

Such a quality does not mean that the individual counsellor must disclose or share all experiencing with the members of the group. Rather, being genuine means that the individual has the choice of whether or not to share with others, but continues to act, verbally and nonverbally, in a way that is congruent with the internal experiencing. This occurs because group leaders who are genuine are comfortable with themselves in all their interactions. They have little need to change when they are with different people, but are able to continue in the same role, regardless of the individual with whom they are interacting.

Genuineness involves spontaneity. While being tactful, effective group leaders do not constantly weigh what they say to members. They do not put a number of filters between their inner lives and what they express to others. They are aware of when they are holding something back as a form of self-protection (for example, because they fear not looking good) and when they are doing it for the member's sake. Rogers points out that being genuine permits the helper to express negative feelings to others only when these feelings persist or when they are interfering with the helper's ability to work with clients in the counselling process.

Effective group leaders are able to develop warm, caring, deep relationships with others because they prize other individuals-their feelings, their opinions, their persons. Such a feeling is a caring that is nonpossessive with little evaluation or judgment; the other person is accepted with few conditions. This warmth or caring is not widespread in our society. Many people experience a certain amount of fear toward allowing themselves to care for other individuals. Their fear is based on the idea that if one freely experiences such positive feelings toward another, the individual may become trapped and therefore vulnerable. Other persons may take advantage; they may make demands that are difficult to reject; they may reject feelings by failing to reciprocate. As a result, many keep their distance, rarely permitting themselves to get close to someone. Effective group leaders are less vulnerable to such fears because they recognize that the risk involved is worth the value to be gained. They therefore respond to others more freely, developing a close relationship with those who share their interests and values. They have wide freedom of choice in developing such relationships because of their ability to care and their relative lack of fear towards caring. They are not nearly so concerned with how many close friends they have, but with the quality of those friendships.

The ability to form warm, caring relationships is partially based on a trustworthy type of behaviour on the part of the group leader. Group members must believe that the group leader is there to promote the well-being of the members, rather than of the leader himself. They must believe that the group leader will maintain appropriate, ethical standards and that they will not be used or taken advantage of in some way.

Corey suggests some specific ways by which the group leader can increase his or her trustworthiness. These include such things as striking contracts with clients and living up to the provisions of the contract; maintaining confidentiality; being sensitive to the other's needs and feelings; demonstrating genuineness, sincerity, and openness; being realistic, but optimistic about others' abilities to come to grips with their problems in living; using carefully and in the interest of others whatever social- influence power one has; and avoiding behaviour that might indicate the presence of such ulterior motives as voyeurism, selfishness, superficial curiosity, personal gain, or deviousness.

It is important that the effective group leader have a basic trust in the members of the group. As was pointed out earlier, the need to feel little vulnerability in establishing a relationship with the group members is essential in establishing the kind of facilitative environment in which group counselling can be most effective. Certainly, group leaders cannot expect group members to have a basic trust in the leader, unless they perceive that the leader also has a trusting attitude toward them.

Trusting behaviour itself is defined by Johnson as "the willingness to risk beneficial or harmful consequences by making oneself vulnerable to another person. " In a sense, such trust means that the group leader will not put some type of invisible barrier between self and the group members, keeping them at arm's length so that they will be unable to get a clear view of the leader's personal weaknesses and failures. Without a mutually trusting relationship, little can be achieved in the group counselling situation.

Sensitivity is also a major factor in contributing to counsellor effectiveness within the group. Being sensitive involves a cognitive as well as an emotional response to each group member and makes possible a deeper and more spontaneous response to needs, feelings, conflicts, and doubts. Everyone has some measure of sensitivity to other people. Without this, no one could exist for very long in modern society. Some people develop high degrees of sensitivity as a normal process in their growing up, while others have to work to sharpen their capacities. In either case, counsellor sensitivity is so important for the helping process itself, that Rogers named the quality of empathy first among his three "necessary and sufficient conditions" for effective helping relationships.

During the process of group interaction, both the group atmosphere and the emotional being of the various members are continually in a state of flux. Because the group consists of living, responsive organisms, group members are reacting at any given moment to the stimulation of the discussion; whether that stimulation is in the form of verbal responses from the leader, from the group leader's expressions and movements, or from internal, reflective thinking going on in the member's own personal, subjective world.

Both the internal processes and the external stimuli have a profound effect on the quality and substance of the interaction among the members of the group, as well as between the members and the group leader. Fortunately, group members do indicate that these changes and responses are occurring in their words, body language, and overall behavioural patterns, as well as by gestures and voice tone. The effective leader is one who is able to discern these minuscule, but nevertheless significant, responses on the part of the group members and to assimilate these changes into his or her own perspectives and understanding of the group.

Sensitivity is similar to *empathy* as Rogers described it. His description involved sensing the other's private world as if it were one's own, but without ever losing the "as if" quality. He suggested that to be able to sense the other's anger, fear, or confusion *as if it were one's own*, yet without one's own anger, fear, or confusion getting bound up in it was a necessary condition for therapeutic effectiveness to occur. Thus Rogers specified two critical conditions: The group leader must be able to experience the member's feelings as the member is experiencing them, in the same way, with the same degree of effect and personal meaning; and the group leader must also be able to maintain an individual identity and remain sensitively aware of the differences between self and the member.

It is important to see this sensitivity and understanding as a personal quality of the individual who is to be effective as a group leader. In this sense, empathy becomes an attitude of the group leader, an attitude that permeates the type of interaction that the leader has with the various group members. Rather than being simply a specific response pattern to a verbal or nonverbal communication by a group member, this type of understanding becomes the basis for various leader behaviours. The group leader is able to decide what kind of intervention he or she wishes to utilize at a given moment in a particular group by being sensitive to the particular dynamics that are occurring in an individual or a group.

Self-confidence implies an awareness that one possesses specific skills and knowledge that can be helpful for the members of the group in achieving their individual goals. It does not indicate that the group leader is arrogant, perfectionist, or perfect, but that the group leader is aware of what he or she can do as a leader as well as what he or she is unable to do. Such self-confidence also includes an awareness of the leader's influence on others.

This influence does not mean that the leader can dominate and exploit others, which are abuses of power; but that the group leader is aware of the effect he or she has on group participants when encouraging them to get in contact with their own unused power and feelings. Such self-confidence results from the group leader's recognizing that he or she does not need to keep others in an inferior position in order to maintain power.

While group counselling is serious business, since the members are there to bring about a change in themselves, there are some humorous dimensions. The ability to laugh at oneself and to see the humour in one's own human frailties can be extremely useful to the group leader. There are times when appropriately used humour can be as helpful as many other types of counsellor behaviours, if not more so. At times, people take themselves so seriously that they miss an opportunity to put into perspective the importance of their problems.

Occasionally, groups will exhibit a real need for laughter and joking, simply for release of the tension that has built up. Such a release should not be viewed as an escape, but as part of a healing process. The leader who can enjoy humour and infuse it effectively into the group process has an invaluable contribution to make. Humour, as a therapeutic attitude, is certainly not sarcasm, ridicule, or cynicism. Rather, therapeutic humour stems from empathic listening and reflects a positive outlook on life.

Sometimes it results in the leader spontaneously laughing with one or more of the group members; at other times the leader is provoking laughter in others. Such humour is spontaneous and natural, not artificial or contrived. Sometimes it consists of no more than a raised eyebrow, a smile, a gesture. When it occurs therapeutically, it brings the members of the group closer together by establishing an additional bond of genuine caring for each other and confidence in the helping nature of human rapport.

The group leader's sense of humour may allow the leader to take the members' irrational ideas to ridiculous extremes, to reduce them to absurdity, and to employ paradoxical intention as a means of helping those members see the ridicule of their own ideas, not the ridiculousness of themselves. Likewise, humour can be a means of expressing the joy and satisfaction of connecting with and caring about each other. Such humour, as long as it is not used to derail an important immediate dynamic, to express anger or to ridicule another person, or to conceal a person's deep feelings, has curative value all by itself. On the whole, humour is an essential part of healthy group life. Group members need to learn to laugh at themselves and at each other. The ability to laugh is not only a valuable skill to be carried into life outside the group, but is also good in and of itself. The visible bubbling-up of joy, of freedom, of well-being, is often the first sign that a group has become truly therapeutic.

The ability to be flexible in organizing and responding to the group is essential to the effective group leader. Such flexibility is based on self-confidence, a sensitivity and understanding of the group, and a self-awareness. As such, the flexibility results in the group leader's being able to respond to and with the group members, rather than expecting them to simply follow in the direction that the leader had planned to take.

Such flexibility is most effective when the leader also has the ability to be spontaneously creative, to be able to develop new ways of dealing with problems as they arise. Even the capacity to approach each group with fresh ideas is not easy to maintain, particularly if the counsellor leads groups frequently. Group counsellors must somehow avoid becoming trapped in ritualized techniques or a systematic presentation of self that no longer is lively and vibrant. By being willing to suspend the use of established techniques and by approaching a group with new ways of doing things, a group leader is unlikely to grow stale. In many ways flexibility of behaviour means that the group leader is letting the group members "lead" the direction of the group. By responding to the expressed needs and wishes of the group members as well as to the dynamics of the group as they occur, the group leader is able both to direct the group process and to allow the group to have some say in the experiencing that occurs.

Such willingness to follow the direction of the group largely results from the self-confidence, sensitivity, and self-awareness mentioned earlier, as well as a sense of trust in the group process. Such a sense of trust is based on the belief that when a group is facilitated rather than directed, the group will recognize for itself the unhealthy elements in its process, clear them up or eliminate them, and move on toward more positive processes.

This flexibility does not mean that the leader has no specific goals for a particular group. Rather, the leader trusts the group to participate effectively in finding the direction by which the group goals will be met. Such an approach focuses on establishing a particular type of facilitative environment in which group members can experience and deal with those feelings, attitudes, and behaviours which have been creating problems for them without providing the total direction the group is to take.

Willingness to self-evaluate

A crucial leadership attitude is that of continually evaluating one's own contribution to the group process, both during and after each group session. Corey and Corey point out that leaders need to be able to ask themselves questions such as: What kinds of changes are resulting from the group? What are the therapeutic and antitherapeutic forces in the group? The skill of self-evaluation rests to a large degree on the leader's knowledge of and sensitivity to what is happening in the group.

9

Future Trends

The viability of guidance as a major helping service depends not only on the profusion of societal problems, complexities, and needs; it must be seen as an effective response.

The many publics—pupils, parents, legislators, the community at large, and educators-must view guidance as a profession that provides a need service, available from no other source. Two factors determine whether or not this will occur. The first is the sensitivity and perceptiveness of guidance workers in discerning the *real* problems and needs, particularly those of which the general public is only dimly aware. The second is the effectiveness in communicating goals and results to this same public. Obviously something positive has to happen in the lives of those who come in contact with guidance. Identifying needs and publicizing results will not alone accomplish the task of ensuring the support of guidance services. But guidance already has the means to ensure that it has a significant impact, and the dynamic nature of the profession, documented throughout this book, practically guarantees that it will enlarge and improve on present approaches and techniques.

Thus, the question needs to be faced, will the guidance professions able to respond effectively to the two major tasks? My position is that it will; the motivation, competency, and imagination of those who will do the job are already plentiful.

In fact, a recurring theme in earlier chapters is the inventiveness guidance workers have repeatedly demonstrated not only in dealing with current needs but in anticipating emerging or hidden ones. Failure will come only if enthusiasm falters, and pressures and challenges are allowed to cause a futile search for security through ingratiatingly taking on a myriad of insignificant and irrelevant tasks in the attempt to become indispensable rather than be professional. Predictions are hazardous but necessary. The task is made easier by the post-Bicentennial climate of taking stock and looking to the future. A positive orientation towards the future is essential in the midst of the present confusions and dilemmas:

America is wallowing in a period of disappointment and disillusion. The idea of progress is till alive, but it is not well. There is an emerging 'new pessimism', not only in foreign policy but in domestic affairs. Government is viewed as, inevitably, bumbling and corrupt. Other social institutions are considered obsolete and ineffectual. But, Elam's view is not one of long-term pessimism. Hopeful signs both of society in general and schools in particular can be drawn from the position that ours is a "self correcting society" and the schools are "a major instrument in shaping the future".

The bases for optimism are substantial. Resources re being depleted, but there are avenues available utilizing selective growth and alternative energy resources that can, if used fully and promptly, head off disaster. The nation's collective ingenuity can find new ways to cope with destructive trends.

Scientific and social innovations and breakthroughs have served to improve the quality of life in past years and have the potential for equally or greater success in the future.

We are only beginning to use our intellectual potential for progress on all fronts; education, especially, stands to gain enormously from new developments in both the cognitive and affective areas. But we may need to experience a "socioquake" and thus arrive at new ways of viewing man in relation to the environment rather than patching up the old perceptions and practices. With an assumption of constructive and positive changes, what are major directions for the next several decades? A review of even a handful of the significant themes required a look at political, economic, social, and educational aspects.

There is a continuity in the international political alignments among power blocs, even as new nations strive for status and recognition, and energy resources modify relations among countries. International politics will be based on power balances and energy resources, but there will be a greater recognition and acceptance of the concept of interdependence of nations.

The related worldwide problems of growth, crowding, and inadequate resources will be faced; cooperative efforts will be made to slow down the population explosion, increase worldwide food production, and enhance the self-sufficiency of third-world countries. Economic problems, primarily inflation, and unemployment, will continue to cause hardships for individuals, while increasing both the cost of services and the need for them. Cooperation among nations will be emphasized, while reduced energy resources and needs of undeveloped countries heighten problems in this country.

The trend of a rising median population age will continue, and the effects will be felt in every aspect of life. Not only will there be a shift in the emphasis of guidance and counselling, but retirement policies and benefits, education, housing, medical care, and the world of work will be dramatically affected. Work and the work setting are changing in ways that will have profound effects in the years ahead.

There will be an increased demand for job security as protection against the fluctuations in the economy. At the same time, however, more humane and stimulating working conditions will be sought. The work week and work day will be shortened, and variations such as splitting job and self-selected work hours will be tested. The increasing age of the labour force and the steady trend for more female participation will affect the workplace in many ways not yet known to us. Changes in education will range from introducing new financing plans to establishing programs for lifelong learning. As the proportion of school-age individuals decreases, the cost of public education rises, and the needs and political power of older persons become more visible, we may see a higher quality of schooling. It seems certain that there will be provisions for lifelong easy entry and exit in educational and training programs.

New school models will merge education and life-family, community, and work-in ways that will make education more significant. Writz predicts that "some kind of provision for enterprising the earning and learning of a living, for interweaving for interspersing the earning and learning of a living, for interweaving employment and self-renewal, is going to have to be recognized as the essential condition for an effective career as worker, citizen, or human being". A host of trends are encompassed by the need Shane describes as "how to remotivate youth to feel that life is good, that it is worth living, and that it can bring enduring satisfaction". Many of the problems of today stem from the lacks this statement implies; some young people seek solutions in fads, cults, drugs, or deviant life-styles.

The educational institution will play a significant part in building new values and purpose, but the next several decades will be marked more by questions and searching than by answers and solutions. If we translate the societal trends into guidelines for counselling and guidance, a general picture of increased pressure for services emerges. The need to make the most use possible of human and material resources leads to a greater concern for individual awareness of potential and opportunities.

The increasing interdependence among nations could enhance concern for problems that are common to different cultures and bring guidance workers in different countries closer together to pool strategies and techniques.

Developing and underdeveloped countries can profit from learning about what is done in other areas if they have the opportunity to adapt principles and strategies for local uses. It would be well to avoid an attitude that what is done in technologically advanced countries is best for others. A cooperative approach to unique needs of each culture would be true implementation of the spirit of guidance. Many of the cutbacks that appear to be inevitable will very likely cause disruptions in established patterns of travel ,recreation, and day-to-day living. New modes may actually be growth-producing-there may, for example, be less dependence on commercial entertainment-but the changes may call for difficult adaptations.

The changing age of the population has obvious and important implications for guidance. Not only will there be a shift to include expanded services for those in their middle and later years, but new types of help will be needed, e.g., assisting mid-life and older persons with educational and work planning. The changing world of work offers some of the most direct implications for guidance and counselling of any aspect of life. Even though efforts are being made to adapt work to individuals and to develop new patterns of work hour and sharing jobs, the central problem of finding meaning and fulfillment will demand increased attention.

Perhaps a combination of meaningful leisure activities and income-producing work will needed. Whatever the eventual solutions, it seems that some kind of human development services both the workplace and in the community will be needed. The changing world of work offers some of the most direct implications for guidance and counselling and aspect of life. Even though efforts are being made to adapt work to individuals and to develop new patterns of work hours and sharing jobs, the central problem of finding meaning and fulfillment will demand increased attention. Perhaps a combination of meaningful leisure activities and income-producing work will be needed. Whatever the eventual solutions, it seems that some kind of human development services both in the workplace and in the community will be needed.

The increasing need for accountability and making the most productive use of resources will make education give additional emphasis to helping all pupils understand and utilize their full potential. Questions are being raised about the assumed benefits of large schools, and there is a shift emerging that emphasizes compulsory education, not just compulsory attendance. These and other trends imply that help will needed to make the school a place for learning and development attuned to the needs of the individual and the community.

The task of helping youth to find challenge, meaning, and stimulation in school programs, work, and productive community life is made even more demanding by the changing social and economic conditions. This is a school-community problem that demands the best efforts of practically everyone, but it is one in which guidance personnel have a unique opportunity for effective leadership and service. A brief and general review of major trends slights a multitude of specific issues, problems and directions of critical significance for guidance workers (e.g. licensure, ethics, preparation, and affirmative action), but it gives the backdrop against which they will be worked out. Moreover, the major trends contain an formation of an increasing need for guidance and counselling for helping all individuals in lifelong growth and development and to give guidelines for dealing with the specific questions and problems.

A major point of this book is that new strategies, techniques, and technology are vital of effective delivery of services today. The future will make even greater demands on the creativity and inventiveness of guidance workers. Two factors support this prediction-accountability and financing. From the counsellor's point of view, the major reason is to provide better-quality help to more people; improving the quality of life ranks above the demand for hard evidence of effects and adjusting to cope with financial limitations. But the realities of the situation require a consideration of the most effective use of personnel and material resources to achieve desired goals.

Tomorrow may usher in strategies that are unknown today. The past few years have witnessed a proliferating of approaches, technology, and strategies.

Some are destined for a brief meteoric life before falling into oblivion. Others are sure to become major styles of guidance in the future. The problem that counselors face is how to tell the difference. There is no quick or easy way; research and evaluation provide the most valid answers. Intuition may seem a trusty guide, but it is often so entangled in personal commitment to an approach or enthusiasm for a cause that its value is doubtful. Moreover, the attitude that what is new is new is good and what is old is bad leads to a distorted view that inhibits a thoughtful and perceptive selection of the most effective means. This naive position, coupled with a tendency to partially try out and quickly dispose of new approaches, not only creates discontinuous development but often relegates to the scrap heap potentially valuable methods and materials. There is much faddishness in U. S. guidance, abetted by an affluence that permits spending of enormous sums on new developments that are discarded even before rigorous testing can be completed. This luxury is fast disappearing. It will take careful evaluation and use of both the old and new to fashion the guidance of the future.

Productive elements that will gain additional use in the years ahead are reflected in earlier chapters. Consultation is one. Together with psychological education and "giving guidance away", it represents a new taking shape for many years. Paraprofessional and computers also have great potential. The needs survey, a new label for holding guidance close to what the public wants, is obviously here to stay.

It has never disappeared since the concept of guidance first surfaced at the turn of the century, but since then it has fallen on hard times. Accountability is of course not new; the only surprising things is that it took so long to emerge as a major consideration in the helping services. A number of other strategies have been endorsed in the preceding pages; the movement toward lifelong learning and guidance, and integrating the school with the community and workplace are the most significant. The separate elements are not new, but the synthesis brings into being a strategy of tremendous importance. One front along which the profession advances does not involve largescale movements nationwide in scope-it is in the day-to-day work of the counsellor who may, for example, develop a better way to help a counselee explore goals, make decisions, and carry out plans, or devise a new mode of working with groups of pupils or parents. It could be any of the multitude of things the counsellor does. Shared with colleagues, these activities have a ripple effect that eventually makes a difference in school guidance.

Reflections on programs naturally lead to speculation about the practice of guidance five, twenty, or thirty years ahead. What will it be like? Is it possible to look into the future with any certainty? Some trends appear to be fairly clearly indicated by current developments. One of these is licensure. There almost certainly will be some type of widespread provisions for licensure, which will have an impact on school counselors. Effects will be felt more definitely by those in non-school gettings, however, as it is predicted that employment in an educational institution will enable the counsellor to practice regardless of licensure status.

Accountability will be given more attention in all settings. Evidence of positive effects will be needed to ensure the continued existence of school guidance services as well as to maintain support for programs in other settings. Moreover, counselors will be expected to expand services with little additional financial support.

The counsellor's role will be more clearly defined, partly because of accountability and partly because of the use of new strategies such as outreach and psychological education, which give the work a visible structure and purpose. Increasing attention will be given to the needs of special groups, e.g., mid-life and older persons, minorities, the handicapped, and women. Moreover, we will see at least the beginning of the implementation of lifelong learning and school-community cooperative approaches.

Changes in public education, particularly the expanded infusion of career education, will make the school a more dynamic and realistic learning environment. At the same time the "basics" will be increasingly emphasized. All of these changes will offer counselors opportunities to serve in new ways and to build a solid position in education. More processes and personnel will be utilized to expand the reach of guidance services. Paraprofessionals are one example, particularly peer counselors. After their slow start in the past decade, computers will be used with increasing frequency.

As school budgets are examined, questions will be raised about the necessity for guidance services. The predicted outcome, however, is that there will be an increase in the support for services because the offer ways to deal with the most pressing school and community problems.

The impact of the social, economic, and political trends described will have a more pronounced effect on guidance and counselling than in the immediate future. It is predicted that more definite patterns of those trends given for the next five years will have emerged, e.g., licensure regulations will be crystallized, career education will be the major mode in public education, and guidance roles will be more clear-cut and more widely understood. Computer technology will be used, and counselors will have much more time to devote to the personal, effective, and decision-making needs of youth.

Lifelong education and school-community cooperation will be realities, and counselors will work with all ages in both school and community.

There will be increases in the number of counselors needed; preparation standards will provide for differential staffing, with high levels of technical and human-relations competency for those in supervisory positions. At the same time there will be increased attention to prevention of problems and the provision of easily available community-wide services. School counselors will be regarded as logical persons to coordinate all school-guidance and pupil-personnel services, and will provide leadership for community-wide coordination strategies.

Disregarding the gloomy projections of those who question the likelihood of civilization lasting into the 21st century-such apprehension would have been equally appropriate in any approach of recorded history-it is not only possible but essential to look ahead to try to discern a reasonably accurate, if tentative, outline of the shape of guidance. Leaders in the field, such as Berdie, Harris, Morgan, and Walz, show a substantial consensus about major developments in the future. Four characteristics stand out. First, the counsellor will go where people are; outreach will be major strategy, and there will be considerable use of support persons. Marple describes a thought provoking fantasy of the future in which "Friendship Centers" alter the lives of people nationally and internationally. But typically, no clear-cut definition of the arrangement of such a center is given; but the implication is that location and type of housing will be of less importance than what happens in the community.

The second major prediction is that services will be available lifelong; the school-age emphasis will have disappeared. Guidance will be provided over the whole range of individuals and groups; no social strata or subculture will be favoured over any other. Along with this breadth, helping agencies and institutions will collaborate far more than they do today, and guidance workers will have a more comprehensive knowledge of and better working relationships with, colleagues in other settings. Much of the counsellor's work will emphasize prevention; while crisis help will be provided, the major thrust will be the change agent's task reducing or eliminating destructive features of the environment that generate problems.

The counsellor's increased versatility will require a sound background in theory, research, and techniques, the quality of preparation will rise. Facilitating personal development, building effective working relationships, and gaining an in-depth understanding of various cultures will be given higher priority. Preparation programs will utilize input from the school, the community, and the working world, and measure student progress on the basis of competency.

Other aspects of the role in the years ahead involve legal status, ethical practices, professional organizations, and counsellor's supply and demand. Prospects are good for increased professional status and the attendant legal and ethical responsibilities. Professional organizations will again the prestige to induce employers to upgrade hiring standards. Some form of licensure will be in operation; counselors will participate in setting qualifications and examining applicants. It is very probable that counselors will be completely in charge of this process.

Index